FROM THE MARROW-BONE

John F. Deane

From the Marrow-Bone

THE RELIGION OF POETRY: THE POETRY OF RELIGION

the columba press

First published in 2008 by
the columba press
55A Spruce Avenue, Stillorgan Industrial Park,
Blackrock, Co Dublin

Cover by Bill Bolger
Origination by The Columba Press
Printed in Ireland by ColourBooks Ltd, Dublin

ISBN 978-1-85607-614-2

Acknowledgements

'The Jesus Body, the Jesus Bones' was delivered, with some changes, to a conference for Priests of the Dublin diocese, Citywest, May 10, 2007.
'Thoughts from the Marrow-Bone' and 'Dipped Again in God' were presented, with some changes, to a conference of the Augustinians in Kilkenny, May 16, 2007.
'The Three Strange Angels' was presented as a talk at the UCC Conference, 'One World: Three Perspectives', 26 May, 2007.
'Look Back in Quietness' was published in the Spring edition of *An Sionnach*, ed. David Gardiner.
'Dream of a Fair Field' was published in *The Furrow*.
'Pressing the Ground Humbly' was published in *Testo*.

Contents

Introduction: Thoughts from the Marrow-Bone   7

PART ONE

The Jesus Body, the Jesus Bones   13

Pressing the Ground Humbly: The Making of a Poem   30

The Bestial Floor: Poetry in an Age of Violence   41

Dipped Again in God   64

The Three Strange Angels   89

Song of the Suffering Servant   105

Dream of a Fair Field   107

PART TWO

Hierusalem, My Happy Home   115

Poet as Outlaw : Robert Southwell   117

This Glow-worm Faith: William Alabaster   128

The Nativity Ode: John Milton   137

My Fruits are Only Flowers: Andrew Marvell   152

Such Great Felicity : Thomas Traherne   166

Joseph Mary Plunkett   181

The Fly in Marmalade: William Butler Yeats   183

The Sails are blowing Southward: Austin Clarke   204

Mayo Theology: A Poem for Enda McDonagh   221

A Shy Believer: Denise Levertov   224

Look Back in Quietness: Gerard Smyth   235

Thoughts from the Marrow-Bone

Dag Hammarskjöld, former Secretary General of the United Nations, and essayist, wrote in *Markings*, in W. H. Auden's translation: 'God does not die on the day when we cease to believe in a personal deity, but we die on the day when our lives cease to be illumined by the steady radiance, renewed daily, of a wonder, the source of which is beyond all reason.'

Philip Larkin once notoriously said: 'Foreign poetry? No!' iterating a prejudice amply seconded by Kingsley Amis. While working with The Dedalus Press, I regularly found such a reaction. I have more recently encountered another, more febrile, prejudice: 'Religious poetry? No!' Being foolish, I once tried to market a book of religious poetry translated from Swedish: 'Religious poetry, and in translation! no! no! and again no!' The failure even to admit the possibility that such work is of value seems to be symptomatic of a whole failure of the imagination, a failure that permeates not just contemporary poetry but society as a whole. Belief in the supernatural – out! out! out! I am speaking, of course, about the closed mind.

To think imaginatively is one of the most crucial functions of the human brain; it is the ability to think of what does not exist, to see beyond the immediate and obvious to the possible. I feel it is this sense of seeking what is beyond the immediate satisfaction of the ego that is anathema to contemporary society. It is the same failure that hinders so much contemporary poetry from knowing 'the roll, the rise, the carol, the creation!' Religious thinking, and religious poetry, move in a world of symbols, shifting from something known to the unknown, seeing in symbols something other than those symbols. Therefore it is the imagination at its most perfect work. If religious faith has been dumped as not being compatible with the economic and technological advances of our age, then a whole culture and sanity have been dumped along with it.

Where today the words of Arthur O'Shaughnessy?

We are the music makers,
 And we are the dreamers of dreams,
Wandering by lone sea-breakers,
 And sitting by desolate streams; –
World-losers and world-forsakers,
 On whom the pale moon gleams:
Yet we are the movers and shakers
 Of the world for ever, it seems.

If the religious imagination in the church in Ireland has been suppressed down the decades in favour of authoritative control, then the loss of that sense of authority may well release vision in individuals again; and that vision ought to provide motive and energy to work towards a new and more whole society, even a more whole church. Perhaps, then, hope is not yet lost.

Is the poet no longer a dreamer of dreams? And is that why poetry no longer moves and shakes anybody or anything? – because it conforms too much to the demands of a merely secular society. Our loss becomes the poverty of the mind that cannot see through objects in the natural world to what lies beyond them; the mind stays in the object and nothing further is suggested, not intimations of human potential, nor of immortality nor infinity. It is the imagination that works through things to focus on them as potential symbols. In our world of rush and push one of the great things lacking is time for contemplation. This great and beautiful world lies before us and we have a choice of response: do we try to grasp, consume and make our very own what lies before us? Or do we stand back from it, admire its beauty and indulge in contemplation of that beauty? If the first, then we destroy what we love, like the goose and its golden eggs; if the latter, then we allow the beauty and wonder of the world to enter our own spirits and take possession.

There is a too-easy notion that 'religious poetry' is soft-centred and unquestioning, whereas the opposite is the case: it is, instead, probing and seriously demanding. The priest-poet Pádraig J. Daly writes of the difficulties he faces in his ministry:

Sorrow
I am eating, drinking, sleeping, dreaming sorrow.
Yesterday I followed a small child to its grave.
Today, an old man.

I watch one I have grown to love,
Beautiful as the wind, languish;
And I flounder in the grief around her.

I sit with husbands in little smoky visiting rooms,
Parsing your reasons;
With broken mothers, with dismayed children.

Your people mutter bitterly against you;
How can I carry them?

(from *The Last Dreamers*, Dedalus)

The word 'imagination' when it comes to the question of religion, often slips away further, and too thoughtlessly, into the word 'mystical'; Elizabeth Jennings wrote, in *Every Changing Shape* (Carcanet): 'In the history of English poetry, the word 'mystical' has perhaps been used most appropriately and with most clarity in the criticism that has accumulated around the seventeenth-century so-called Metaphysical poets. The great representatives of this group of poets are, in fact, not metaphysical at all; on the contrary, they are mystical poets. Vaughan, Herbert and Traherne were not primarily interested in the nature or study of being, the true meaning of metaphysics; they were concerned with making direct contact with reality or God, and with expressing this in their verse.' If we are to dismiss, in our time, the functions of the imagination, then *ipso facto* we must dismiss the poets Jennings mentions here, along with so many others: Hopkins, Eliot, Dickinson, R. S. Thomas, Edwin Muir ... all poets of the religious imagination.

As we dismiss the myth of a unified society, unified in its physical and spiritual concerns, and as we turn more and more to the immediate and urgent satisfaction of our economic demands alone, we develop a sense of individuality, an ego-tripping that eschews the good of the whole, and of others, individuals or society. The ensuing sense of disconnection with the world, when we grow aware of it, brings with it a feeling of dread. And yet it is also the function of the imagination to discern the relationship of the individual to the course of history, to ensure we do not, as individuals, fall subordinate to the collective will; I believe it is most truly in good religious poetry (as opposed to devotional or sectional verse) that the solution to this seeming contradiction may be found. In religious ritual, in our time, the distrust of the imagination is discernible; where the circling and meditative spirit of Gregorian chant has been replaced by the raucous clinking of guitars to a plethora of clichéd verses; where, in the teaching of religion, any sense of cultural reference must be avoided in case it impinges on some other cultural demands, and where the religious imagination corkscrews into social conscience. So many of us move awkwardly through a faith structure that has become drained of real meaning; only the surface rituals remain, and these are now void of imaginative power.

Late in his career William Butler Yeats wrote:

A Prayer for Old Age
God guard me from those thoughts men think
In the mind alone;
He that sings a lasting song
Thinks in a marrow-bone;

From all that makes a wise old man
That can be praised of all;
O what am I that I should not seem
For the song's sake a fool?

I pray – for fashion's word is out
And prayer comes round again –
That I may seem, though I die old,
A foolish, passionate man.

This is a plea for the enabling imagination, as is, I believe, Samuel Beckett's beautifully strange and cryptic piece, *Imagination dead Imagine*. This begins: 'No trace anywhere of life, you say, pah, no difficulty there, imagination not dead yet, yes, dead, good, imagination dead imagine.' The piece explores a white 'rotunda', everything still, everything white, scarce any movement, any life. The search goes on for enabling energies, energies to be found not in frantic bursts of action to appropriate the world, but in eager and patient contemplation, in the openness to all experience and, I believe, in the openness to religion, and to religious poetry.

Ireland's current unease, even disease, springs too from a failure of imagination in government. Today the 'conservatives' insist that an economy leaning towards the richest and already powerful will, ultimately, work to the best interests of all, including the impoverished and marginalised. Our experience points to the opposite being the truth. To distract and deceive the voter, even to bribe with promises of tax cuts and all sorts of financial concessions, has become the way of political speeches and presentations, the governing folks failing to imagine that the voter is indeed capable of intelligent choice and rational persuasion. What we have long lacked is true democratic government. Conglomerates, large corporations, international banking concerns, all of which so easily get government support and subsidy, simply do not enter another country with the charitable purpose of bettering the lot of the people; they drain the area dry, take what they need, and vamoose. Government, it appears, cannot see beyond the immediate profit for which it yearns. Wendell Berry writes, in *Another Turn of the Crank*: (Counterpoint): 'If you have eyes to see, you can see that there is a limit beyond which machines and chemicals cannot replace people; there is a limit beyond which mechanical or economic efficiency cannot replace care.' *If you have eyes to see*: but perhaps we have lost that seeing power, we have lost it because we have grown scared of the ideal of a people living in wholeness, in the unification of the spiritual and the material, we have banished imaginative living.

Local communities have suffered greatly under this 'conservative' approach: witness the imposition of so much over-the-top housing hammered onto the edges of small villages, the plague of holiday absent-landlord cottages along our coastline; witness the Rossport struggle, village people taking on the might of an uncaring oil company, Shell. To quote Wendell Berry again: 'To put the bounty and the health of our land, our only commonwealth, into the hands of people who do not live on it and share its fate will always be an error. For whatever determines the fortune of the land determines also the fortune of the people.' And is it not a wilful failure of imagination that our government, on the mere word of a severely discredited regime, refuses to examine aircraft using our airports that even the heron knows are ferrying prisoners to torture in other countries?

Those of us who cling to some form of contemplation, to a belief in the power of the imagination, are often accused of holding to something out of date. I wonder whether what we cling to is something not 'out of date', but 'out of place'. It is the society we move in that is destroying itself; it is the poetic imagination, allied with some faith in a unifying belief, that is required. There are many who instantly baulk at the word 'religion', who recoil at the use of the word 'God'. The demands of a serious poetry that applies imaginative exploration of the deepest levels of human living, may appear too much for the merely rational approach to life; where are our 'foolish, passionate men'? Religious poetry, meaningful spiritual rituals, together with an openness to faith itself, lead of themselves inevitably to a more whole person, and to a more unified society.

The Chaplet
I can go back, quiet as a ghost, from here
where sweet coals whisper in the grate, I can go back –
while hailstones sputter against the panes outside – to see her
standing in the doorway, snow falling softly, an old-woman's
spotted apron holding her, and know that she
is watching too, ghosting inwards and going back, visiting
her losses, as if she could find a way
to string it all together, to a sentence, making
sense, and I can sit remembering –
and shaping, the way a sonnet shapes –
that dusk her rosary burst asunder and beads
spilled skittering all-which-ways on the stone floor
as if her prayers and aspirations left
nothing in her shaking hands but a thread, bereft.

(from *The Instruments of Art*, Carcanet)

The Jesus Body, the Jesus Bones

In the summer of 2000 I was lucky enough to have been offered a short residency on the island of Gotland in Sweden and flew from Dublin to Stockholm. We had to wait for a small plane to take us out to the island, about forty minutes' flight from Stockholm. As a group of us waited for that flight the weather got wilder; a storm was gathering, the winds grew in anger and the rain began to fall. It was announced that our flight would be the last one out of the airport that night. As we walked across the tarmac in failing light, I watched a young girl (who was clearly somewhat mentally challenged) and her father ahead of me; she was nervous, she had a doll in her hand, and the father urged her on, almost pushing her up the small steps onto the aircraft. He settled her into her seat but she was crying. She was very scared.

During the flight our small plane was tossed about on the clouds and the girl cried out loud, adding to my own sense of fear and sympathy; her body rocked in distress and her fingers bruised that half-forgotten doll. I remember thinking that, like the whole of creation, she shared in the suffering body of Jesus. Later, as I eased myself into bed on the island, a bell chimed midnight from a dark tower nearby; for some reason, a memory of my serving Mass one morning on Achill Island came back to me, the memory associating itself with the child and with the body of Jesus. It was one of those strange and stirring moments when many things seem to come together in one's head: a moment, if you like, of inspiration, an epiphany. And, as it has been a life's effort to understand my world and my Christianity through the medium of poetry, I spent my time in Gotland working on something. Here is the poem:

Acolyte
The wildness of this night – the summer trees
ripped and letting fall their still green leaves,
and the sea battering the coast
in its huge compulsion – seems as nothing

to the midnight chime from the black tower,
reiterating that all this tumult
is but the bones of Jesus in their incarnation.
I have flown today onto the island,

our small plane tossed like jetsam on the clouds;
I watched the girl, her mutilated brain,
the father urging, how her body rocked
in unmanageable distress, her fingers

bruising a half-forgotten doll; hers, too,
the Jesus-body, the Jesus-bones. Once
in early morning, the congregation
was an old woman coughing against echoes

and a fly frantic against the high window;
the words the priest used were spoken out as if
they were frangible crystal: *hoc – est – enim –*
The Host was a sunrise out of liver-spotted hands

and I tinkled the bell with a tiny gladness;
the woman's tongue was ripped, her chin,
where I held the paten, had a growth of hairs;
her breath was fetid and the Host balanced

a moment, and fell. Acolyte I gathered
up the Deity, the perfect white of the bread
tinged where her tongue had tipped it; the
necessary God, the beautiful, the patience.

I swallowed it, taking within me
Godhead and congregation, the long obedience
of the earth's bones, and the hopeless urge
to lay my hands in solace on the world.

This sense I have always had, that the world is one, and that
it is graced through by the death and resurrection of Jesus, must

have come to me from the wonder and beauty of the island on which I was born and reared. As I grew to relish that world, that earth, I also grew to an awareness of my Catholic heritage, but it was the words of Paul that stuck somewhere in my consciousness:

> Now there are varieties of gifts, but the same Spirit; and there are varieties of services, but the same Lord; and there are varieties of activities, but it is the same God who activates all of them in everyone. To each is given the manifestation of the Spirit for the common good. To one is given through the Spirit the utterance of wisdom, and to another the utterance of knowledge according to the same Spirit; to another faith by the same Spirit, to another gifts of healing by the one Spirit, to another the working of miracles, to another prophecy, to another the discernment of spirits, to another various kinds of tongues, to another the interpretation of tongues. For just as the body is one and has many members, and all the members of the body, though many, are one body, so it is with Christ. For in the one Spirit we were all baptised into one body – Jews or Greeks, slaves or free – and we were all made to drink of one Spirit. (Paul: 1 Cor: 12)

Into one body, the Jesus body. This is, I suppose, that 'communion of saints' we spoke of in our creed; it is the prayer of Jesus himself, 'that they all may be one, as thou, Father, and I, are one'. One God. One creation. One people. And Paul also wrote (Rom: 18):

> I consider that our present sufferings are not worth comparing with the glory that will be revealed in us. The creation waits in eager expectation for the sons of God to be revealed. For the creation was subjected to frustration, not by its own choice, but by the will of the one who subjected it, in hope that the creation itself will be liberated from its bondage to decay and brought into the glorious freedom of the children of God. We know that the whole creation has been groaning as in the pains of childbirth right up to the present time. Not only so, but we ourselves, who have the first fruits of the Spirit, groan inwardly as we wait eagerly for our adoption as sons, the redemption of our bodies.

The redemption of our bodies, and of the earth itself. Those bodies, that earth, that have been riddled through with the very flesh and blood of Jesus who died and was born again. If our hope rests on the resurrection of Jesus, and on the resurrection of our body, then it appears, too, that the whole earth will be resurrected in some way. The Catholic Church has always appeared to me to be in denial of so much that is physical in our being, it has been so alert with exclusions that gradually, down all the years in which I have been asking questions, I find myself now on the side of the world against that old form of church. I hesitate to call myself a Christian, a Christ-person, though this is what I want to be, because that name is so full of virtue, love, self-sacrifice, that I feel myself unworthy of the name. I believe the name of Christian is one to be earned, not to be merely conferred on a mewling baby by baptism, to be earned only by a lifetime of effort. I believe, then, in the Jesus body, the Jesus bones.

With the admixture of a rural 50s Catholicism and the physical beauty of Achill Island, perhaps it was inevitable that I turn to poetry. It is in a poetry that refuses to baulk at the reasonable and successful, and passes beyond into the unreasonable, the wonder-full, that I find the deepest search into faith and how that faith may respond to the terrible demands of our time. To walk along a lazy, wet bog road on Achill Island, an island that has been riddled through with Christian faith, with time, beauty and the depredations of time, to idle on that track under an enormous sky, is to know something of the long reaching of God into one's life:

Towards A Conversion
There is a soft drowse on the bog today;
the slight bog-cotton scarcely stirs; for now
this could be what there is of universe, the far-off
murmuring of ocean, the rarest traffic passing, barely

audible beyond the hill. I am all attention, held
like a butterfly in sunlight, achieve, a while,
an orchid quiet, the tiny shivering of petals, the mere
energy of being. Along the cuttings

bubbles lift through black water and escape, softly,
into sunlight; this complex knotting of roots has been
an origin, and nothing new nor startling
will happen here, save the growth of sphagnum

into peat; if this is prayer, then
I have prayed. I walk over millennia, the Irish
wolf and bear, the elk and other
miracles; everywhere bog-oak roots

and ling, forever in their gentle
torsion, with all this floor a living thing, held
in the world's care, indifferent. Over everything
voraciously, the crow, a monkish body hooded

in grey, crawks its blacksod, cleansing music;
lay your flesh down here you will become
carrion-compost, sustenance for the ravening roots;
where God is, has been, and will ever be.

To mention God in poetry today, to bring God into any conversation, is to feel oneself placed at once as appearing hopelessly
out-of-date. Faith, and particularly the Catholic faith, is seen as
something once widely held but no longer to be taken seriously,
like the penny farthing bicycle, like tansy as a cure for hysteria.
Progress in economic terms has put faith into a box of old curios;
the world can and will do without faith. If so many of the wars
of history can be ascribed to differences of faith, then the world
will be better off without religion. Catholic teaching has not kept
pace with scientific or economic or any other kind of progress,
including developments in the equality of men and women, and
therefore the church has lagged behind the world, behind a creation unified in the death and resurrection of Jesus. If the central
sacraments are still insisted upon in the life of an individual,
baptism, marriage, extreme unction, and if the Catholic rituals
of bringing the dead to church, of saying Mass for the dead, of
Christian burial, are still carried out, it is done so often simply
out of a sense of tradition, a kind of insurance, a method of chan-
nelling grief. Three or four nods to Catholic faith, but serious living looks elsewhere.

I think it has been the negative and divisive stance of the

Catholic Church that has been alienating me over the years, together with the hierarchy's stress on glory-robes, authority and privilege. In my early years priests were always a scary presence, judgemental and domineering, and everybody knows how that posture has been undermined by revelations of corruption. The sense of exclusivity, not only keeping women out of any real role in ministry, but insisting that any form of ecumenism be ruled by Catholic dogma, that liberation theology, particularly in Latin America, was somehow against the church's authority, the official church standing, as it seems to me, always by the powerful and privileged and leaving the works of justice on behalf of the poor and oppressed to voluntary groups and non-governmental agencies: all of this has stirred either anger or indifference to the church. I never hear the church speak out forcefully against the violence of our times; where are the voices now against the war crimes being perpetrated by Israel, by Bush and Rice and Rumsfeld, by Sharon and Olmert, by the fanatics of another domineering faith currently in the ascendant ... In other words, how can I hold to a church that denies in so many ways the possibilities of love, that love which moves towards the unification of all mankind in brotherhood and sisterhood?

John Donne wrote it down well:

The bell doth toll for him that thinks it doth; and though it intermit again, yet from that minute that that occasion wrought upon him, he is united to God. Who casts not up his eye to the sun when it rises? but who takes off his eye from a comet when that breaks out? Who bends not his ear to any bell which upon any occasion rings? but who can remove it from that bell which is passing a piece of himself out of this world? No man is an island, entire of itself; every man is a piece of the continent, a part of the main. If a clod be washed away by the sea, Europe is the less, as well as if a promontory were, as well as if a manor of thy friend's or of thine own were: any man's death diminishes me, because I am involved in mankind, and therefore never send to know for whom the bell tolls; it tolls for thee ...

If the Christ has been crucified, entombed and returned to

life, then in that faith must all our hope lie. And hence our universe is impregnated with the fact of the incarnation of God, the
fact of the God's taking of flesh and bone, its partaking in our
world and in our living, and hence the need for oneness and the
hope that all of the earth, bone and fragment, hill and ocean
depth, must partake of that wonder. I find the detailed implic-
ations of this belief difficult to frame in prose and so have tried
to explore it in a series of poems, because poetry does not stop at
the great blank wall before which reason comes to a dead end.

Mappa Mundi
Let this then be your diary and yearbook: make
  a frame of oak on which to fix
a sheet of finest vellum, stretched, like skin; draw

freehand, a not quite perfect circle; use black
  ink, some red, for the heart, let's say, for the Red
Sea; blue for rivers, veins, and brown-egg shapes

for mountain ranges, and for faith; focus it all
  towards the centre, Christ, his bones stretched wide
in crucifixion, colour him too insistent red

to confute the non-believers. Puce, for wars, but let it not
  predominate. Have angels flutterfly above
and devils snarl, scarlet, in the guts. Remember

that something within the frame of bones grows wiser
  as the bones grow heavier, the same that shifts
your being gratefully towards cessation. Now see

how down the long avenue the cherry trees once more
  have sifted all the juices of the earth
into extravagant blossoming, a canopy for wedding feasts, a
  Bach

cantata in the key of white, but in you, memory
  or the doleful rhythms of experience, hold the heart
from lifting in exultation, chill winds being possible

and unseasonable frosts. Remember, too, how the monks
  laboured years over their charts, finding in the corners
place for monsters, for the slithery ladder and the sulphur

lakes beneath. If there is time, etch in gold leaf your fabled
   places,
   Samarkand and Valparaiso, the pancreas, the afterlife.
Something within the frame of bones is in no rush

to clothe again the hard-won nakedness of spirit. Fig-leaf.
   Rue.
   When you are done, step back, and gaze awhile
into the mirror, note contour-lines about your face

and the curious light still shining in your eyes.

I point again to a belief in the harmony of all nature, and
man's place in that harmony. We are in great danger, in our
time, of destroying that harmony. To damage our world is to
damage our selves; not to cry foul when our ecology is threatened, when military powers are given free hand to undertake
any kind of warfare they feel they can get away with, when
over-the-steeple wealth is put on display for its own sake …
then humanity is sliding down a loose-shale cliff towards the
abyss. When wealthy nations take unto themselves the right to
cheat and lie and torture, all in the name of a 'war on terror' and
the church does nothing about it … And I cannot help but remember how the church in the Unites States stood behind
George W. Bush when he went for re-election, even though his
hands are bloodied and the Republican Party stands accused of
dealing in death, then I lose faith in that church and its mission
to be 'one, holy, catholic and apostolic'. We have been, simply,
invited to love; in George Herbert's great poem 'Love', the God
invites the soul to come and sup at God's table but the soul
draws back, conscious of sin; then Love reminds the soul that
Jesus Christ supped with sinners, prostitutes and tax collectors
and it is not the worthiness of the soul that counts, but God's
own infinite giving, his mercy. When we grow aware of this
invitation, it is not of our own merits we must think but of God's
overwhelming and unquestioning gifts of grace to us. We must
howl and scream and gesticulate against the inhumanity of our
times; it is of no earthly use to climb into an armour-plated pope
mobile and wave out of ermine glory to the common people,
massed in their hope of hearing a new message of peace and

love and sharing, a message wrung from the immediacy of our era. If there is a balance, then all of us must put on the scales even more and more of what is good and beautiful to counteract the evils that war and violence are placing on the other side.

If all of this comes across as a certainty in my life, then I am sorry; it is not so. I am conversant with poetry; I have been immersed in Catholicism; yet now I am lost and, like so many others, am seeking passionately for the truth. How desperately people are seeking, too, everywhere, all over the world. There are endless signs and symptoms of this search and I have to say that the answers we are so often given are the negative, the Thatcherite ones: 'Out! Out! Out!' The only certainty in my life, after my passion for poetry, after love and family, is that a man lived once, an anointed one, a Christ, and that his name was Jesus, meaning saviour. To him I cling, to his words, and his example. And to the hope that he offered to a (then, too) confused and violent world. I cling to the Jesus body, the Jesus bones. It is the urgency of the quest, and the imagery left on my soul by Achill Island that spirit my writing, often against what I feel has been an original inspiration. The God intrudes. Often I am grateful, and often not. But then I realise, if the Bones and Body of Jesus are firm in the flesh of creation, then everything I write is stronger the closer it comes to those sacred bones.

> Take your pen, you urge, and write: God.
> But I resist and write
> sea-mew, fuchsia, city, moon.
> You insist, write: God. I say –
> I have no pen now, I use PCs.
> Then type out: God, you say, translate me
> into this your century.
> I type out: God; and then delete, type
> sea-mew, fuchsia, city, moon.
> And when I hear you laugh I know again
> you are the letters of every word I use, you
> the source and form of every poem. But,
> I plead, the people mock and say that God
> is not fit subject for our century. So I write again
> sea-mew, fuchsia, city, moon. And you say
> yes! you have written me down once more.

When I was growing up I suffered a severely repressive education in morality, emphasis almost always on sexual affronts. As the world today appears indifferent to such a morality, many disturbing questions rise in me. Questions to which I have no answers; I see a generation growing up in almost complete sexual freedom; I am aware of the potential diseases that this may bring, I am aware too of the values of family life and the fruits of stabilities in human relationships that may be lost in such an approach to loving. I hear around me only the same negative moral voices that I heard decades ago and the pointlessness of an undeveloping morality from the mouth of the church hurts me still. Our technologically wizard younger generations have no time to consider questions of morality or faith; their duty is to themselves, to technology, to worldly possessions and 'success'. And what do I have to oppose to such attitudes should I, indeed, wish to oppose them? I believe, because of the Jesus body, the Jesus bones, that everything in the body of creation is good and that humankind has yet a great deal to discover in that body, that the search is good, and that a human balance will prevail. That is, however, a view depending on one's faith in the inherent goodness of a humanity that moves without the guidance of a progressive church. And so, once again, I propose ... Christ.

In the hidden sutures of my own mind I grow aware, too, of death. How can we not be aware of it, we who have been grieving witnesses to the terrible power of modern technology to destroy human life and the infrastructures of an ancient nation. How suddenly did Israel, backed up by Britain and the regime of George W. Bush, rain death down on the innocent lives of children, in Southern Lebanon, in Palestine, in Quana. And how imperfect the most highly-boasted techniques of mass destruction in their pinpoint accuracy fail so abysmally; death, overlord and ever-present cackling ghost, death indiscriminate and carefree, hovering over their precision-guided bombs. What is there to offer the generations in opposition to such inhuman terror? Christ, again Christ, Christ only.

I want to push further down this uncertain yet sustaining lane. I assert, in all humility and with all the stays of vagueness, insubstantiality and wilfulness, that I try to call myself a Christian, a Christ-follower, and eschew Catholicism as it is currently conceived. And if, as Joseph Mary Plunkett touched on, 'I see His blood upon the rose, and in the stars the glory of His eyes,' then I must partake more closely, and perhaps more foolishly, in the great sacrament of communion with that Jesus body. Hence the great moment of the Mass still means a lot for me, that moment of transubstantiation, and then of taking that sacred body within my own. If there is even a scintilla of truth in that, then the substance of the being of Jesus enters my substance; 'Body of Christ,' the priest says, and I answer fervently, 'Amen!' 'Blood of Christ', he offers, and I agree again, 'Amen!' And then, when I walk down a beautiful country lane, the world around me is transubstantiated, too, the great sacrament extending into the landscape with which I am in league.

Kane's Lane
The substance of the being of Jesus
sifts through the substance of mine; I
am God, and son of God, and man. Times I feel

my very bones become so light I may
lift unnoticed above Woods's Wood and soar
in an ecstasy of being over Acres' Lake; times again

I am so dugged, so dragged, my flesh
falls granite while a fluid near congealed
settles on my heart. The Christ – frozen in flight

on the high-flung frame of his cross –
leaves me raddled in the grossest of mercies
and I walk the length of Kane's Lane, on that ridge

of grass and cress and plantain
battening down the centre, I sex my tongue
on the flesh juices of blackberries, cinch my jaws on the chalk

bitterness of sloes, certain and unsettled,
lost and found in my body, sifted through a strait
and serpentine love-lane stretched between dawn and night.

To make the statement that sets one quite apart from so many of one's contemporaries, especially when that statement is made with a modicum of doubt and a deal of uncertainty, must appear a very foolish thing. The lane I have travelled is not in itself a scientific one, quite the opposite, it partakes of the craziness of the imagination and of the foolishness of a trust in the movements of the heart and the track of poetry. That statement is a belief in the truthfulness of the gospels, made in my mind even more truthful because of the inconsistencies and contradictions between the four evangelists. I trust in the actual existence of Jesus, and in the value of his words and example. I trust that, if the God was crazy enough to stir out of eternal restfulness to create a world filled with the doubtful wonder that is humanity, then that God is a poet, and a hugely masterful one. Because, alongside reason and its offshoots, there is the invisible door in the invisible wall that one must open and go through for a full faith in Jesus as incarnate God; here I can do no more than hope. But poetry can go beyond that hope; poetry can take the invisible key, open the door that is not there in the great blank wall of reason and step out into the wonder and beauty of what is beyond. This is the ultimate power of the Jesus presence in the whole of the created world; this is the finest power of poetry. Down the centuries, the great poets have taken this key and opened that door: Donne, Herbert and Marvel, Milton, Blake and Hopkins, Eliot, Dickinson and Thomas, and many, many more. The trust is in the Word; and the word is, ultimately, love. Whether or not this love is radiated by the Catholic Church is a matter of personal decision; for me, the church does not mediate that love. I go back to what I already mentioned, the morality and greatness of a life devoted to family, to the love of one person, to the treasure that is marriage.

Your Name
A warm rain falls outside, sowing its dust-motes
softly onto soft ground; I will sit here
beside you while you sleep. All my thoughts again, will be
concerning you. Your body lies
easeful, your breathing gentle as the fall of dusk.
You have gifted life and death to me
and given both your name, and with that name
I will go down proudly to my grave, my lips
holding to these exceptional words: I have loved.

The dark blue of the walls around us, here
where we have lived, will be the colour
waiting for me when I close my eyes. You
to me are truce in the long war, a tent
fixed firmly against the waging desert storm.
I will have laid the jewel of my death
in your kindly palm, or you
will have laid yours in mine, the hand
closing over it will wait, in warmth, in quietness.
They will speak of me, when they speak,
in terms of you, the way they say a stream
meanders through its chosen country. Remember
how we found each other, hurt, migrating birds
resting on a green island; remember
how we kissed, under the unblinking eye
of Mars. Here now I write your name in sand-dust
and it will blow about this favoured earth forever.

I sometimes wonder how deep was the faith of the people of my generation, and of the generations before them, when they followed without demur every rule and regulation of the Catholic Church. I have spent a week in Drumshambo, Co Leitrim, and during three days of that week the local people were offered their annual 'mission'. This triduum was known as the days of the Portiuncula, after the little church in Assisi founded by the great St Francis. In the earlier decades, crowds overran Drumshambo and assisted at every Mass, penitential service, confession, prayers, blessings … It was a festival atmosphere, something like the crowds that now throng the Galway races, with obvious differences. There were stalls erected and people bought their religious objects, the rosaries, medals, scapulars, holy water, holy pictures … and took them to be blessed on the final evening. And the priest thundered at them, sinners that they were, outlined the fires of hell, the sufferings of purgatory, the narrow and strait way that would lead to heaven. They worked for plenary indulgences, for themselves and for the souls in purgatory. And they went home purified, full of resolutions and hope, and went back to their difficult lives.

But was all of that really faith? Was not a great deal of it a matter of custom, of tradition, of fear? There were half-held convictions, supported by the authority of Rome and their local priesthood, convictions that we have seen fall away so fast and so easily. How we trusted in those men who dressed in gorgeous robes and processed about our churches, chanting in a foreign tongue, performing rituals of which we had only a general understanding. There was security there; there was an absence of personal responsibility; there was a path, signposted and with cleansing stations, to follow. Ireland is, I believe, currently in a phase of adolescence, being a young country in its freedom, and for the first time in its history finding itself with a great deal of money to spend. We are still far from maturity. It is easy to blame the church now for taking that responsibility from us, for holding us in the palm of her hand, for threatening and cajoling us down the path she insisted we must take. But that will not do; nor will it do for the church to fall back, as she appears to be doing, on those same old simplistic rules and sanctions and threats, withdrawing into a fortress and refusing to admit the modern world and its advances and its sorrows. Who will guide the country through its adolescent and foolish phase? Or what country should we take as example to follow? The church itself must constantly work with the world towards a common maturity; it, too, appears to be in an adolescent phase, in denial of its need to grow up, in its constant iteration of objections and refusals. To be vocal and authoritative in this world the church, too, must accept the oneness of all people in God, the oneness of all the creation in God, and strive, with the original Jesus, to convince the world of love, of the Jesus body, the Jesus bones.

We are witness, in our time, to an evil that grows in tandem with technological advances and economic wellbeing; that evil is selfishness, the opposite of the love and service that I am speaking about. It is clear and is shouted about often enough, God knows, that technological advances and economic wellbeing are showing the way to bring ease and health to regions that are yet in dreadful straits. The fact that the 'developed' world is turning those assets to its own egotistical ends, again proves the point that I am hoping to make. I am offering a picture of our world: I am offering words that go too far, yet that is where poetry must go, and that is where I find my hope:

Lank yellow cranes, like migratory birds, stilted, are feeding in the shallows of our suburbs and our village outposts and this building frenzy seems a part of our adolescent rush yet this, too, is part of God's creative urging; the finely-speckled breast of a mistle thrush, proud yet startled in the shadow of an old ash-tree, this, too, is listed with our hurrying in the one, ongoing annals of the world; yet soon branch and bole of the ash-tree will lift naked out of mud, like lopped limbs in a war zone; men in daffodil-yellow hard hats move like robots carrying wooden planks; earth shakers, world movers. Beyond this frenzy it is easy to lose heart, and I have been figuring, in a place apart, if this is stitching or unstitching of the world. Times now I feel like hosting requiem before our ocean juggernauts, road juggernauts, sky juggernauts and before mosquito jets masterful in their economies, their deconstructions; in our economic victories such spiritual defeat!

I stand before him and he says: 'Body of Christ' and I chew on flesh, he says 'Blood of Christ' and I taste a bitter, small intoxication; I take the substance deep into my substance and can say I, too, am Jesus; and I pray – that after all, through the Jesus body, the Jesus bones, the deaf will hear the breezes siffling through the eucalyptus trees, will hear the breaking of waves along Atlantic's shingle shores; that the blind, after darkness and the shadows that darkness throws, will see the moonlight play like fireflies along the undersides of leaves, that those of us botched in brain and limb will be gazelles across an intimate terrain and that the tears of the too-old woman, inward-dwelling, wheelchair-locked who lost her lover-man to death some twenty years ago will step out giddily again into blue erotic light.

The Jesus Bones
It was full summer and the skylarks soared
over the wild meadow;
across ditch and hedgerow the dogrose
was draping its pink-rose shawl while the flowering
    brambles reached

dangerous fingers
towards the flowerbeds. A bat lay dead on the garage

window-ledge, amongst webs
and husks; it was curled up tight, perfect as a babyfist

though flies already
had laid their eggs in the sacred caverns of the ears;
I touched the fur and brushed the unresisting skin of night.
The holly leaves hymned in the sun

and small birds flitted through it;
it was shaping in torsion – all of us subject to corruption – a
    green
promise of clusters of the most scarlet of all berries; tree, I
    imagined,
of the knowledge of good and evil, its bitter roots

driving into the humus of our sleep. I would be, at times,
animal, thread of the skein
of earth, free of the need of redemption. Once I crept along a
    ditchtop,
in a tunnel of rhododendron, on earth mould,

leaf mould, on blossom-droppings, the tiny hardnesses
stippling palms, and knees;
this was everyday adventure,
the eyes of blackbirds following and their alarm calls,

with the strange and beetly
insects frightening me, their throbbing, their pebble-eyes.
I could fall silent there, hidden on the pulsebeat of the earth,
    mind
vacant, body stilled. Part of it. To receive.

And watched the fox slip by the drain outside,
there, uncareful, in daylight,
each russet hair sun-burnished, the breathfilled brush
like an old guardianship, a queen's train, that sorrowing eye

rounded where a moon-sliver shape of white
startled me; her long tongue lolling, the teeth were visible
in a grim fox-smile. My breathing stopped and a tiny shiver
    of fellowship
touched my spine. A moment, merely. Then

she was gone. A magpie
smattered noisily in the trees: *one for gloria, for hosanna*. If, in
    our waking,
we could mould it all into a shape, beautiful and at peace
the way the electrically burnt heart of Jesus

found rest in the rock tomb
though we are many, seam and femur, root-system,
belly, spleen. Night, and the moon dressed the storm-black
    clouds
in scarves of buttermilk-white while a solitary star, as if
    hastening, sat

over the eucalyptus tree. We –
not animal enough and cruel beyond thought –
go scattering blood over the earth
as we might scatter water off our fingers,

big-headed man, articulate, stitching and unstitching
mindlessly as we pass. The Jesus bones
have been nailed into the timber of the tree, the blood
in its revolutions

pouring through the puncture-holes, this man,
of localised importance, this Jesus-fox, who broiled fine fish
on a nest of stones by the lakeshore; this
rag-and-bone man, this stranger, this lover, giver, priest.

Pressing the Ground Humbly
The Making of a Poem

Poetry began, for me, as a puzzle remote from my actual living. Though, for examination purposes, I had to learn texts by heart (Wordsworth, Milton, Shakespeare) they were never explicated to me, either what they were doing as poems or why they were written in peculiar forms. It took a friend offering me, when I was almost thirty years of age, the works of Gerard Manley Hopkins, for me to find that the music and rhythmic patterning of poetry, along with the imagery and linguistic excitement, touched on areas of experience far beyond the everyday, yet intimately tied to that everyday, that poetry that I actually understood, both in terms of what it was saying and the way it was saying it, opened up new and relevant insights into the way the world shifted itself along. And with Hopkins, that primary learning for me was associated with religious questioning.

I was born and reared on an island where Roman Catholicism was prevalent as rain and wind. That great myth of Jesus the Christ, unquestioned, entered my soul with every breath. Many years later, when one close to me died, when my faith did not succeed in finding any consoling answers, the hurt I experienced took that breathing away. I found myself seeking out other myths.

With the excitement of the discovery of poetry like a fever upon me, I found myself trying to probe language for myself, to see if it could lead me out of myself and into the world again. I began to reach back, for sustenance and theme, to the ancient stories; not only for theme, perhaps, but for shape and form. My early attempts, I now know, were an effort to impose such shapes and myths on my world. I was approaching poetry from without. It was a failure. My reasoning was too much involved; the myths I used, the themes I touched on, were impermeable, nothing additional, no 'poetry', no music or imaginative lift would pass into the words.

And then I wrote a piece, or a piece was written through me, where I attempted to understand the incomprehensible and the unacceptable, a night when my wife, already quite ill, was distracted enough to leave the house in the middle of the night, searching for who knows what. I had been reading, in translation, the poetry of St John of the Cross and, of course, his notion of the 'dark night' surfaced at once. I went to that individual poem, used the form, the rhyme pattern, the movement, but applied it instinctively to what was happening in my own life. For the first time I found that the mundane (though highly charged) details of everyday living impinged on my efforts to write; this was a response to a reading and to a sorrow, it was not an imposition of already acquired relevance onto experience.

On a Dark Night
On a dark night
When all the street was hushed, you crept
Out of our bed and down the carpeted stair.
I stirred, unknowing that some light
Within you had gone out, and still I slept.
As if, out of the dark air

Of night, some call
Drew you, you moved in the silent street
Where cars were white in frost. Beyond the gate
You were your shadow on a garage-wall.
Mud on our laneway touched your naked feet.
The dying elms of our estate

Became your bower
And on your neck the chilling airs
Moved freely. I was not there when you kept
Such a hopeless tryst. At this most silent hour
You walked distracted with your heavy cares
On a dark night while I slept.

The words flowed through me and out of me, it was what I call now 'inspiration', for the moment of the writing I was permeable, but it was through the work of another that the poem had happened. I felt that, by leaving myself open, for that period, by 'earning' the inspiration through waiting, reading, and suffering, it was the first moment of the actual making of poetry in my life. I learned too, though slowly still, that poetry does not start outside oneself; it begins, as W. B. Yeats wrote, 'in the foul rag-and-bone shop of the heart'. It was time to search out those poets who worked with imagination, allowing the surface of the mind – through the workings of the imagination – to be permeated by the rich wonder of the actual experience of living, and to confine my reading to such poets who also sought, not the success of repeated and refashioned earlier work, but an ongoing exploration into the meaning of the world, poets such as the Swedish poet Tomas Tranströmer or the Irish poet Thomas Kinsella.

It is not easy, trying to lay oneself open, to allow the outside in rather than send the inside out. One is continually surrounded, in our time, by poetry that does not achieve greatness, either in depth of reference or in breadth of imagination, and it is rare that one discovers a poetry that combines both. Now, back to my religious faith. When I lost the simplicity of my earlier faith, I found the emptiness of the new world I tried to face almost unbearable. I needed to find my way back into some form of sustaining belief. Reason, it was clear, would not do. Faith, I realised, must go beyond reason. Poetry, I also came to feel, goes beyond reason, too. Could I be open both to belief and to poetry? Could I be permeable in life as well as in verse? Both of these were difficult for one brought up in a strict and all-embracing religious faith, and brought up to regard poetry as 'thoughts decked out in gaudy finery'.

I looked again at the poets I most admired and found that they did start in the heart, that foul rag-and-bone shop, in the heart that had lived through real experiences and that recalled those experiences in vivid detail. I found myself relishing a poem by Thomas Kinsella called 'Hen Woman' which has this description in the middle of the work:

> There was a tiny movement at my feet,
> tiny and mechanical; I looked down.
> A beetle like a bronze leaf
> was inching across the cement,

clasping with small tarsi
a ball of dung bigger than its body.
The serrated brow pressed the ground humbly,
lifted in a short stare, bowed again;
the dung-ball advanced minutely,
losing a few fragments,
specks of staleness and freshness.

The accuracy of detail stunned me, the observation, the lack of intrusion by the poet, the utter immediacy of recognition I experienced; perhaps I was starting on my own work at the wrong end, seeking 'meaning'; perhaps I, too, should 'press the ground humbly', should take the details of the world around me and allow these details their space, without imposition of a philosophy, a willed faith, even a hope. Let the foul rags and bones speak; keep the ego out as long as possible.

The making of a poem begins, I now believe, in the capturing of the physical actuality of one's experience, the everyday normal surroundings of a life. An event, however insignificant it may seem, will impinge and its presence trigger a memory, or prove significantly moving in its own right. Take the hare that simply came round the corner of the house the other day and sat, cheekily and calmly, at the patio's edge. I stood still to watch and admire, and its great rounded eye, that looked black with a tiny speck of white at its centre, touched me as did, of course, the big ears upright in expectation. Its nose twitched; it was all watchfulness. I made some slight movement, some sound perhaps, and it was gone, those massive back legs propelling it into instant flight.

That present moment recalled another, long past, long forgotten and it is here that I believe we all collect, as we travel our life's trackways, moments of some significance that pass into some part of our subconscious, to surface later as an 'epiphany', the opening up of a moment of relevance. Most of us let these moments slide away, back into the treasure-chest stored in our attics, and we think of them no more. But a poet calls on them, for their relevance, their truth.

So then, the hare among the summer grasses, that eye, those ears; and the hare I was taught to kill, decades ago, my father teaching me to shoot. We had practised several times, focusing at first on the lid of a saucepan nailed to a stick and posted down at the far end of a field, against the safety of a hedge. But what was it that had brought this memory so vividly back to me today? I believe it was the thinking about the world as I see it right now that brought that picture back to me.

If a poet begins from the actual and tries to maintain his or her hold on actuality, that is necessary in itself, but to write something of value then the work must also contain the truth of the poet's view of life, a *Weltanschauung*. Verses, light verse, Sunday poetry, all of these are very common and some of them can satisfy on a superficial level but great poetry brings with it a view of actuality, a personal and integrally presented view that does not claim to be the ultimate in philosophical or theological research, but does claim to be a totally honest interpretation of living, however personal that may be. And I do not mean that this must be valid, sensible, or remarkably wise; after all some of the great poets held views of life that were distinctly off the mark. It is the integrity of the vision and the honesty of the approach that give the thinking, in poetry, its value.

The Rowan Tree
There is a sense of this as imposition,
the greening, blossoming, and the curt showing
of scarlet berries. Till nudity returns

and stillness, the dark flesh gleaming under rain
and the solitary robin visible again in its singing
of the grace to be found in endurance.

From the rowan tree at the front door I recognised the image of that belief I have in nature and its necessary ongoing movement and our corresponding requirement to know and to accept endurance. Now I have always been trying to understand this world in terms of a possible afterlife, in terms of a loving God. In this age I have been trying to reconcile, in my own mind, this loving God with the horrors of our time, the wars, the drugs, the human trafficking, the greed … If my own disgust is with the propensity for wars and domination, then anything to violence hurts me deeply. This sense of hurt, along with the impetus of nature to suffer, to endure and out of that endurance to find new growth and beauty, finds a need for love and grace in our world to be a deeply human, even religious, necessity. It was the sighting of the hare, at a time when such thoughts on our world were flailing about within me, that brought back my memory of the rifle my father had put into my hands.

I have a dream, a foolish dream! And it is that the world will come to recognise that war and violence serve no purpose, that (perhaps even in our time!) the potential, indeed the proven, destruction of innocent and uninvolved human life as well as the clear destruction of the environment, is inevitably disproportional and that the only way forward is the total abolition of war. A dream ... of course, but it is something that occupies a great deal of my thinking. If a poem is to remain true, however, then the merely selfish dreams of the ego must not intrude. The integration of one's *Weltanschauung* to the poem must be of the original essence of the experience and therefore of the poem. These are vital points in the making of a poem: the ego, and the intrusion.

A poem springs from introspection, from the ego examining itself and its experiences. And so a poet is very often self-absorbed, seeking within him- or herself for clarity and understanding. Without such self-absorption nothing individual can emerge. Look at Keats and his necessary introspection, look at R. S. Thomas and his probing of the twentieth-century soul out of his own experience; look at the mighty 'terrible sonnets' of Gerard Manley Hopkins with their rooting about in the dark recesses of his own suffering. Then look again at how the individual idiosyncrasies of the personality in each case have been erased, so that there is no self-pity, no swagger, no egomania; the ego has been erased and the vital truth of the experience remains. A poem that retains any trace of the ego-magnifying, the self-propulsion towards success, the lobster-like long reaching pincers of the self-aggrandising ego ... any trace of this will reduce the final work to a mere shadow of what it ought to be. This does not mean that the 'I' in a poem is not allowed, by no means; but it does mean that all traces of the individual sentimentality be erased, and that the 'I' that is left is a generalised 'I', one available to, and recognizable by, everyone.

Flotsam
High tide by afternoon, Atlantic
purring like an old tom-cat under the sun,
this swollen moment
of plenitude before the turn;

the years have taken on themselves
the plenitude of dreams
passing swift as dreams; my hair
holds like tufts of fine bog-cotton, my skin

crinkles like the gold of gutter-leaves;
the ribs of splayed half-deckers
are the days of my well-loved dead
cluttering low tides of memory and still the world

holds me where I stand, brittle and yet
breathless with wonder; I have been
submerged in the happiness of everyday concerns,
gifted every now and then

with word-inebriation; and therefore
whether my fall is to be hard
or whether I am to drift away in silence
I would that you could say of me, yes

he lived, and while he lived
he gathered a few, though precious,
poems
lacquered with brittle loveliness, like shells.

We are at a point where the individual soul has faced up to individual experience, probing its roots for meaning, and where this meaning moves beyond the individual experience to a wider, universal relevance. And how to focus on this relevance? What are the mechanisms that allow the individual experience acquire a breadth of meaning that leaves the ego far behind? I think these mechanisms are many: among them the excitement of language itself, the music behind the words, the rhythms, and of course the imagery that draws the experience into the universal. In other words, the original experience, purged of the ego after the ego has plunged into the depth of the experience, is mated with another movement, even another experience, and out of this is born a child, the poem itself.

In the case of my own memory of the hare and my father's teaching me to shoot, there surfaced, too, a sense of my reluctance, even at that tender age, to take my father's advice. This appears to me to be reduced to the word 'love', in a new awareness of the meaning of that word. In order to make a proper hit on the hare, my father told me to try and 'love' the spot at which I was aiming, by which I believe he meant that I must get rid of other notions, such as excitement, nervousness, suddenness and that, by focusing closely on the actual shoulder of the hare, I could hold myself ready and gentle enough not to jerk or react foolishly. Fine, I understand. I had seen many cowboy movies where the cool hero sights his target with just such a 'love' and thereby always wins. Yet along with that came my actual 'love' of the hare, for I had seen the beautiful creature in many postures, in its alertness and its playfulness; I had watched it at coursing meetings as it leaped and arrowed its terrified body away from the dreadful jaws of the chasing hounds; I had seen it leap in the great pleasures of a spring day, almost boxing its companions in the delight of its physical being; I had admired it, I had 'loved' it. And then, too, I have always 'loved' the beauty and freshness of the natural surroundings where I had been brought up. This definition of 'love' became the mate, in my memory and my present imaginings, that gave impetus to the creation of the poem. So, actual physical surroundings, the presence of, and the actual depletion of, the examining ego, and another impetus from which to approach the experience.

At this stage what I have is lines, notes, notions of what I am searching for. There is, then, whether one wishes to admit it or not, the question of audience. We have long ago poured a great deal of icy water on Shelley's 'poets are the unacknowledged legislators of the world' so that we do not expect poetry to 'make anything happen'. Yet it seems to me that the greatest poetry down the centuries has still aspired to communicate, to reach some audience instead of lying in a drawer at home, or in a glass case in some collector's library, or being discussed in a lecture theatre by a small group of over-bright students. In our time there is a great deal of poetry that approaches the nihilism attendant on the loss of faith in any myth, including the Christian one, and some of that poetry, in its effort to touch on some general human and shared perception, touches on the incommunicable in an almost incommunicable way: I think of poets like John Ashbery. Yet under this abstraction there still lies the will to communicate, however difficult, even impossible, that aim seems to be. Poetry readings are widely common in our age and often take the place of the bookshop that hesitates to stock any serious poetry; hence the need to communicate with an audience grows stronger; nobody wants to sit in wholly bemused silence before an uncommunicative speaker. And the greatest sin of all is a wilful obscurity, an I'm-superior-to-all-of-you kind of stance that does great damage to the notion of real poetry.

It is in the formal and metaphorical bases of a poem, I believe, that the deepest communication will occur, not necessarily on the surface of the poem that touches on the poet's individual experience. It is here that a poem moves 'beyond reason' into the richer area of complete being. Form, imagery, rhythm, even line-endings in 'free verse', all of these play a vital role, giving the language of the poem its urgency and its levels of communication. For it is true that a poem communicates on several levels, and the first one is simple comprehension, essential to a living audience. Yet only in the final labours of drafting the poem do these considerations take centre stage. Faithfulness to the rag-and-bone shop of the original experience, along with integrity in the view of a life's foibles and directions, it is this that will bring the poem to a head. In the case of my own poem it began with a simple note and I wrote: 'The hare has come from somewhere onto the new-mown lawn and danced and leapt for the joy of living.' I took up that notion of joy in living and wrote: 'if the mind could settle to such quietness and accept the impetus to dance ...' And something began to settle in my being. Though not yet on the page. All these days, too, I am pondering the manifold violence, the wars in Iraq, Darfur, The Lebanon, Palestine ... and the notion of the abolition of war suddenly clicked into focus with the memory of the hare. I wrote, hopelessly! 'to raise a wall of poetry against their guns' and then, I think out of the simple line I next wrote 'I have fallen in love again with the earth', I found I could put myself in the hare's place and see the world through that great round eye. The poem began. The title was obvious at once: 'The Eye of the Hare', that original 'the' to be later dissolved. It went, though loosely written in lines of breathing-length: 'I saw a hare, amongst the grasses and the vetch,/ all attention; I saw the ears, like watch-towers,/ I knew the power of the hind legs; I remembered father and/ concentrate, he said, love the enemy, focus/ on the shoulder-muscles where the bullet bites;/ do not jerk on the trigger. I practised/ with a saucepan lid at the meadow's end,/ by the hedge, and became expert, shooting a hole/ eye-perfect through it. But the more attention/ I paid to the hare the more I began to relish its view/ of the world, its greenness under sunlight,/ how it relishes the fresh fruits of the grasses,/ and I turned away from violence, and felt absolved.'

At this stage there begins a great pleasure, that of finding the real poem amidst the throwings. I search first for the instinctive image-pattern that may be there and find a double one, that of loving what one sees, and that of turning away and escaping from trouble. A mental note to draw out the fullness of both of these, followed by a search for a line that feels perfect in the context of the whole and I found 'I saw the ears, like watch-towers, and I knew ...' and this gave me a feel and a rhythm. I shaped the other lines around these. The division into couplets happened easily when I noticed the first four lines, with breaks after the second and fourth. And I shaped the other lines into couplets, too. The search for words becomes instinctual at this stage, when one allows the music of other words to dictate: such as that line 'a green world (giving me the sure long eee sound) easy under sunlight, (giving me the music of sss) of sweet sorrel and sacred herbs. . .'

Eye of the Hare
There! amongst lean-to grasses and trailing vetch
see her? – vagrant, free-range and alert;

I saw the eager watch-tower of the ears, I knew
the power of legs that would fling her into flight;

concentrate, he said, and focus: you must love
the soft-flesh shoulder-muscles where the bullet bites,

caress – and do not jerk – the trigger: be all-embracing, be
delicate. I had no difficulty with the saucepan lid

down at the end of the meadow, lifted, for practice,
against the rhododendron hedge, I could sight

its smug self-satisfaction and shoot a hole
pea-perfect and clean through. Attention to the hare

left me perplexed for I, too, relish the vision
I imaged in its round dark eye, of a green world

easy under sunlight, of sweet sorrel and sacred herbs –
and I turned away, embarrassed, and absolved.

This is a poem springing from my absolute love of nature
and my horror of violence. It stands among my other poems
with a certain personal relish, in that here God does not 'intrude'. The word 'mystical' has been used of my work and I do
not accept it, it is a word greatly abused and often simply refers
to just such a love of nature. It also suggests a certain mystery
and abstraction from the common crowd and this I utterly reject.
For me the true meaning of the word resides in the notion of a
special contact with the transcendent, a mystic being one who
revels in the direct experience of his or her God. And as my
perennial search is for a poetry that clarifies belief and thereby
gives a real meaning to my own existence, most of the time that
God does 'intrude'. In the poem quoted the only concession
made to that faith is the final word 'absolved'. I also believe that
a poem may well contain within itself the principle of its own
contradiction, by which I mean that a poem does not give answers to life's questions; it asks the question and may perhaps
be in itself an answer. But because it is not a wholly autonomous
life-view in itself, then the leaving of a question or an unease
may well form part of its poetic truth; in the case of the poem
quoted, the word 'embarrassed' places me in just such a position.

The Bestial Floor
Poetry in an Age of Violence

George Herbert's major lyric and mini-drama, 'Love', contains the bones of what human living, faced with a loving and personal God, is about: the movement from guilt to acceptance of weakness, the human struggle to see God, or Christ, or Love, as overwhelmingly kind and generous.

Love

Love bade me welcome, yet my soul drew back,
  Guilty of dust and sin.
But quick-eyed Love, observing me grow slack
  From my first entrance in,
Drew nearer to me, sweetly questioning,
  If I lacked anything.

A guest, I answered, worthy to be here.
  Love said, You shall be he.
I the unkind, ungrateful? Ah my dear,
  I cannot look on thee.
Love took my hand, and smiling did reply,
  Who made the eyes but I?

Truth Lord, but I have marred them: let my shame
  Go where it doth deserve.
And know you not, says Love, who bore the blame?
  My dear, then I will serve.
You must sit down, says Love, and taste my meat:
  So I did sit and eat.

There is a process of arguing and of reasoning, of demur and cajolement, going on in the poem, between 'Love', or God, and the soul. Here is the rational Christ, the offering of love, the urging of whole-hearted acceptance as a reasonable response though it is a kindness freely offered. The first lines of the gospel of John read: 'In the beginning was the word, and the word was with God and the word was God'; we are faced with, among the multitude of other magnificent notions, Christ as the spoken word that gives form to God, Christ as reason.

In his lecture (so summarily hijacked over one phrase in it) given by Pope Benedict XVI in September 2006, in the University of Regensburg, we are presented with humanity as a unified whole and therefore we 'work on the basis of a single rationality with all its dimensions'. In other words, there is not one reasoning for Irish people and another reasoning for Swedes, Americans and Lebanese. Our relationship with a reasonable God must exist on a level of common reasoning. The Pope was quoting a Byzantine Emperor who argued that any use of violence to spread faith is self-defeating, faith being a free gift of God, unenforceable. The aim of the first part of his talk was to show that violence is against the rational nature of God, of our own souls and of faith freely given.

There is a movement corollary to this, that of mystical experience. This is equivalent to experience of the source of faith itself. An analysis of the great poets of this experience, such as Teresa of Avila, John of the Cross, William Blake, insists that the experience of the source is one that arrives in full and complete freedom as a gift perfect in itself, suggesting, too, that truly great poetry begins rather as a listening than a speaking, in being receptive to 'the fine delight that fathers thought'. Benedict's insistence on the evils of 'voluntarism', the view that urges that God is not amenable to human reason, that the transcendence of God must be maintained and that knowledge of him is forever unattainable, leads him to urge more strongly that God is Logos, knowledge and reason. This is redeemed, however, by his quoting Paul in Ephesians that God is love, that love transcends knowledge, 'perceiving more than thought alone'. If this is so, he argues, yet this love remains a love of the God who is Logos.

When it comes to poetry, it must not be forgotten that the receptivity required of the poet can move language, image, rhythm etc all together into the area of the transcendent. The listening of the poet reaches, in great poetry, beyond reason and touches on the area of love. All this is exemplified in the poem by Robert Southwell, 'A Child My Choice', that Jesuit p↖ hanged in 1592 under the persecutions of Catholics during Elizabeth's reign. The poem holds in thought the notion that faith is a gift, that it is a gift received by deliberate choice, and that it is given freely by a loving God and is to be answered by a freely returned love. The delight Southwell takes in the innocence of the Christ as a new-born Child, an innocence that will inevitably lead to suffering and death in this world, gives the poem its original urge and potency: The short, carefully modulated phrases of that poem, capture the sense of argument and reason in building up to the final prayers of the poem. This is no emotional outburst, it is a thoughtful and clarifying outline of faith, finding, in contradiction, truths and, in difficulties, certainty. It is a poem that in no way diminishes Pope Benedict's call for reason and faith together, but it adds so much more, moving, the way love moves, into the gloriously transcendent.

The perceived and argued harmony between faith and reason Benedict names as the source and sustenance for centuries of European culture. In spite of wars, persecutions, witch-hunts, the slaughter of heretics, the intrinsic acceptance of this harmony lasted until comparatively recent times. It is the basis of a great deal of poetry written down those years, as, for instance, this 'Holy Sonnet' by John Donne:

Since she whom I loved hath paid her last debt
To Nature, and to hers, and my good is dead,
And her Soule early into heaven ravished,
Wholly on heavenly things my mind is set.
Here the admiring her my mind did whet
To seek thee God; so streams do show their head;
But though I have found thee, and thou my thirst hast fed,
A holy thirsty dropsy melts me yet.
But why should I beg more Love, when as thou
Dost woo my soul for hers; offering all thing:
And dost not only fear lest I allow
My Love to Saints and Angels things divine,
But in thy tender jealousy dost doubt
Lest the World, Flesh, yea Devil put thee out.

The reasoning: *since, so, but though, but why* ... moves with the

, with the consciousness of general acceptance
, even though the playful Donne is not far from
ion, the tenets of the Christian faith, moved on a
ilt-for-two until the rush of the earth in its courses caught up and overtook. Pope Benedict goes on to examine
the reasons why this harmony fell asunder. Firstly, the principle
of *sola scriptura*, faith only as it is found in the biblical Word,
found space in the Reformation in the sixteenth century, and in
the works of Immanuel Kant who decided to set thinking aside
to make room for faith, denying reason access to belief; secondly, the reduction throughout the nineteenth century of the richness of faith to the mere moral message of Christianity. Here the
Pope speaks of the historical-critical exegesis of the New
Testament, faith shrinking to the space of empirically verifiable
facts and provable truths. Technology bumps up against faith,
leaving a damaged vehicle behind. The whole question of God,
in scientifically verifiable insistence, is a non-question. And all
the adjuncts of faith, man's place and purpose in a scheme of
things, must also be relegated to the recycling bin. The major
loss in this approach is the linking of ethics to religion, 'ethics
and religion lose their power to create a community and fall
prey to arbitrariness'. This, for me, represents a most central and
serious point and offers, perhaps, a clue to the hoped-for solution to society's problems.

Pope Benedict further points to the de-Hellenisation of
Christianity, the claiming of the right to 'return to the simple
message of the New Testament prior to that inculturation, in
order to inculturate it anew in their own particular milieu'. He
sees that as a false premise, the New Testament having been
written in Greek and necessarily being impregnated essentially
by Greek culture.

The conclusion to all of this? Pope Benedict calls for a new re-
coupling of faith and reason in our time. 'All that is great in
modernity must be acknowledged unreservedly.' Yet there are
great dangers for the world in many of these advances and only
a full gathering together of faith and reason and the vast hori-
zons that this would open up, gives hope for the future. Only in
this way will a contemporary dialogue between faiths throughout the world become possible. 'A reason which is deaf to the

divine and which relegates religion into the realm of subcultures, is incapable of a dialogue of cultures.'

What this comes down to appears to me to be of vital importance for our era. It is in no way a call to permeate society's institutions, nor its political or civil offices, with theology. Rather it is a call for *universitas*, for the widest possible conversation among all of humanity, for a dialogue to promote a world of peace and justice, a world of love, based on a complementary relationship between faith and reason. It is faith – God, Christ, love – calling to the soul to accept an overwhelmingly generous gift. If faith has become, through the weight of secularist ideology, excluded from basic rational inquiry, then religion has been forced into the private arena. Dialogue, rational dialogue, is required. We cannot simply deplore those who appear on our media with their catch-cries, their unreasoned and highly emotive jingles, about the rules and regulations emanating from religious ur-books, nor can we deplore or ignore those who use television programmes for the promotion of their extreme religious views. Nor can we be complacent with our Christianity and simply expect it to move people by falling back on its often-rehearsed tenets. As well as a dialogue between reason and faiths, we need an imaginative impulse based both on reason and faiths, that will move beyond rational discussion into the area where faith surely begins. I am reminded of William Butler Yeats's great poem that calls for just such an imaginative re-exploration of the Christian myth:

The Magi
Now as at all times I can see in the mind's eye,
In their stiff, painted clothes, the pale unsatisfied ones
Appear and disappear in the blue depth of the sky
With all their ancient faces like rain-beaten stones,
And all their helms of silver hovering side by side,
And all their eyes still fixed, hoping to find once more,
Being by Calvary's turbulence unsatisfied,
The uncontrollable mystery on the bestial floor.

This is what we seek to penetrate, this 'uncontrollable mystery on the bestial floor', this birth of something into our world far beyond our normal ken, allied to the deepest, even the darkest, movements of our being. And it is my belief that only art, in its most perfect presentations, can penetrate into this area and come back laden with truths that remain mysteries, though mysteries that are wholly life-giving. It has been argued that the source of poetic imagination remains the same, whether we are speaking of Teresa of Avila or George Herbert; the experience adumbrated in each poem is unique yet at the centre of every poem is a moment of illumination, that moment when irreconcilables become reconciled. The 'flash upon the inward eye' and the 'fire burning in the heart' arise out of moments of recognition when the 'house is at rest'. Perhaps it is the closeness to the source and the wholehearted giving to that source that differentiates the poetry of the mystic from that of the other poet, but it must be remembered that a poem does not go off into a wholly foolish rant of its own but is a continuity of the experience of real life and the reasoning and awareness of the individual that gives the work its inner dynamism and its power. A poem does not hang in a void; it is that further expedition out of the known world into the unknown.

As I have touched upon Yeats, I want to mention W. H. Auden and his wonderfully apt poem 'In Memory of W B Yeats'; part of it is as follows:

You were silly like us; your gift survived it all:
The parish of rich women, physical decay,
Yourself. Mad Ireland hurt you into poetry.
Now Ireland has her madness and her weather still,
For poetry makes nothing happen: it survives
In the valley of its making where executives
Would never want to tamper, flows on south
From ranches of isolation and the busy griefs,
Raw towns that we believe and die in; it survives,
A way of happening, a mouth.

'Poetry makes nothing happen'; of course not, in the immediate sense, but Auden goes on to say that it is the executive classes who will display no care for poetry but that it survives, 'a way of happening, a mouth'. It seems to me to be untrue to Auden merely to quote that 'poetry makes nothing happen', but that it is a way of happening in itself, and a mouth that opens on the world and speaks, and goes on speaking. And Yeats, of course, was anxious throughout his life about the effects of his own work; did his poetry, in fact, make something happen? Even in 1938, shortly before his death, in a poem called 'The Man and the Echo', he was interrogating himself:

> All that I have said and done,
> Now that I am old and ill,
> Turns into a question till
> I lie awake night after night
> And never get the answers right.
> Did that play of mine send out
> Certain men the English shot?

The play he refers to was 'Cathleen ni Houlihan', produced in 1902; its reception was ecstatic and its revolutionary message well received. How much influence, if any, did the work have on the people who 'went out' at Easter 1916 to establish, by force, an Irish Republic? Of itself it had, perhaps, little effect, but its deeply emotive words and imagery touched strongly on a mood growing in the country, a sense of willing sacrifice and a surge of almost mystical fervour, ably abetted by poetry. The Old Woman of the play is Ireland, who complains of the theft of 'My four beautiful green fields'. She calls for men to help her get them back: 'It is a hard service they take that help me. Many that are red-cheeked now will be pale-cheeked; many that have been free to walk the hills and the bogs and the rushes will be sent to walk hard streets in far countries; many a good plan will be broken; many that have gathered money will not stay to spend it; many a child will be born and there will be no father at its christening to give it a name. They that have red cheeks will have pale cheeks for my sake, and for all that, they will think they are well paid.' The call is to self-sacrifice. It became a bloody self-sacrifice some years later.

The Rebellion of 1916 occurred at a time when it was least expected. England was at war, but a great many of the Irish wished to help in England's war, hoping England would then keep faith with her offering of Home Rule. Yeats himself admitted that the work of earlier poets had greatly influenced him, poets like Davis, Mangan, Ferguson. No doubt their poetry moved through the minds of many Irish still uncertain of England's keeping faith. Even the work of the immensely popular Thomas Moore sang in the minds of the people:

Oh! where's the slave so lowly,
Condemn'd to chains unholy,
  Who, could he burst
  His bonds at first,
Would pine beneath them slowly?
What soul, whose wrongs degrade it,
Would wait till time decay'd it,
  When thus its wing
  At once may spring
To the throne of him who made it?
  Farewell, Erin! farewell all,
  Who live to weep our fall!

Behind the rising of 1916 was the continual call to fight for freedom, and behind that was the renewal of interest in Ireland's mythic and romantic past. James Clarence Mangan's poem 'Dark Rosaleen' has still a strange power to fire the blood; several more poems stir the patriotic soul, 'O'Hussey's Ode to the Maguire' among them. I remember my father going about the house reciting Mangan's 'Woman of Three Cows'. The poetry of Samuel Ferguson digs deep into Irish mythology and his 'Lament for Thomas Davis' speaks a plain language couched in a rousing musical lyricism:

Oh, brave young men, my love, my pride, my promise,
  'Tis on you my hopes are set,
In manliness, in kindliness, in justice,
  To make Erin a nation yet,
Self-respecting, self-relying, self-advancing,
  In union or in severance, free and strong –
And if God grant this, then, under God, to Thomas Davis
  Let the greater praise belong.

And that same Thomas Davis perhaps offered the most rousing song of all with his poem 'A Nation Once Again'. Here, too, a certain obeisance is offered to God in the struggle, as well as in Ferguson's poem in lament. For Davis, speaking of hope, wrote:

It whispered, too, that 'freedom's ark
  And service high and holy,
Would be profaned by feelings dark,
  And passions vain or lowly;
For freedom comes from God's right hand,
  And needs a godly train;
And righteous men must make our land
  A Nation once again'.

Can there be any doubt, then, that poetry, faith, a form of mystical romanticism, stirred in the 'rebels' of the Irish Rising? Joseph Mary Plunkett suffered ill-health all his short life, knowing the fevers of the highs and lows that tuberculosis brings. Mixed with this he knew a strong sense of the universe as displaying in its physical being the very Being of God, along with a powerfully moving love affair, the friendship with another poet involved in the Rising, and a strongly mystical urge that led him to absorption in the works of St John of the Cross, St Teresa of Avila and others, led him to such lines as these:

Thy love is a sword
In the heart of slaughter,
Thy love is a word
Of the high-king's daughter,
A song that is sung
In a mystic tongue,
A fountain sprung
From the Living Water ...

For thy love is a sign
In the Book of Wonder,
A mark divine
On the seals of thunder
That the Spirit's light
And the Water's might
And the Blood red-bright
Have witnessed under.

Plunkett helped Edward Martyn and Thomas MacDonagh to found the Irish Theatre in 1914. Thomas MacDonagh, another signatory of the Proclamation of Irish Independence, and also executed for his part in the rising, had been a close friend of

Plunkett's and had taken a leading part in the build-up to the events of Easter 1916. He, too, was an accomplished poet. He had a love of things Gaelic and joined Patrick Pearse as assistant Headmaster in St Enda's school, a school where Pearse hoped to fire a new generation with love for all things Gaelic, including the language. Here is one of MacDonagh's poems:

On A Poet Patriot
His songs were a little phrase
    Of eternal song,
Drowned in the harping of lays
    More loud and long.

His deed was a single word,
    Called out alone
In a night when no echo stirred
    To laughter or moan.

But his songs new souls shall thrill,
    The loud harps dumb,
And his deed the echoes fill
    When the dawn is come.

If the modesty of the poem, in length, form and contents, is a genuine modesty, the impulse behind the work is in no way modest; the calling up of the harps suggests a long tradition of Irish poetry, song and rebellion, and the coming of the 'dawn' that will remember this modest song, is emotive in the extreme.

Patrick Pearse, in the last month of 1915, wrote of the war in Europe: 'The last sixteen months have been the most glorious in the history of Europe. Heroism has come back to the earth, the people themselves have gone into battle because to each the old voice that speaks out of the soil of a nation has spoken anew. Belgium defending her soil is heroic, and so is Turkey fighting with her back to Constantinople. The old heart of the earth needed to be warmed with the red wine of the battlefields. Such august homage was never before offered to God as this, the homage of millions of lives given gladly for love of country. War is a terrible thing and this is the most terrible of wars, but this war is not more terrible than the evils which it will end or help to end.' So, war that will end evil: we know how that worked. So, too, the warming of the fields with sacrificial blood and, in the same breath, the offering of this blood becomes a homage to God.

My own mother, rest her soul, loved the words of Pearse's poem 'The Rebel' and saw herself, at a safe distance from the actuality of what she spoke aloud, as a fine patriot. And sometimes she would make me say another of Pearse's poems which I had learned, for her, by heart; she would stand me up before her, half-close her eyes and, no doubt, feel part of that strange thing that was, in those years, regarded as patriotism.

The Mother
I do not grudge them: Lord, I do not grudge
  My two strong sons that I have seen go out
  To break their strength and die, they and a few,
  In bloody protest for a glorious thing,
  They shall be spoken of among their people,
  The generations shall remember them,
  And call them blessed;
  But I will speak their names to my own heart
  In the long nights;
  The little names that were familiar once
  Round my dead hearth.
  Lord, thou art hard on mothers:
  We suffer in their coming and their going;
  And tho' I grudge them not, I weary, weary
  Of the long sorrow – And yet I have my joy:
  My sons were faithful, and they fought.

Nineteen sixteen and the Rising, Easter Sunday being chosen quite deliberately as the starting point, was a hopeless venture from the start, so many of the imaginatively-schemed preparations simply failing to come about. It was an event starred about by poetry and romantic ideals of self-sacrifice, liberty and by rhetorical language. It was an event that ended, inevitably, in tragedy and bloody sacrifices, as well as England's error of trying to fight that ephemeral effort by institutional violence. For decades, and perhaps even still today, the Easter Rising rings deeply emotional bells in the souls of the people and the names of the poet-heroes have been used and misused down all the years. Perhaps the poetry did not make anything happen, but it certainly kept the whole thing alive and before the minds of people several generations afterwards.

The famous proclamation declaring an Irish Republic begins: 'Irishmen and Irishwomen: in the name of God and the dead generations from which she receives her old tradition of nationhood, Ireland, through us, summons her children to her flag and strikes for her freedom.' It later states that the Provisional Government 'will administer the civil and military affairs of the Irish Republic under the protection of the Most High God, Whose blessing we invoke upon our arms ...' making it clear, of course, that Ireland and the Catholic faith were closely allied and that there is such a thing as the 'just war', aided and abetted by God himself. And were my parents wrong, then, in seeing 'the struggle' as a necessary work, in seeing war and uprisings and violence as a necessary part of our human living?

St Augustine was the one to originate the 'just war' theory: 'The natural order conducive to peace among mortals demands that the power to declare and counsel war should be in the hands of those who hold the supreme authority.' And 'A just war is wont to be described as one that avenges wrongs, when a nation or state has to be punished, for refusing to make amends for the wrongs inflicted by its subjects, or to restore what it has seized unjustly.' The causes for going to war were vital: 'We do not seek peace in order to be at war, but we go to war that we may have peace. Be peaceful, therefore, in warring, so that you may vanquish those whom you war against, and bring them to the prosperity of peace.' St Thomas Aquinas agreed, pointing out conditions: on whose authority, just cause and rightful intention. Later theologians added that the war must be fought as a last resort and in a proper manner (without killing the innocent). There are direct combatants and indirect combatants, (helpers, in any way, of the combatants) and then there are non-combatants. The killing or wounding of enemy combatants falls under the natural law idea of self-defence. The indirect killing of non-combatants or neutrals is permissible according to the principle of double effect. But such killing must be unintentional and unavoidable. Direct killing of such people is murder, that is, when it is intentional and avoidable.

St Augustine's argument was from the natural order of peace, to the right of rulers to declare war to maintain that peace. St Thomas agrees and stresses the common good of the people as a whole. The church has, down the centuries, even promoted wars such as the Crusades and approved of military orders. Soldiers such as Martin of Tours and Joan of Arc have been declared saints. If an individual can defend himself against unjust aggression, so can the State. Over the centuries, war attained a certain romantic glory; I think of the Hussars of so many Russian tales, of the heroes heading off to war to the cheers and waving handkerchiefs of the relieved multitude; and let me here quote two poems that contributed to this vague and unreal sense of the glory of war. The first is by Alfred Lord Tennyson, and was written during the Crimean War, about 1856, when 247 men out of 637 who charged into battle were killed or wounded: I offer just two stanzas, telling stanzas, however.

The Charge of the Light Brigade
'Forward, the Light Brigade!'
Was there a man dismayed?
Not tho' the soldiers knew
Someone had blundered;
Theirs not to make reply,
Theirs not to reason why,
Theirs but to do and die:
Into the valley of Death
Rode the six hundred.

When can their glory fade?
Oh, the wild charge they made!
All the world wondered.
Honour the charge they made!
Honour the Light Brigade,
Noble Six Hundred!

And then there is the rousing Battle Hymn, still sung in churches all over the world, a fine piece of loudly rhetorical writing allied to a clumping stepping-along rhythm and melody that fires the blood and wears God like a pennant on a spear: written during the American Civil War and published for the first time in 1862: Julia Ward Howe's

Battle Hymn of the Republic
Chorus:
Glory, Glory Hallelujah, Glory, Glory Hallelujah,
Glory, Glory Hallelujah, His truth is marching on.

Mine eyes have seen the glory of the coming of the Lord;
He is trampling out the vintage where grapes of wrath are
    stored;
He hath loosed the fateful lightning of His terrible swift
    sword,
    His truth is marching on. *(Chorus)*

I have seen Him in the watch fires of a hundred circling
    camps;
They have built Him an altar in the evening dews and
    damps;
I can read His righteous sentence by the dim and flaring
    lamps,
    His day is marching on. *(Chorus)*

He has founded forth the trumpet that shall never call re-
    treat;
He is sifting out the hearts of men before His Judgement Seat
Oh! Be swift, my soul, to answer Him, be jubilant, my feet!
    Our God is marching on. *(Chorus)*

In the beauty of the lilies Christ was born across the sea,
With a glory in his bosom that transfigures you and me;
As he died to make men holy, let us die to make men free,
    While God is marching on. *(Chorus)*

To labour the point a moment, let me repeat a line from each of these two poems: 'Theirs not to reason why, Theirs but to do or die': this blind acceptance of foolish valour was seen as virtue; and 'As he died to make men holy, let us die to make men free', links the death of Christ with death of soldiers in war. If the line has been changed now to 'let us live to make men free', it does not sit right with the original inspiration.

I have always felt that war is unacceptable in Christian terms; the most simple and basic Christian values, love of God and love of one's neighbour, preclude it. And then, of course, the generalities and imponderables of the just war theory are inapplicable in actual situations. It goes without saying that the so-called and inevitable 'collateral damage' destroys the notion that non-combatants must not be injured. Witness Vietnam, witness the Twin Towers, witness Iraq. And here it appears to me is the kernel: Christ established a new law, the love of one's enemies. We move at once into a realm beyond reason, we move into an area in which those without belief in Christ simply cannot be comfortable, we begin to cherish and forgive instead of hating and seeking revenge. It was Christ's clear rejection of physical force and any notion of revenge that brought him to Calvary and his death. St Augustine failed to equate Christian love with his sense of a just war; he skipped over the difficulty. And it does not appear that St Thomas was able to draw a distinction between war in the abstract and war in its horrible reality. During the era of Constantine, the church developed its just war theory as it became more and more identified with the Roman conquests.

Poetry finds it difficult to approach the vastness and abstraction of the general notion of war, but poetry succeeds powerfully in focusing on details that bring home the personal tragedies involved. If Julia Ward Howe wrote her Battle Hymn in 1861, and Tennyson lauded the Light Brigade in 1857, Walt Whitman wrote his anti-war poem in the decade between 1860-70:

Come up From the Fields, Father
Come up from the fields father, here's a letter from our Pete,
And come to the front door mother, here's a letter from thy
    dear son.
Lo, 'tis autumn,
Lo, where the trees, deeper green, yellower and redder,
Cool and sweeten Ohio's villages with leaves fluttering in the
    moderate wind,

Where apples ripe in the orchards hang and grapes on the
    trellis'd vines,
(Smell you the smell of the grapes on the vines?
Smell you the buckwheat where the bees were lately
    buzzing?)
Above all, lo, the sky so calm, so transparent after the rain,
    and with wondrous clouds,
Below too, all calm, all vital and beautiful, and the farm
    prospers well.
Down in the fields all prospers well,
But now from the fields come father, come at the daughter's
    call.
And come to the entry mother, to the front door come right
    away.

Fast as she can she hurries, something ominous, her steps
    trembling,
She does not tarry to smooth her hair nor adjust her cap.
Open the envelope quickly,
O this is not our son's writing, yet his name is sign'd,
O a strange hand writes for our dear son, O stricken mother's
    soul!
All swims before her eyes, flashes with black, she catches the
    main words only,
Sentences broken, gunshot wound in the breast, cavalry
    skirmish, taken to hospital,
At present low, but will soon be better.

Ah now the single figure to me,
Amid all teeming and wealthy Ohio with all its cities and
    farms,
Sickly white in the face and dull in the head, very faint,
By the jamb of a door leans.

Grieve not so, dear mother, (the just-grown daughter speaks
    through her sobs,
The little sisters huddle around speechless and dismay'd,)
See, dearest mother, the letter says Pete will soon be better.
Alas poor boy, he will never be better, (nor may-be needs to
    be better, that brave and simple soul,

While they stand at home at the door he is dead already,
The only son is dead.

But the mother needs to be better,
She with thin form presently drest in black,
By day her meals untouch'd, then at night fitfully sleeping,
    often waking,
In the midnight waking, weeping, longing with one deep
    longing,
O that she might withdraw unnoticed, silent from life escape
    and withdraw,
To follow, to seek, to be with her dear dead son.

And if I may intrude my own voice as a poet, I want to offer a piece written during the Israeli destruction of the Lebanon; illustrating what I believe is one of the strengths of poetry, that focuses on a fact or event in its intimate detail and from that abstracts, in the way a poem can, to an emotional, rational and supra-rational grappling with the world:

Cedar
In what year of war did Jehovah
abandon them? A man
riding a Yamaha XS 400 model 1982
has taken his two daughters from the ruins of their house,
has left the battered bodies of his wife and mother
among the rubble and tries to flee
across the baked, beloved fields of Lebanon;
into a hole somewhere, please God, the two
children, terrified, big eyes filled with tears, fingers
gripping hard but the bike will scarcely move, it sputters,
    skids, one
child before him, one behind, both tied to him
with light-blue clothes-line round their waists, the bike
slithers out into the day and turns, please
God, north on a cratered road, the sky itself so beautiful, such
an immaculate creation, and the children's voices wail
louder than the stop-go reluctant coughing of the bike till an
Israeli F16, inaudible, well-nigh invisible, so high

above, oh God please God, draws
a gash of fumes across the sky
and father, daughters, bike explode into shards
of flesh and chrome and are lost
in the bleak inheritance of the Old Testament
while only the back wheel of the bike
a Yamaha XS 400 model 1982
spins in uproarious speed and will
not stop, will not
stop

The poetry that came from the first and second world wars, and from the conflicts in countries suffering under communism, all of these are well known. The horrors of these wars are well-documented in poetry. But it is the utter and indiscriminate havoc of contemporary war instruments that underlines the whole obscenity of war. The Second Vatican Council allowed for 'the right of a nation to defend itself by a discriminate and pro-portionate use of force as a last resort'. Proportionality is added as an issue. When is a so-called defensive war legitimate? Israel, for example, and the Bush Administration's designation of North Korea, Iran and Syria as an Axis of Evil ... claim they are working to defend their lives and territories, but again the 'col-lateral damage' is significant, especially in Israel's case where the lives of women and children are continually being de-stroyed. In Iraq the ongoing destruction of civilians on every side is a scandal and a disgrace to humanity, as well, of course, as being a desperate tragedy. The contemporary war-cry of de-fensive war and pre-emptive strike is no more than an excuse for aggression and is wholly unacceptable, in reason, or in Christian terms; it is an affront to God and an affront to human beings. Further, the almost unlimited strength of contemporary air power dictates that even more ethical restraints be applied to air force. The targeting of civilian infrastructure will affect ordinary citizens for years after the end of hostilities and amounts to war on non-combatants. We have witnessed Hiroshima and Nagasaki, as well as Dresden and Baghdad; ethical standards of propor-tionality must be re-examined. The utter savagery of today's warfare contradicts everything human love could ever believe in. Gerard Smyth captures civilian dismay in a fine poem in which the irony of the Jewish Old Testament figure of Rachel suffers the violence of Israeli war-mongering in The Lebanon:

War Widow
The price of land is blood, she says.
The woman in black headdress
animated by the Furies
on the ten o'clock news
live from the scene, in the country of cedars.

Shaking her fist, demanding justice
she stands in the rubble of the latest blitz,
in the tatters of a murderous time.

She is the mistress of unstoppable words.
Another Rachel crying to the Lord
who must, wherever He is, feel the voltage
of her declaration that the army exacting
annihilation has not depleted her fortitude,
cannot destroy her courage.

We must be aware of the success of a few non-violent revolutions in our time, but the list of violent conflicts far outweighs them. Reason admits that when sustained attempts at non-violent action fail to protect the innocent against real injustice, then legitimate political authorities are permitted as a last resort to employ limited force to rescue the innocent and establish justice. Poetry and the arts might go further and outlaw, for the sake of a full humanity graced by Christian love, all forms of violent action or reaction. But how, how might this be possible? And here I begin to touch on the wildest dream, the most foolish hope, the most sacred imaginative pulse of our living, that a commitment to resist evil and injustice, violence and hatred, by means of an active labour towards the emphasis of what is true, beautiful and humanly meaningful in our life be developed on a much wider basis. I speak of creating an atmosphere throughout the world where violence of any kind becomes as unacceptable in every community as slavery now is, or child pornography, or rape. A commitment to art forms that develop and insist on the beauty of the world in which we live and which we can better, is not an impossible thing. Foolish it may seem in this age to suggest it; but Christ chose the foolish and the poor to confound the wise and wealthy. Let the world of reason be confounded by the world of imagination, no, not confounded, let it be imbued with the values of the artistic imagination.

The warrior hero is really the Christ, and this was already signalled in an Anglo-Saxon poem of the 8th century, attributed to Cynewulf. In 'The Dream of the Rood', Christ climbing onto the Cross for the good of humankind becomes the great saving, rescuing hero; here are a few lines from that poem in which it is the Cross itself that speaks:

> I saw
> the Ruler of mankind rush with real courage to climb
> on me and I did not dare (my Lord had warned!)
>
> bend down or break, though I saw the broad
> surface of earth shiver. How simple – the Lord knows –
> to smite His enemies! but firm and stout I stood
>
> unmoving. The hero stripped, though He was God
>   Almighty!
> robust and resolute, mounting onto the gallows
> spirited, in the sight of many, to redeem mankind.
>
> I wavered while the warrior embraced me, clasped me
> and I did not dare bend down towards the ground,
> fall on the earth's surface, I must stand fast.

If this is the ultimate in non-violent alternatives then it can be seen as the duty of national governments and organisations to give the arts, and I speak specifically of poetry, the serious consideration that they demand. Here are words of Thomas Merton, a prayer that may be added to our hopes: 'Help us to be masters of the weapons that threaten to master us. Help us to use science for peace and plenty, not for war and destruction. Show us how to use atomic power to bless our children's children, not to blight them. Save us from the compulsion to follow our adversaries in all that we most hate, confirming them in their hatred and suspicion of us. Resolve our inner contradictions, which now grow beyond belief and beyond bearing. They are at once a torment and a blessing; for if you had not left us the light of conscience, we would not have to endure them. Teach us to be long-suffering in anguish and insecurity, teach us to wait and trust. Grant light, grant strength and patience to all who work for peace ... grant us prudence in proportion to our power, wisdom in proportion to our science, humaneness in proportion to our wealth and might. And bless our earnest will to help all races and peoples to travel, in friendship with us, along the road to justice, liberty and lasting peace.'

All of this, I believe, sits quite kindly with Pope Benedict's reason underscored by faith. Everything calls conclusively for a total abolition of war. The total abolition of war. If this goes beyond what reason apprehends, it is the point where poetry enters. I would see a world saturated with the imaginative and Christian values of poetry and the arts, each move towards war in such a context being seen for what it is, a crime.

And so, to poetry. If a simple notion of balance be introduced, with evil and violence weighing down one side, then it is up to poetry to be added to the other side, and this poetry to be always better and stronger. If in 1916 an atmosphere, a mood was created with the help of poetry, so too in our time we can begin to create an atmosphere, an awareness where the smallest things and events of our everyday lives can be seen in the light of eternity. If our daily lives, by the grace of God, do not come in contact with evil and war, yet we can take part in such a movement, by seeing the small things as glorious in the light of poetry. Here is a poem exemplifying what I mean; it is by Eva Bourke:

> *I woke to Svatoslav Richter*
> I woke to Svatoslav Richter playing Bach:
> the English Suite VI.
> The early morning spilled over
> the city's cornices and sills.
>
> It was October, still mild
> with the smell of vegetal decay;
> trees in the street were turning colour,
> golden, russet, flaming-red,

passers-by chatted and laughed
below my window.
Bach was on the air, each note rose
out of the black body

of the radio, weightless, clear
and unerring on its way.
In the terraced gardens above the city
evil was unheard of,

fear and hate stood still and listened,
pain and despair halted
their progress through hospital wards
and listened.

The left hand knew precisely
where the right was going and vice versa,
justice was justice,
truth and love were one,

soul rested against soul
beneath the wild cataracts.

I move back to the poem of George Herbert's I quoted at the beginning, about God's invitation to the hesitant, reasonable soul to ditch reason and to give itself wholly to the overwhelming love of God. In response to that poem I have written one of my own, a response, too, to the call for the total abolition of war. I call it

The Poem of the Goldfinch
Write, came the persistent whisperings, a poem
on the mendacities of war. So I found shade
under the humming eucalyptus, and sat,
patienting. Thistle-seeds blew about on a soft breeze,
a brown-gold butterfly was shivering on a fallen
ripe-flesh plum. Write your dream, said Love, of the total
abolition of war. Vivaldi, I wrote, the four
seasons. Silence, a while, save for the goldfinch
swittering in the higher branches, sweet, they sounded,
sweet-wit, wit-wit, wit-sweet. I breathed
scarcely, listening. Love bade me write but my hand

held over the paper; tell them you, I said,
they will not hear me. A goldfinch swooped,
sifting for seeds; I revelled in its colouring, such
scarlets and yellows, such tawny, a patterning
the creator himself must have envisioned, doodling
that gold-flash and Hopkins-feathered loveliness. Please
write, Love said, though less insistently. Spirit, I answered,
that moved out once on chaos … No, said Love,
and I said Michelangelo, Van Gogh. No, write
for them the poem of the goldfinch and the whole
earth singing, so I set myself down to the task.

Dipped Again in God
Against Walls and Fortresses, for Christ and Poetry

To be a Christian does not mean undergoing a process of learning a set of rules, guidelines, commandments and spending one's life obeying them – thereby reaching the promised land, heaven; or by disobeying them to find oneself thrown into eternal misery. To be a Christian is to continue on a voyage of discovery that ends only at death, for Christ and the mystery of God are unknowable in their wholeness until we enter onto the vision of God. To be a Christian is to dwell in strangeness and magnificence; it is also to dwell, without fear, in the valley of shadow and suffering, and from within the strangeness and suffering it is to relish, all the more and ever more, the ordinary.

To be a Christian is to live justly, without anger or despair, to offer and to accept mercy, to work without expectation in the shadow of a willing God and to express in one's days the word of God that you have been given to translate.

It is when the sense of discovery and growth comes to a halt, when the Christian living congeals like the fat of mutton in a cold pan, that humans come to rely on dogma, holding fast to what they have; it is when the church becomes frozen in its own waters and those waters cease to flow: then the consequences are a holding to what one has against the other, against the stream of Protestantism, against Islam, against, against, against. Luther, for instance, found Christianity congealed under a weight of dogma; he worked for reform, but the Roman Church fought against him; his only hope for purification was to break away. Christianity is not a fortress; it is a plain, and it is an adventure to cross that plain. And the adventure is mirrored in our poetry. Faith, then, is not a sword turned outward; it is a walking stick, a staff, to help us forward; faith must be linked with imagination and have its own jagged edge.

The poet William Butler Yeats spoke wonderfully of the imagination; here is a passage from his essay on *The Philosophy of Shelley's Poetry*: '... if a powerful and benevolent spirit has shaped the destiny of this world, we can better discover that destiny from the words that have gathered up the heart's desire of the world, than from historical records, or from speculation, wherein the heart withers ... I have observed dreams and visions very carefully, and am now certain that the imagination has some way of lighting on the truth that the reason has not, and that its commandments, delivered when the body is still and the reason silent, are the most binding we can ever know.' Armed with such a defence for the workings of poetry, I can approach Christianity from a poet's perspective.

To begin at the beginning, baptism. I would wish to see this sacrament as the blessing on an exciting and indeed an overwhelming journey, an adventure into the wonderful, rather than the cleansing of anything from a clearly sinless soul. As James Alison says in his wonderful book *Undergoing God*: 'Christian worship is predicated on the understanding that there is nothing left to achieve. It has already been achieved, once and for all. The struggle is over; the kingdom has been inaugurated and obtained. I can't get over how difficult it is for us to pause and sit in this for long enough. We are not building ourselves up for something which is going to happen; we are beginning to be swept up into the rejoicing that is emanating out from something which has already happened.' Our baptism, then, is the first step we take, or that is taken on our behalf, on that inward journey of possession, on that circling through life which is a seeking for that which is already found, an adventure towards the purchase of a territory which is already ours.

Sometime in the ninth century an Irish poet wrote on the margins of a manuscript by Sedulius of Liège an epigram in Irish which has been translated and rhymed by Frank O'Connor:

To go to Rome
  Is little profit, endless pain;
The Master that you seek in Rome,
  You find at home, or seek in vain.

The journey has been mapped and treasured by poets over the centuries. That the journey has been an adventure is not always celebrated; often the adventure has been a dangerous and difficult one, a journeying in the hands of a demanding God, a journeying through the coils of earth's traps and loveliness, a journey from the empty tomb, back again to the tomb.

The journey, early in the history of Ireland's poetry, begins naturally enough with an excited questioning. This poem is from about 600 AD, was written in Latin and I offer my translation:

Quis Est Deus?
Who then is God
and where is God,
and where does God come from
and where His dwelling place?

Tell me has He sons and daughters,
this God of yours, has He silver, gold?

Does He live forever,
is He beautiful,
tell me if many people
gave nourishment to His son?

Tell me if His daughters
are beautiful, are they loved
by the world's men?

Is God in heaven
or on earth?
Is He in the ocean,
in the rivers,
in the mountains
or in the valleys?

Please give to us
tidings of Him:
How is He to be seen,
how loved,
and how discovered?

Is He to be found
in old age, or found
in youth?

And while we are at it, St Patrick is reported to have written the most wonderful of prayers, suitable for beginnings, suitable for the start of a journey, suitable for the ongoing pursuit of that journey. It is the armour the soul puts on to get her through life; and its early sense of the soul fighting a battle is yet rich with a sense of the great wonder and beauty of a world rich in the presence of Christ:

I gather strength today
through the invocation of the Trinity;
the Source and Sustenance of our being,
the Name and Nature of the Source
and the Breath that gives it being.

I gather strength today
through the power of Christ's birth and baptism,
through the power of His crucifixion and His burial,
through the power of His resurrection and His ascension,
through the power of His coming on the Final Day.

I gather to myself today
strength in the love of Cherubim,
strength in the obedience of angels
and in the service of archangels,
strength in the hope of resurrection,
in the prayers of patriarchs
and the foretelling of the prophets,
strength in apostles' preaching
and in confessors' faith,
strength in the innocence of virgins
and the actions of prudent men.

I gather strength today
through the great power of heaven,
light of the sun
and radiance of the moon,
strength in the lightning flash
and splendour of the fire,

in the swiftness of the winds
and in the depths of ocean,
stability of the earth
and steadfastness of rock.

I gather to myself today
the strength of God to guide me,
the power of God to uphold me,
wisdom of God to lead me,
the eye of God to watch for me,
ear of God to hear for me,
the word of God to speak for me,
the hand of God to guard me,
God's way to stretch before me
and the shield of God to shelter;
the Godly hosts to save me
out of the snares the devils set
and out of temptations of viciousness,
out of the clutches of those who wish me harm,
however far they be, however close,
singly, or in multitudes.

I call to myself today
God's strength against all evil,
against all cruel force and merciless
that may attack my body and my soul,
against incantation of false prophecy,
against the black laws of the heathen,
against the false laws of heresies,
against the lies and shams of idols,
against the spells of women, smiths and druids,
against those webs of knowledge that entrap the souls of men.

Oh Christ I pray protect me
against poisons, burnings, drownings,
and against all wounding powers
that I may reap abundant harvests of rewards.

Christ be with me, Christ before,
Christ behind and Christ within me,
Christ beneath and Christ above,

Christ on my right hand, Christ on my left,
Christ in my sleeping, and in my rising,
Christ in the courtyard, Christ at the wheel,
Christ in the heart of everyone who thinks of me,
Christ in the mouth of all who speak of me,
Christ in the eye of all who see me,
Christ in the ear of all who hear me.

I gather strength today
through the invocation of the Trinity;
the Source and Sustenance of our being,
the Name and Nature of the Source
and the Breath that gives it being.

The adventure begins, the invocations finished, God the guardian through the power of the Christ. We are still, at this stage, in a primitive state of Christian imagery in Europe and the pilgrimage inwards is visioned often in the journey by sea where dangers are perpetually threatening. With the invocation of God's help as in the poem above, the voyage may be undertaken. Saint Columbanus wrote in Latin still, and came from Ireland to the continent sometime towards the end of the sixth century. In exile in Italy he founded the great monastery of Bobbio. His 'boat-song' is really an exhortation to his companions to persist in the journey towards the discovery of the Christ waiting within. Storms come, but they must continue on the journey:

En Silvis Caesa
Look now, cut out of wood, how the sharp keel
cuts through the waves and glides greasily on the Rhine –
  Heave, men, let our resounding echo sing out – heave!

Rough breezes blow, wild rains wreak havoc,
but the true strength of men conquers and conquers storms –
  Heave, men, let our resounding echo sing out – heave!

For clouds melt away with study, and the storm yields,
striving overcomes everything, persistent labour conquers all.
  Heave, men, let our resounding echo sing out – heave!

Only endure, preserve yourselves for better things,
you've suffered worse, and God will end these too.
Heave, men, let our resounding echo sing out – heave!

Thus the hated enemy behaves, wearing down the heart
tempting and shaking the innermost heart in frenzy.
Oh men, remembering Christ now, keep on, heave!

Stand firm of soul, spurn the enemy's foul tricks,
and duly seek defence in the weapons of virtue.
Oh men, remembering Christ now, keep on, heave!

A firm faith will conquer all, with blessed application,
and breaks at length the darts of that old yielding enemy.
Oh men, remembering Christ now, keep on, heave!

King, too, of all virtues, source of all, highest power,
promises victory to the determined, reward to the victor.
Oh men, remembering Christ now, keep on, heave!

Out of dogma and static virtue emerges, inevitably, an em-
battled extremism, a fundamentalism that will not look beyond
itself and its own liens, its self-inflicted chains. A fundamental-
ist, of any persuasion, is one who has come to the pier and
walked out to the end, has become aware of the immensity of
the ocean and of the boat waiting to carry him out on that ocean
on a voyage of discovery but who decides, instead, that it is
comfortable and safe to remain on the pier; anyone passing him
by and stepping aboard that boat thereby constitutes for him a
threat and a reproach; and so, let him build a fortress at the root
of the pier. A like analogy to a modern-day train station would
also apply. Christianity is an inexhaustible source of wonder
and glory; it is not to be limited by dogmas, commandments,
rules and orders.

The Irish religious experience reached a delighted and delightful apotheosis in the eighth, ninth and tenth centuries,
roughly, with the expansion of monasticism both at home and
abroad. The delight of the solitary monk in the midst of his natural surroundings is one of the great uplifting glories of Irish
poetry.

I am enriched by forest trees about me
where the blackbird sings so sweetly;
immersed in my books and bookish things
I relish the melodies that rise around me.

From groves of bushes the cuckoo calls
in its grey hood echoing back to me;
God's grace be with me where I write
with bird and bush and high forest trees.

The hermit's life where he or she comes to live in the love and the praise of God is itself a voyage of discovery. The richly illuminated manuscripts of those times are testimony to a labour of love, the colours and patterns of joy and suffering, the tracings of love and loss and the reaching deep down into the Bible for light and encouragement, all of these are part of the adventure. At about this time, in England, the Anglo-Saxon writers were also taking the Christian adventure as a voyage, a difficult one, it is true, but a voyage of discovery none the less. Here is a small part of 'The Seafarer', firstly the very beginning where the difficulties of the voyage are outlined.

May I relate a truthful tale from my life, tell
of a journey, how in long labour-filled days
I suffered whole hours of hardship, felt

bitter anguish, bore terrible anxieties,
was occupied so often in watches of the night
on a ship's prow in severe and pounding seas

when we tossed under cliffs and when my feet
were frozen and fettered with the chains
of frost. Cares festered in my heart and great

hunger came harrying my mind, oh I was a man
wearied by the sea.

The description is wonderfully evocative and clearly drawn directly from experience. The writer goes on to contrast his life with that of those who live in luxury and ease:

Still, how could you know –
or anyone who lives in luxury and ease on land –

> how I, wretched and anxious, with the sea icecold …
> How wrong
> it seems to you who live in the comfort of cities,
> how little you know of journeys, terrifying, long;
>
> when you're lazy, lusting for wine, how can you see
> why I wearily pursue the ocean paths.

Gradually the real message of the journey becomes clear:

> Earthly goods will not stand a man eternally; always
> something takes him at the appointed time: disease
> or age or violence will carry him away;
>
> so, in proud assemblies, nothing can equal praise
> from the living, for those lordly men who have achieved,
> before their death, their due of good works, whose days
>
> passed magnanimously on earth, in spite of the malice
> of enemies, whose bravery faced with evil is well known
> and brings honourable mention to men's lips. And this
>
> praise lives afterwards among the angels, in the glory
> of eternal life, with hymns of joy among angelic hosts
> for ever.

The invitation to live the more difficult life may not offer the most pleasing prospects; the adventure will be demanding and dangerous, but it contrasts wonderfully, and with good reason, with the life of ease and laziness. The poet concludes:

> Let us think then where our true home lies
> and learn how we may sail thereto, and learn to win
> God's grace against the fateful meeting where man's life
>
> will be blessed by the Lord's love in the port of heaven,
> by Him who has honoured us though we sin and sin again,
> the Prince of Glory, the great Captain for ever. Amen.

Already, so many centuries ago, poets were urging people out and on, to shake themselves from lethargy and the laziness of settled things, and make a life of goodness and of seeking for themselves. About 1375 a poem called 'Pearl' appeared, a vision poem whose subject is ostensibly a young girl who died before the age of two, and the dream of her father, the poet, who goes in search of his lost pearl. It is a carefully constructed and elaborately metered poem, bringing the father to a great river where he sees his pearl, happy on the other side, in Paradise. When he tries to cross he is flung back to earth, not yet fit for Paradise. The poem is far more than an elegy, it is the search for the comfort to be found in faith in Christ; it is doctrinally virginal, emphasising merely the loss that we are aware of in our humanity, a loss that Christianity will relieve when we are found capable of living it as fully as we can. A seeking, therefore, not a sermonising.

Written about the same time is the wonderful 'Piers Plowman' of William Langland. The poet lies down somewhere in the Malvern Hills, in Worcestershire, and dreams; he has a vision of a tower set on a far hill and of a dungeon set in a dark valley; these are symbols of heaven and hell and between them he sees a 'fair field full of folk', people like himself, struggling with their living. Piers, a humble ploughman, appears to the dreamer and offers himself as a guide to the discovery of Truth. A finely drawn out and complex narrative, the poem yet exists as an adventure, a pilgrimage, a journey towards finding out the fullness of the Christian vision, rather than a telling of something already known and explored.

Many beautiful poems appeared about this time, poems of love and praise, poems of hope and joy, all of this before the terrible religious persecutions began. Take this one as an example of close physical awareness of the Christ-child, a poem of utter simplicity and wholehearted love:

The Virgin's Song
Jesu, my sweet Son dear,
  On the poorest bed you are lying here,
And it grieves me sore;
And that your cradle is like a bier,
Ox and ass sole friends, I fear,
  Well may I weep, therefore.

Jesu, sweet, do not be wroth,
Though I have neither patch nor cloth
  That you I might enfold,
  To wrap you in so you might rest,

The rags I have are none the best;
But lay your feet against my breast,
  And keep you from the cold,
  And keep you from the cold.

We may pass over the next two centuries, an era fraught with tensions between England and the papacy, and between Roman Catholicism and Protestantism, an era that saw martyrs on both sides. I think of 'blood guilt' and the dangers of 'zeal'! It appears that when it comes to faith and dogmas it is we who are the angry ones, we humans, and that it is God who is reaching out to us, offering himself as the sacrifice that we require for our own reassurance and our vengeance. God does not need us; nor does he need or require vengeance. Let me move into the seventeenth century.

Ben Jonson struck the beginning of the new century with some force. Born in 1572 he was the son of a clergyman. He never knew his father and worked, unhappily, as a bricklayer for his stepfather for a time. In 1598, after a spell as a soldier and involvement in a drama company, he killed a fellow-actor and was sentenced to death, which he escaped by claiming 'benefit of clergy', a privilege established in the 12th century whereby Christian clerics were exempted from criminal prosecution by secular courts. He was, however, imprisoned where he converted to Roman Catholicism, returning to the Anglican Church ten years later. When he was released he forfeited his possessions and was branded on the thumb as a felon! Religious vacillation was common at this time, and Jonson's explosive temperament and awareness of his own genius made him both petulant and sarcastic, as well as occasionally rueful and contrite. He died in 1637 and was buried in Westminster Abbey; a plaque simply read 'O Rare Ben Jonson'!

In poetry, Jonson's reputation is often overlooked in favour of his dramatic works, but he wrote a great deal of poetry and was highly influential on the group of poets who came after him, the 'Cavalier' poets whose work rejoiced in linguistic niceties and clever love conceits. Jonson wrote several magnificent love poems, too, alongside several poems of religious power that show his awareness of the Christian life as a salutary reminder of the vicissitudes and betrayals of this life. He used such poems as an exploration of his deeper and most private self, at a time when religious questions were becoming a matter of life and death, literally, and a question of the possibility either of preferment at court or of incarceration.

To Heaven
Good and great God! can I not think of thee,
But it must straight my melancholy be?
Is it interpreted in me disease,
That, laden with my sins, I seek for ease?
O be thou witness, that the reins dost know (the inner thoughts)
And hearts of all, if I be sad for show;
And judge me after: if I dare pretend
To aught but grace, or aim at other end.
As thou art all, so be thou all to me,
First, midst, and last, converted One, and Three!
My faith, my hope, my love; and in this state,
My judge, my witness, and my advocate.
Where have I been this while exiled from thee,
And whither rapt, now thou but stoop'st to me?
Dwell, dwell here still! O, being every where,
How can I doubt to find thee ever here?
I know my state, both full of shame and scorn,
Conceived in sin, and unto labour born,
Standing with fear, and must with horror fall,
And destined unto judgment, after all.
I feel my griefs too, and there scarce is ground,
Upon my flesh t'inflict another wound:
Yet dare I not complain, or wish for death,
With holy Paul, lest it be thought the breath
Of discontent; or that these prayers be
For weariness of life, not love of thee.

In the midst of his personal battles and angers, Jonson was aware of the Christian adventure on which he was also embarked. To be a Christian means to transform the pattern of our desires towards new perspectives, the perspective of Christ; and this is echoed well in Augustine's phrase: 'You have made us for Yourself, O God, and our hearts are restless until they rest in

You.' This restlessness comes from the desires we cultivate in our life; it is desire which confers energy; when the desires are fulfilled, if ever they are, that energy dissipates and new desires must be found to take their place. Jonson is aware that melancholy attends the misdirection of desire; he protests in this poem, but basically to himself, that his desires are not properly oriented. It is a request, please 'be all to me'! but the poem is aware that this is not yet so. One is exiled from God in so much as the ultimate aim in life veers from the fulfilling of what must be our ultimate desire, to partake in the Divine life itself. Jonson is scared of the judgement, yet his whole life – his angers, his killing, his sarcasms, the frightening religious battles going on around him – has grown aware of death. His longing is to turn his whole life towards 'love of thee'. Behind a poem like this is an awareness, confused by the times, that the great Christian adventure is one that transcends the present and grief and all desires that are bound too closely to the earth, that the adventure partakes of the growth of creation itself to the perfection to which God intended it. Whatever stunts that growth is what we may truly call 'evil'.

The ship, *Mayflower*, left Southampton in August 1620. She took some sixty-six days to reach the New World, off the tip of Cape Cod, and while still just anchored, one Susanna White gave birth to a child she named Peregrine, a Pilgrim. Most of those on board that famous ship were Pilgrims, bringing with them a religious Puritanism they wished to give free rein to in a new territory. England had become ice-bound in dogma against which the Puritan movement was part of a sweeping revolt. It was, of course, allied to a revolt against the ruling society; the Puritans themselves had taken power within England in a wave of bloodshed, killing the king, winning a civil war and brutally conquering the neighbouring people of Ireland. Intolerance, of course, breeds an even greater intolerance. As we know from one of the greatest poets of their arrival in Massachusetts, Anne Bradstreet, women were wholly suppressed to male domination. Nothing new, I'm afraid, in terms of religious intolerance. The Puritans hoped to found a 'city upon a hill', an example to all of capitalist excess and religious extremism, though they did not see it in those terms. The Puritan aspect of the *Mayflower*'s voyage needs to remain distinct from the Pilgrim aspect, although both sets of travellers shared many of the same ideals. But it is, in historical terms, a prime example of dogma fighting dogma, the battles that ensue, and the separation that necessarily follows for survival. How important, then, to remember the whole openness of the Christ experience, and the ongoing difficult but wonderful growth of Creation that overtops such rocks flung in its path.

Edward Taylor was born under the Puritan ascendancy in England, in 1642 and at the age of 24 made his way to Massachusetts. He spent his life as a minister in the town of Westfield, where he died in 1729. The poetry that he wrote he saw as one of the ways in which he could praise the Lord, developing his metaphors and using psalms and everyday experience as sources of meditation. His high seriousness and the carrying over of forms and metres from the English poetry tradition have made him appear less exciting as a poet than Bradstreet, but the work is sincere and his slight drawing back from the utter strictures of a damning Puritanism is welcome.

Meditation

What Love is this of thine, that cannot be
  In thine Infinity, O Lord, confined,
Unless it in thy very Person see,
  Infinity, and Finity conjoined?
  What hath thy Godhead, as not satisfied
  Married our Manhood, making it its Bride?

Oh, Matchless Love! filling Heaven to the brim!
  O're running it: all running o're beside
This World! Nay overflowing Hell; wherein
  For thine Elect, there rose a mighty tide!
  That there our veins might through thy Person bleed,
  To quench those flames, that else would on us feed.

Oh! that thy Love might overflow my heart!
  To fire the same with Love: for Love I would.
But oh! my straitened breast! my lifeless spark!
  My fireless flame! What chilly love, and cold?
  In measure small! In manner chilly! See.
  Lord blow the Coal: Thy love enflame in me.

It is pleasing to see the emphasis on love, and the response of the soul, another favourite topic of religious poetry about this time, George Herbert being the one who wrote best in this area. The whole notion of repentance was one dear to the Puritans, a repentance that was offered to this God of Love, often in fear and in awareness, as in the above poem, of how poor the response of the soul is to God's love. The Christian journey is even the more wonderful when the possibility of repentance is examined in this light; if God is love, and his love is so overwhelming, it is not God who needs us to repent or do penance, it is ourselves; repentance is a way in which the freely given gift of God is returned to the person who has spurned it for the moment, and it is an earnest of the soul's continuing the exploration, through the world of love and grace, of that infinite love. The Christian way, then, is one of enthusiasm, of fire; it is not a cold and removed reasoning thing, not a narrow road without turn or obstacle, it is a joyful and demanding journey of allowing the greatest possible love to permeate the human soul.

William Wordsworth, in the magnificent Tintern Abbey poem, writes of the excitement of the human position in the world, aware of something, a 'motion and a spirit', that impels both man and earth along. In the earlier stages of his career, Wordsworth accepted and wrote out of a pantheistic religious sentiment that gave to the world about him a sacred power which he did not identify as a personal God. The poem is an expression of his awareness of human disharmony after and around the French Revolution, in a world that he wishes to see in harmony with itself. He worked, alongside Coleridge, to place human beings in that wished-for natural harmony where, they hoped and at times believed, the human might grow aware of, and participate in, such harmony. Up to this, the natural world had more often been portrayed as something inimical to civilised human living. Christianity, too, appeared to have nothing to do with or to say about the natural world and Wordsworth's explorations and faith moved to a vague and ultimately unsatisfying 'something' that nevertheless produced a series of poems richly orchestrated and deeply moving, though perhaps suffering from an excess of rhetorical noise. The influence of this 'romantic' poetry, however, is with us still; the excitement of the 'discovery' of the beauties of the world in which we live, adding to the wonder and value of a more deeply aware Christianity. It is not difficult to recall how much earlier faith had treated the physical world as, at best, a distraction to the soul's journey, and, at worst, a source of corruption and sin. Wordsworth and others were clearly also reacting to eighteenth century rationalism. We do not court poetry for its philosophy, but its 'mood' and power to penetrate beyond rationalism will have a deep and lasting effect on one's outlook on the world. Attempts have been made to place Wordsworth's religious outlook in a Christian context and in an evangelical Anglicanism setting, but it is the richly outward-looking and exploratory excitement in the work that has had a lasting power. Here is a passage central to this poem:

Lines
Composed a Few Miles Above Tintern Abbey,
on Revisiting the Banks of The Wye, During a Tour, July 13, 1798

> These beauteous forms,
> Through a long absence, have not been to me
> As is a landscape to a blind man's eye:
> But oft, in lonely rooms, and 'mid the din
> Of towns and cities, I have owed to them
> In hours of weariness, sensations sweet,
> Felt in the blood, and felt along the heart;
> And passing even into my purer mind,
> With tranquil restoration: – feelings too
> Of unremembered pleasure: such, perhaps,
> As have no slight or trivial influence
> On that best portion of a good man's life,
> His little, nameless, unremembered, acts
> Of kindness and of love. Nor less, I trust,
> To them I may have owed another gift,
> Of aspect more sublime; that blessed mood,
> In which the burthen of the mystery,
> In which the heavy and the weary weight
> Of all this unintelligible world,
> Is lightened: – that serene and blessed mood,

In which the affections gently lead us on, –
Until, the breath of this corporeal frame
And even the motion of our human blood
Almost suspended, we are laid asleep
In body, and become a living soul:
While with an eye made quiet by the power
Of harmony, and the deep power of joy,
We see into the life of things.

The poem speaks of 'feelings', 'sensations', 'blessed mood', 'the mystery', 'this unintelligible world' … All of this was important at that time in moving faith, in whatever form, a little further away from set dogmatism to remain more concerned with the mystery and its wonder. This has done no little good for Christian awareness. He later speaks of 'gleams of half-extinguished thought, With many recognitions dim and faint'; none of which can make an impression on the closed mind whose ideas and ideals are formed and set in stone!

For I have learned
To look on nature, not as in the hour
Of thoughtless youth; but hearing oftentimes
The still, sad music of humanity,
Nor harsh nor grating, though of ample power
To chasten and subdue. And I have felt
A presence that disturbs me with the joy
Of elevated thoughts; a sense sublime
Of something far more deeply interfused,
Whose dwelling is the light of setting suns,
And the round ocean and the living air,
And the blue sky, and in the mind of man;
A motion and a spirit, that impels
All thinking things, all objects of all thought,
And rolls through all things.

If Wordsworth's poetry urges the imagination to pass beyond the merely rational into a less definable religious mode, John Henry Newman, in 'The Dream of Gerontius', takes the Christian adventure back into remarkably traditional mode, yet does so with a successfully imaginative treatment of the soul's journey, this time after death. If Elgar's setting of the long poem to music has helped it to survive into our own times, yet the poem, in the context of which I speak, remains fruitful to exploration in itself. Newman's life straddles the nineteenth century, (1801-1890). He converted to Catholicism and was made a cardinal; hence it is obvious that in the Victorian age his Christian outlook would be conservative. He came to Ireland in 1854 as rector of the newly-established Catholic University of Ireland. His poem 'Lead Kindly Light' has made a fine hymn, and 'The Dream of Gerontius' was a late work, one of the rarest of poems, moving as it does into the realm of the other world. As a convert from Anglicanism to Catholicism, he was influential on the life of Gerard Manley Hopkins.

Lead Kindly Light
   Lead, kindly Light, amid th'encircling gloom, lead Thou
   me on!
The night is dark, and I am far from home; lead Thou me on!
Keep Thou my feet; I do not ask to see
The distant scene; one step enough for me.

   I was not ever thus, nor prayed that Thou shouldst lead me
   on;
I loved to choose and see my path; but now lead Thou me on!
I loved the garish day, and, spite of fears,
Pride ruled my will. Remember not past years!

   So long Thy power hath blest me, sure it still will lead me on.
O'er moor and fen, o'er crag and torrent, till the night is gone,
And with the morn those angel faces smile, which I
Have loved long since, and lost awhile!

   Meantime, along the narrow rugged path, Thyself hast trod,
Lead, Savior, lead me home in childlike faith, home to my
   God.
To rest forever after earthly strife
In the calm light of everlasting life.

The hymn is fairly based on traditional Christian devotion and in many ways harks back to the poetry of writers like Herbert and Vaughan with their pleas that God might take over the individual will and give such grace as might overwhelm the natural bent of selfishness. There is a journey to be undertaken; in younger years human beings often take byways and sideroads; darkness and difficulties beset the strait path, this 'valley of tears' but if God leads, then the journey, however hazardous, will be a successful one. For me the basic strength of the hymn lies in the simplicity of its direct appeal to God, and in that phrase, 'one step enough for me'. The stress, too, is, for that Victorian age, in the salvation of the individual soul; this is the aim, the end of all religion. Newman, however, takes this journey further into the realms of afterdeath. Again, in 'Gerontius', the question is of the salvation of the individual soul but the intrinsic interest of the work is in the sense of what happens after death, and in that marvellous sense that, though there is no longer any movement, yet the journey continues. Newman succeeds in making that strange journey of the soul both believable and traditionally Catholic, the adventure is a real adventure, in the poem, and the tension continues.

'Gerontius' can be taken to mean 'old man'. At the start of the poem we are in the dying man's room and hear his pleas, hear, too, his terrors and the prayers of those around him for the safe passage of his soul from this world to the next. The second part is the more interesting; the soul 'wakes' to a new consciousness of itself and of its still terrifying journey onwards.

> This silence pours a solitariness
> Into the very essence of my soul;
> And the deep rest, so soothing and so sweet,
> Hath something too of sternness and of pain.
> For it drives back my thoughts upon their spring
> By a strange introversion, and perforce
> I now begin to feed upon myself,
> Because I have nought else to feed upon.
> Am I alive or dead? I am not dead,
> But in the body still; for I possess
> A sort of confidence which clings to me,
> That each particular organ holds its place
> As heretofore, combining with the rest
> Into one symmetry that wraps me round,
> And makes me man; and surely I could move,

Did I but will it, every part of me.
And yet I cannot to my sense bring home,
By very trial, that I have the power.
'Tis strange; I cannot stir a hand or foot,
I cannot make my fingers or my lips
By mutual pressure witness each to each,
Nor by the eyelid's instantaneous stroke
Assure myself I have a body still.
Nor do I know my very attitude,
Nor if I stand, or lie, or sit, or kneel.
So much I know, not knowing how I know,
That the vast universe, where I have dwelt,
Is quitting me, or I am quitting it.
Or I or it is rushing on the wings
Of light or lightning on an onward course,
And we e'en now are million miles apart.
Yet … is this peremptory severance
Wrought out in lengthening measurements of space,
Which grow and multiply by speed and me?
Or am I traversing infinity
By endless subdivision, hurrying back
From finite towards infinitesimal,
Thus dying out of the expansed world?
Another marvel; someone has me fast
Within his ample palm; 'tis not a grasp
Such as they use on earth, but all around
Over the surface of my subtle being,
As though I were a sphere, and capable
To be accosted thus, a uniform
And gentle pressure tells me I am not
Self-moving, but borne forward on my way.

The whole is an intriguing and beguiling exercise in imaginative faith; the soul, having passed through death, is taken by an
angel and 'carried' towards the judgement seat of God, passing
angels and demons on the way. Newman's faith here is based on
the often stated Creed but in it there are placed no barriers, it is
like a river that the soul floats on, making its way towards God.
Nowhere is there a dam built on this river, there is no freezing of

creed or creeds, the river does not have to break its bank to find alternative ways. It is a Christianity of openness and charity and therefore a richness in the hard fortress of Victorian rigidity. The soul, having lost all sense-awareness, is moved onwards towards God, through its necessary purgation, all the time being encouraged by an angel, who explains the 'stations' of this journey as they reach them:

> We have gained the stairs
> Which rise towards the Presence-chamber; there
> A band of mighty angels keep the way
> On dither side, and hymn the Incarnate God.

The soul at length finds itself so close to the presence of God that its own impurity makes it wish for the final phase of purification, in purgatory; the angel says:

> Now let the golden prison open its gates,
> Making sweet music, as each fold revolves
> Upon its ready hinge. And ye great powers,
> Angels of Purgatory, receive from me
> My charge, a precious soul, until the day,
> When, from all bond and forfeiture released,
> I shall reclaim it for the courts of light.

The whole poem is not used by Elgar in his setting of the work, but it is all worth the reading, the imaginative and warm focus of the poet working well in an almost impossible area, the whole poem taking the view of the Christian soul on a long pilgrimage to the uttermost moment of that journey.

One of the first poets to express grave doubts about the whole Christian way was Thomas Hardy. Born 1840 he married Emma Lavinia Gifford whose death in 1912 had a severely traumatic effect on the poet. He tried spiritism and struggled all his life with agnosticism. The echoes of Wordsworth's supernatural forces are found in Hardy, though these forces are not benevolent here but alert with caprice and, at best, indifference. All through this searching he retained a devotion for Christianity in its rituals, particularly when it came to small local community life. Some of his poems bring a sense of fun to religious ritual though all of them come from a soul sincerely searching for a deeper truth that might redeem the journey of living. He died in 1928.

The Oxen
a Poem for Christmas 1915
Christmas Eve, and twelve of the clock.
   'Now they are all on their knees,'
An elder said as we sat in a flock
   By the embers in hearthside ease.

We pictured the meek mild creatures where
   They dwelt in their strawy pen.
Nor did it occur to one of us there
   To doubt they were kneeling then.

So fair a fancy few would weave
   In these years! Yet, I feel,
If someone said on Christmas Eve
   'Come; see the oxen kneel

'In the lonely barton by yonder comb
   Our childhood used to know,'
I should go with him in the gloom,
   Hoping it might be so.

This is undoubtedly a carry-over from the delights of childhood Christmases yet there is a real sense of longing and even of belief in the work. The mind is not closed off; where doubt enters the whole Christian journey it is still vital that that doubt does not take upon itself the utter blockage that militant atheism might take. Doubt is a natural condition. And here is a piece that has a delicate humour in it:

Afternoon Service at Mellstock
On afternoons of drowsy calm
We stood in the panelled pew,
Singing one-voiced a Tate-and-Brady psalm
To the tune of 'Cambridge New'.

We watched the elms, we watched the rooks,
The clouds upon the breeze,
Between the whiles of glancing at our books,
And swaying like the trees.

So mindless were those outpourings! –
Though I am not aware
That I have gained by subtle thought on things
Since we stood psalming there.

It is an easy thing to say, I am a Christian. But it is not an easy thing to be. In fact, I feel one never can say I am a Christian in the sense that word ought to convey, namely I am now like Christ. One *becomes* a Christian, and this is a process that goes on to the very last moment of one's life. It is a demanding and often difficult and painful process, but it is the only process worth giving one's entire energies to, and it is a process that must not create barriers along the way, barriers of doctrine, doctrinaire tendencies, dogmas, fortress beliefs … Christ came to give freedom, not to set up dividing walls or barbed-wire barricades, a freedom that demands tolerance and selflessness, and the willingness to accept even the remote possibility that we may be, at times, wrong in our certainties! A stanza from Mary Coleridge underlies the demanding aspect of Christ's arrival in the flesh; she was a great great niece of Samuel Taylor Coleridge; she was a novelist and poet, who lived from 1861 to 1907:

I saw a stable, low and very bare,
    A little child in a manger.
The oxen knew Him, had Him in their care,
    To men He was a stranger.
The safety of the world was lying there,
    And the world's danger.

T. S. Eliot's great poem, 'The Journey of the Magi' takes us right back to the beginning, the epiphany, the opening up to the world of the Incarnation, 'the world's danger'. Eliot's achievement in this poem is to be able to ask, at the end of the poem, if what the magi were witness to was a birth, or a death; he brings us back, indeed, to the empty tomb from which our own Christian faith takes its course. The speakers of the poem tell of the difficulties of their journey during the very worst time of the year; many of the encounters they had along the way are suggestive of the crucifixion, the three trees, the men playing at dice with their pieces of silver. When they return home they are no

longer content to remain in their own ways, in the 'old dispens-
ation', their own people have now become alien to them, clutch-
ing at the old gods. The journey, beginning from a death, and
from our hope in the resurrection, brings us to a position where
we are not content with the old barriers, we are forced to move
on, onwards, and forever.

Finally, there is a poem by D. H. Lawrence that delightfully
sums up both his own thematic concerns in the fiction, and the
sense of ongoing journey that leads through life to life. He wills
to know that his own life 'is moving still with the dark earth, and
drenched with the deep oblivion of earth's lapse and renewal.'

Shadows
And if tonight my soul may find her peace
in sleep, and sink in good oblivion,
and in the morning wake like a new-opened flower
then I have been dipped again in God, and new-created.

And if, as weeks go round, in the dark of the moon
my spirit darkens and goes out, and soft strange gloom
pervades my movements and my thoughts and words
then I shall know that I am walking still
with God, we are close together now the moon's in shadow.

And if, as autumn deepens and darkens
I feel the pain of falling leaves, and stems that break in storms
and trouble and dissolution and distress
and then the softness of deep shadows folding, folding
around my soul and spirit, around my lips
so sweet, like a swoon, or more like the drowse of a low, sad
    song
singing darker than the nightingale, on, on to the solstice
and the silence of short days, the silence of the year, the shadow,
then I shall know that my life is moving still
with the dark earth, and drenched
with the deep oblivion of earth's lapse and renewal.

And if, in the changing phases of man's life
I fall in sickness and in misery
my wrists seem broken and my heart seems dead
and strength is gone, and my life

is only the leavings of a life:
and still, among it all, snatches of lovely oblivion, and
    snatches of renewal
odd, wintry flowers upon the withered stem, yet new,
    strange flowers
such as my life has not brought forth before, new blossoms of
    me –

then I must know that still
I am in the hands of the unknown God,
he is breaking me down to his own oblivion
to send me forth on a new morning, a new man.

When Mary Magdalene looked into the sepulchre she saw two angels in white sitting at either end of the stone where the body of Jesus had lain. The tomb is empty; the whole of creation breathes with a new and wonderful, and a demanding, excitement. Mary turns and sees Jesus who says to her 'Why are you weeping?' The empty tomb; the whole world stretching away from that incredibly beautiful and challenging moment. This is not an ending; it is a beginning, the beginning of the Christian adventure, the only journey worth the effort, the only adventure that is certain to end, and to begin again, only at death.

The Three Strange Angels

Here is St Paul, from the Epistle to the Romans, Chapter 8:

> It is my belief that the sufferings of this present time are not worth comparing with the glory that is to be revealed to us. For the creation waits with eager longing for the revealing of the sons of God. For the creation was subjected to futility, not willingly, but because of him who subjected it, in hope that the creation itself will be set free from its bondage to corruption and obtain the freedom of the glory of the children of God. For we know that the whole creation has been groaning together in the pains of childbirth until now. And not only the creation, but we ourselves, who have the first fruits of the Spirit, groan inwardly as we wait eagerly for adoption as sons, the redemption of our bodies. For in this hope we were saved. Now hope that is seen is not hope. For who hopes for what he sees? But if we hope for what we do not see, we wait for it with patience.

The whole of creation, and that means the physical universe in which we live, together with all the human beings who have occupied a place in that universe, along with all the other creatures, animate and inanimate, develops, through suffering, towards the culmination of God's most wonderful plan. This is one of the many passages of scripture that has intrigued and cajoled me over the years. It seems clear to me, yet I have never heard it distinctly addressed by Christian apologetics. It states, it does not suggest, that the whole of creation was 'subjected to futility' and I presume that the one who subjected it thus was humanity in the persons of Adam and Eve; in other words, that force of entropy that moves everything forward through time by the facts of its need to use up energy and thereby its diminution of energy. So the whole of creation waits, as we do, for the freedom of the glory of the same humanity. The whole of creation groans in expectation and it is this hope that saves us. As I read this text the whole of creation, and not just humanity, forms part of the one body, the Jesus Body, and all of creation, not just humanity, forms the limbs of that one body, the Jesus Bones.

It goes further and steps, kindly, into my own demesne for Paul says that 'what is seen is not hope'; we hope for what we do not see and this hope saves us. Poetry gathers up the straws of what we do not see and therefore should, and does, empower the Christian adventure. And poetry leaps with delight on the creation itself, wallowing in the physical details and not eschewing them (as my church led me to believe I ought to do) and pushing reason beyond itself into the realms of the unknown and unreachable, into that which sacrament signifies.

It took centuries, up to the time of Shakespeare and beyond, for poetry to relish the physical details of our world. Up to then it was the simplicity of a faith that insisted humanity care for the spiritual to the detriment of the physical and no wonder, given the miserable physical conditions in which so many generations suffered. One of the first of the poets to open up to the world was a little-known and little-appreciated optimist, Thomas Traherne whose work was done around the middle of the seventeenth century, and therefore before the Romantics who, perhaps, took their love of the physical world to extremes. Traherne wrote: 'Thus all the world is yours, your very senses and the inclinations of your mind declare. The works of God manifest, His laws testify and His word doth prove it. His attributes most sweetly make it evident. The powers of your soul confirm it. So that in the midst of such rich demonstrations you may infinitely delight in God as your father, friend and benefactor, in yourself as His heir, child and bride, in the whole world as the gift and token of His love. Neither can anything but ignorance destroy your joys, for if you know yourself, or God, or the world, you must of necessity enjoy it.'

'The whole world as the gift and token of His love': is not this great, good news? In that floppy book we had in secondary school, *Apologetics and Catholic Doctrine*, in its 1923 edition, you will read: 'A Sacrament is an outward rite instituted by Christ to signify grace, and to give the grace it signifies.' An 'outward rite' because it can be perceived by the senses; and the compiler of this textbook, one Most Rev M. Sheehan, goes on to say that Christ 'wished us to know with certainty and through the evidence of our senses the exact moment His grace is given to us'. Here again is a passage from Thomas Traherne, a moment of awakening while he was still a student and struggling with doubt and darkness:

> Another time, in a lowering and sad evening, being alone in the field, when all things were dead and quiet, a certain want and horror fell upon me, beyond imagination. The unprofitableness and silence of the place dissatisfied me, its wideness terrified me, from the utmost ends of the earth fears surrounded me. I was a weak and little child, and had forgotten there was a man alive in the earth. Yet something also of hope and expectation comforted me from every border. This taught me that I was concerned in all the world, and that in the remotest borders the causes of peace delight me; and the beauties of the earth when seen were made to entertain me; that I was made to hold a communion with the secrets of divine providence in all the world ... The comfort of houses and friends, and the clear assurance of treasures everywhere, God's care and love, His goodness, wisdom and power, His presence and watchfulness in all the ends of the earth were my strength and assurance forever.

The sacraments indicate the grace they confer because 'in each, words are used which clearly point to the spiritual effect produced' and 'the meaning of the words is enforced or illustrated by the ceremony itself'. It is up to the poet to relish the sensual things of the word and behind those things to touch on what is not seen but known 'as in a glass darkly'. In other words, a good poem is a sacrament, a sacrament of the most incredible hope and excitement in a world of war, suffering and inequality. Poetry sees the world itself as sacrament; it knows the world as eucharist. And perhaps one definition of poetry can be found in those words of Traherne: 'I was made to hold a communion with the secrets of divine providence in all the world.'

Now, if I am making huge claims for the wonders of poetry, and I am doing just that, I am not making such a claim for my own work; I see it as exploratory, an effort in a militantly secular age to say 'No sir! there is more!' Here, then, is a poem that touches on the poverty, both physical and – at least on the surface – spiritual, of a family I knew on Achill Island. You will recognise the myth behind it, that of Ruth and Boaz, one of the great love stories of the Bible; mine is an attempt to touch what is beyond the visibly obvious in a person's living:

Call Me Beautiful
Broad-shouldered, big as a labouring man, Ruth
was egg-woman, slow and inarticulate,
flat-footed in her widowhood and her big sons

slap-witted, dun as she. I was ever dumb
before her, decades of harsh news
in the lines of her face, and a small smile

grateful for neighbourly busyness; each egg,
mucous-touched, she spat on and frotted clean
against black woollen skirts. Crucifix

over the door, painted Madonna on the sill,
her house was an island on chicken-shitted ground
with a harvesting of rushes, her world

not ordered by methodical thinking. Now I know
it is my own need disturbs me, to find
meaning and motive beyond the manifest

ungainliness, to seek the spirit's dance towards
divine friendship, and to vision her rapt
on her knees in a field of corn, gleaning.

There is another delightful tale in the Bible, in Genesis, when Abraham, sitting in some doldrums under his oak trees, suddenly saw The Lord. But it is not Yahweh, or God Almighty, or El Shaddai as we would envisage him or her, but three strangers. Something about these three men as they approached him, touched Abraham deeply; he saw beyond them to what they signified. What do you do with three strangers who suddenly appear nearby? Do you ignore them and let them pass along? Do you invite them in and offer them of your very best? Here's the story:

The Lord appeared to Abraham by the oak tree of Mamre, as he sat at the entrance of his tent in the heat of the day. He looked up and saw three men standing near him. When he saw them, he ran from the tent entrance to meet them, and bowed down to the ground. He said, 'My lord, if I find favour with you, do not pass by your servant. Let a little water be brought, and wash your feet, and rest yourselves under the tree. Let me bring a little bread that you may re-fresh yourselves, and after that you may pass on – since you have come to your servant.' So they said, 'Do as you have said.' And Abraham hastened into the tent to Sarah, and said, 'Make ready quickly three measures of choice flour, knead it, and make cakes.' Abraham ran to the herd, and took a calf, tender and good, and gave it to the servant, who hastened to prepare it. Then he took curds and milk and the calf that he had prepared, and set it before them; and he stood by them under the tree while they ate.

No stinting of generosity here. And no stinting of generosity in return because the Lord promised then that Sarah, though well beyond the age, would bear a son. It went further, Abraham pleading with the Lord that he would spare the innocent of Sodom, that they would not be swept away among the guilty. Indeed the appearance of God, of Yahweh, or El Shaddai or El of Bethel, to men like Abraham was well known to the people of the Middle East and it was often a terrifying experience. Such divine apparitions were known as epiphanies and the great example in the Christian world has been beautifully written of by T. S. Eliot. There is a whole school of thinking that sees the so-called 'inspiration' for a good poem to be an epiphany, that moment of enlightenment when experiences coalesce to form a new revelation of depth and human relevance, a view that has brought the poet close to prophet or mystic.

Back to the bones, the Jesus bones of this world; I see Mary Magdalene, that wonderful morning, standing in the garden, waiting, the body and bones of Jesus having vanished. The mo-ment of the Master's revealing himself to her is the moment of the greatest epiphany. I try to put this into a poem, how we are buried in the earth, how we are drowned under the sea, how we have suffered, waiting, for the freedom of the children of God, how the Christ himself, part of all this, gathers himself out of the Underworld and stands in the garden, waiting, waiting for the moment of his revelation to Mary, and to humanity and the whole of creation.

The Garden, Waiting
We are written down under the skin of the world
the way cloudbones manuscript the skies;

we are written, too, into the drills
of underwater kitchen-gardens, gazing up

towards the many-jointed shoals jittering above us.
Among nightmare predatory shapes, and among

the lurking abrupt murderings where cold
blood drifts like smoke and dissipates, the Christ

comes beckoning, ghostly figure among ghosts;
there will be a gathering of bones, picked to a sheen

and laid jostling together, that have waited, as the heaped
bones lay, in Auschwitz, along tainted air,

waiting, in patience, for re-assemblage, waiting
until the murdered Christ at last

has gathered himself together out of the tomb
and stands, astonished in the garden, waiting.

It seems that in Greek mythology the gods and goddesses appeared at will to Greeks and Trojans, in dreams, around the turn of a road, under trees, and that they appeared, at times, to move in forms very little different from human beings. The world, then, was full of gods, tree-gods, pond-gods, house-gods, sea-gods, the bones of the great creator, or creators, thickening the earth. In the end that was unsatisfactory, it was a way of reverencing the world, perhaps, but without a final and convincing Presence, without a reality behind the epiphany. Now here is a poem by the great lover of the world, D. H. Lawrence, written early in the twentieth century:

Song of a Man Who Has Come Through
Not I, not I, but the wind that blows through me!
A fine wind is blowing the new direction of Time.
If only I let it bear me, carry me, if only it carry me!
If only I am sensitive, subtle, oh, delicate, a winged gift!
If only, most lovely of all, I yield myself and am borrowed
By the fine, fine wind that takes its course through the chaos
   of the world
Like a fine, an exquisite chisel, a wedge-blade inserted;
If only I am keen, and hard like the sheer tip of a wedge
Driven by invisible blows,
The rock will split, we shall come at the wonder, we shall
   find the Hesperides.

Oh, for the wonder that bubbles into my soul,
I would be a good fountain, a good well-head,
Would blur no whisper, spoil no expression.

What is the knocking?
What is the knocking at the door in the night?
It is somebody wants to do us harm.

No, no, it is the three strange angels.
Admit them, admit them.

We are back again with Abraham and those wonderful men standing waiting under the oak tree of Mamre. Admit them, admit them! The wind that Lawrence wishes to be whirled away by can be assumed, from his other work, to be a close alliance with the forces of nature the characters in his novels are carried along with; and it is clear that admitting the strangers is close allied to terror, that frightening, demanding knocking at the door in the night. It is the beauty and challenging wonder of the world itself that shudders the being into consciousness of sacrament: of what I call the Jesus bones. A visit to the famine village on Achill Island will confirm both the sadness and the beauty of that place as well as its unquestioned power to stir the watcher's soul:

Slievemore: The Abandoned Village
You park your car on the low slope
  under the graveyard wall. Always
there is a mound of fresh-turned earth, flowers
  in pottery vases. There is light, from the sea and the wide
western sky, the Atlantic's
  soft-shoe nonchalance, whistle
of kestrels from the lifting mists, furze-scents, ferns,
  shiverings –
  till suddenly you are aware
you have come from an inland drift of dailiness to this shock
  of island, the hugeness of its beauty
dismaying you again to consciousness. Here
  is the wind-swept, ravenous
mountainside of grief; this is the long tilted valley where
  famine
  came like an old and infamous flood
from the afflicting hand of God. Beyond all
  understanding. Inarticulate. And pleading.
Deserted. Of all but the wall-stones and grasses,
  humped field-rocks and lazy-beds; what was commerce
  and family
become passive and inert, space
  for the study of the metaphysics of humanness. You climb
grudgingly, aware of the gnawing hungers,
  how the light leans affably, the way an urchin once might
  have watched
from a doorway;
  you are no more than a dust-mote on the mountainside,
allowing God his spaces; you are
  watercress and sorrel, one with the praying of villagers,
one with their silence, your hands
  clenched in overcoat pockets, standing between one world
and another.
  It has been easier to kneel
among the artefacts in the island graveyard, this harnessing
  of craft
  to contain our griefs;
here, among these wind-swept, ravenous acres

where we abandon our acceptably deceased to the
mountain earth.
In grace. In trustfulness.
This, too, the afflicting hand of God. Beyond all
understanding. Inarticulate. Though in praise.

I see the physical universe as inarticulate, and pleading; I see
it as the part of the poet's task to make the world about us an
articulate pleading, that will lead to praise. The Christian adventure, the end of which we know is eternal glory with the most
generous God, is an intensely difficult, but a wholly delightful
challenge. If a wreathe of withering flowers on a grave speaks
sacramentally of our loss and pain, it is the part of a Christian
poetics to push beyond such signs to discover the deeper ones,
the ones that language itself, in its own mystery, may touch
upon. What I am saying is that Christianity offers, if it is imaginatively lived, a way to travel that is grace-filled in a constant
way; it offers a way forward to all of us by portraying the world
in which we live as sacred in itself and an involvement with the
pulsing of that world to be the way towards holiness. Further,
any religion that has not blocked itself imaginatively, will offer
the same possibilities, clearly in different terms, under differing
circumstances. And sadly we know that religions place the great
walls of dogmas and doctrinaire findings in the way of their
own progress.

The floppy book of Catholic Doctrine states 'that in the
Blessed Eucharist Christ himself – His Body and Blood, His Soul
and Divinity – is really, truly, and substantially, present under
the species (accidents, appearances) of bread and wine'. The
central sacrament, the taking of bread and wine to confer the
grace of Christ's real presence within us, body and bones, the
Jesus Body, the Jesus Bones. This is the bread of our activity on
the earth, our working, our playing, our restfulness, our loving;
and it is the blood of our suffering, our movement onwards towards death, our wars and harryings, our follies and fetishes
and falls. And this is the world of which Paul, in 1 Corinthians
wrote: 'The cup of blessing that we bless, is it not a participation
in the blood of Christ? The bread that we break, is it not a participation in the body of Christ?' If the Eucharist contains Jesus

Christ in the fullness of his divinity and the completeness of his humanity, and if the whole earth is in travail, along with humanity, then the whole earth, too, is eucharist and one with humanity in the Jesus Body, the Jesus Bones. The living, breathing Jesus is in the world as he is in the eucharist. It follows that the earth is sacrament itself, signifier, as Traherne said, of grace and guarantee of that grace.

I want to present a poem, now, by Thomas Hardy:

Afterwards

When the Present has latched its postern behind my tremulous stay,
    And the May month flaps its glad green leaves like wings,
Delicate-filmed as new-spun silk, will the neighbours say,
    'He was a man who used to notice such things'?

If it be in the dusk when, like an eyelid's soundless blink,
    The dewfall-hawk comes crossing the shades to alight
Upon the wind-warped upland thorn, a gazer may think,
    'To him this must have been a familiar sight.'

If I pass during some nocturnal blackness, mothy and warm,
    When the hedgehog travels furtively over the lawn,
One may say, 'He strove that such innocent creatures should come to no harm,
    But he could do little for them; and now he is gone.'

If, when hearing that I have been stilled at last, they stand at the door,
    Watching the full-starred heavens that winter sees,
Will this thought rise on those who will meet my face no more,
    'He was one who had an eye for such mysteries'?

And will any say when my bell of quittance is heard in the gloom,
    And a crossing breeze cuts a pause in its outrollings,
Till they rise again, as they were a new bell's boom,
    'He hears it not now, but used to notice such things'?

Thomas Hardy, too, offers a poetry that takes the earth as sacrament and yet he, along with D. H. Lawrence, would not have called themselves Christians; indeed they both criticised Christianity because of its failure to take on board the physical beauties and the soul-forming qualities of working closely with the world. Hardy's poem works because of its deeply nostalgic awareness, because the accuracy of his grasp on the physical realities is conveyed in such a way we are able to watch with the furtive hedgehog and marvel in the light of dusk as the dewfall-hawk crosses before us. And there is, of course, St Francis of Assisi and his great *Canticle to the Sun*:

> Praised be my Lord, for sister moon and sister stars,
> In heaven you have shaped them clear and valuable and fair.
> Praised be my Lord for brother wind
> And for the air and clouds and good and every kind of
>   weather,
> By the which you grant to your creatures nourishment.

The world is charged, as Gerard Manley Hopkins said, with the grandeur of God. The point of his great sonnet, 'God's Grandeur' is that the world is a visible sign of God's presence amongst us and that, in spite of our best efforts to destroy our planet, nature is never spent and holds within itself the seeds of its own regeneration. Whether or not this is wholly true for the continuance of our planet's health in our day and time does not, of course, affect the worth of the poem; it makes the urgency of our world's seeing the freshness that Hopkins has divined all the more urgent. The reason for this freshness, according to the poet, is that the Holy Spirit gives life to the world, just the way that a hen keeps its brood warm.

> The world is charged with the grandeur of God.
>   It will flame out, like shining from shook foil;
>   It gathers to a greatness, like the ooze of oil
> Crushed. Why do men then now not reck his rod?
> Generations have trod, have trod, have trod;
>   And all is seared with trade; bleared, smeared with toil;
>   And wears man's smudge and shares man's smell: the soil
> Is bare now, nor can foot feel, being shod.
>
> And for all this, nature is never spent;
>   There lives the dearest freshness deep down things;

And though the last lights off the black West went
  Oh, morning, at the brown brink eastward, springs—
Because the Holy Ghost over the bent
  World broods with warm breast and with ah! bright wings.

Is this not sacrament? And the signification of that sacrament
is, among other things, art and among the arts, poetry. The hand
of the Creator is on the world and the Son of the Creator took
flesh and became part of the world, blessing it with his body and
his blood, just as he blessed the bread and wine. And therefore,
too, the earth is sacred and demands our care; it is a logical con-
sequence of this that carelessness with the eco-systems of our
planet is as much a sin as theft from a commercial bank. Must
we not, then, gaze on the forces and the places of our world with
greater awareness, with a huge sense of awe and with greater
care?

Harbour: Achill Island
The winds come rushing down the narrow sound
between islands; from the north the whole
ocean pours through, exploding against boulders,
against landfalls, and courses into quiet
when the tide brims. A seal
lifts its grey-wise head out of the current, a mackerel shoal
sets the surface sparkling as it passes.
After the storm, light across the harbour
is a denser grey, soft-tinged with green; the whip
suddenness of lightning has shone this stolid
stonework fragile for an instant and the downpour
is a chariot drawn by six roan horses
pounding in across the sea. To the eye the water's
stilled now in the bay; stones on the sea-bed
shimmer like opals, cantankerous crustaceans
side-legging across the sand. I stand
awed again that this could be the still
point of all creation, the fruits
of a crazy generosity, yet how we amble through it
as if it were our portion, and our endeavour.

I want to come back to D. H. Lawrence once more, to his sense of the earth, its seasons, its blessings and its miseries; Lawrence often speaks of God, but it is not our God, it is not the God of the Christians but the God that is a pantheistic force in the world, a vague and ill-defined presence or urgency that does not touch on any personal relationships, and therefore is not as meaningful, finally, as the Christ whose flesh and blood permeate, in sacramental form and in actuality, the physical universe.

Pax
All that matters is to be at one with the living God
To be a creature in the house of the God of Life.

Like a cat asleep on a chair
at peace, in peace
and at one with the master of the house, with the
mistress
at home, at home in the house of the living,
sleeping on the hearth, and yawning before the fire.

Sleeping on the hearth of the living world,
yawning at home before the fire of life
feeling the presence of the living God
like a great reassurance
a deep calm in the heart
a presence
as of a master sitting at the board
in his own and greater being,
in the house of life.

The beauty of this poem is manifestly moving but ultimately the vagueness of phrases such as 'God of Life, the living God, the living world, the fire of life', is unsatisfactory. It is a pleasing kind of pantheism that is acutely aware of the veins of the living earth, its growth, its decay, its tantrums and tantalising loveliness. But we who are Christians are more blessed to know the person of Jesus whose being floods the earth with grandeur and with grief. Suppose that same world of sacrament familiar to and beloved by Lawrence to be permeated by the bones of the Son of God, so permeated that to be part of it is to be filled with grace, so filled with grace that the world itself becomes source and sustenance of our living and, as St Paul stated, will share in the same bodily resurrection that we as Christians expect; does that not give us cause for celebration, reason for continuous gladness even in the teeth of the hounds, and cause for gratitude to the provident Creator? That Christianity be not locked into the bleak negativity of dogma, then, seems to be ever more vital in our time. If Catholicism had been more an adventure than a set of handcuffs in the days of Martin Luther, if it had been more open to and accepting of the natural world, we might today be more unified than we are. What, then, of these bones: what of the Jesus Body, the Jesus Bones? The poem I offer here touches on some of the great flood catastrophes of recent times, as of Indonesia and New Orleans, and of the first, mythic flood of Noah and his friends. How much we are part of the earth, out of which we came, and to which we will return; however, this is not an unalloyed view of grace and glory; it is a view of our living wholly alert to the ongoing sufferings to which the flesh is heir, sufferings both of human contrivance and natural disasters:

The Jesus Body, the Jesus Bones
Supposing the God to be moody and resentful
he has made us yet – earthen vessels of spittle and clay – in
　　likeness
of himself, longing to crucify and to be
crucified. Once I danced, my girl-child born,

on deserted streets, the way God must have danced across
　　his vast
echoing ballroom, everything now poised
to begin; but we begin, and begin again. Homes, up beyond
　　their eaves
in flood-water, lie still

as ranked coffins after war, corpses
floating, ceiling-high. This is a bleak and weakening
　　framework
of streets and intersections,
basements, hallways, embarrassed kitchens, slumped

like the fluid
interstices of the brain. How the mind, receiving warnings,
   will slew
away, unwilling. After the first flood,
God's stir of bitterness appeased, a silence moved over the
   waters;

do poplars breathe or hold for forty days
their breathing? and raptors, do they soar so high and live on
   dreams
for forty nights? We have lain,
fallen into earth, and softening. This evening

on the slow hills, such downpour-music, such culvert-chords
   and drain-strings;
the rooks, vested in solemn black,
announce their raucous vespers; rains have ended, the tipsy
fingers jittering at our windows

ceased, and in the after-loneliness
moths that had tangoed to the candles' flames grew precious
for the brevity of their hours. At last
high and lumbering things, elephant, emu and giraffe

came cautiously out into the air
from the rough-wood ribs of the ark, wood-lice and earwigs
in quick-step from the mud; all animal things
stepped, as perhaps each dawn they do or every dusk,
   astonished

at the washed aspect of the world.
Within our bones the folded feathers and frame of a grateful
   spirit
wait and sulk, that will lift one day
with the potency of resurrection out over the muddied earth.

I am, I know, facing into theology with the wild abandon and
the licence to kill of a poet and what I have said may not meet
with approval. But what I am pleading for is the imaginative
freedom applied to Christianity and to faiths in general that
lurks behind poetry. What I am offering, I think, is the extreme
but reasoned (poetically) hope that all is well, and all manner of

thing shall be well. For a poem to be good it must be true, but that truth must be only to itself; there must be no stealth or preaching, no dishonesty or fabrication, there must be commitment (in this case to language, also) and harmony and an openness to experience that is not contorted or manipulated. All of which must also be applied, I believe, to the working-out of one's faith – in my case, to the working-out of a commitment to Jesus. If Joseph Mary Plunkett saw the blood of Jesus upon the rose, and in the stars the glory of his eyes, then what I see as the sacrament of the world is no more than an extension of that note, no more than an introduction to the concept of the mystical body. And if we are to participate in that sacrament and receive the grace it signifies, then we are taking part in eucharist and our destiny is magnificent beyond our capacity to grasp magnificence.

Eucharist
I stand before him and he says
'Body of Christ' and I chew on flesh; he says
'Blood of Christ', I taste a bitter, small inebriation;
I take the substance deep into my substance and can say
I, too, am Jesus; and I pray
(thanks to the Jesus body, the Jesus bones)
that the deaf will hear the breezes
siffling through the eucalyptus trees,
will hear the breaking of waves along Atlantic's shingle
    shores,
that the blind, after darkness and the shadows that darkness
    throws,
will see the moonlight play like fireflies
along the undersides of leaves,
that those of us botched in brain and limb
will be gazelles across an intimate terrain and that the tears
of the too-old woman, inward-dwelling, wheelchair-locked
who lost her lover-man to death some twenty years ago
will step out giddily again
into blue erotic light.

Song of the Suffering Servant

They called me Princess, Sarai; I was beautiful, but barren.

I have been long uprooted, following my man,
old Abram building altars and ever heading south;

I have suffered him, his mumbling to himself, his taking
the mutterings as gospel; times we pitched a tent

in the shade of the terebinth and I mingled resin in the wine
to take away the bitterness; it is no small thing the people

turn away from God, he said, my own people
moiling in darkness in which they live and the earth

falling away from them, bit by grit by bit, into blown dust.
To walk in quietness through the sand is to hear

the shush shush shush of the suffering soul;
I am a stranger on the face of earth, I live

in tents; daily I accuse myself, of unfocused longing.
On scatter-days my words are anger, sometimes

resentful silence; when I feel that it is old God herself
has become infection in the air, and Abram growing bitter

as lime or lemon, fidgety for children. A son, he said,
no mention of a daughter, (oh yes I would have liked

a daughter); he never said, but he glanced blame
at me. Sarai. Old lady. Barren. Came that day of haze,

Abram sitting idle under his oak tree, three
strangers lift like spectres from out the sun; I see

small disturbances of sand-dust and something stirs

uneasily within me; three male strangers, grave of face

and I knew (my man, big-husband, doing his big-man thing
again) it would mean pain for me; God does not shift

soul-spaces without purpose and the weight falls,
as it always does, on God's most loved, on woman.

I made bread for them, apricot cinnamon cakes
but they ignored them in favour of burnt flesh; I heard

child-promises and I giggled at the designs of God.
Now I have learned: wonders may be found in a dull place

and terror is possible in the visitation of strangers, of God
the Creator, who laid the heavens out before her

like a camel-hair nap, in wadis, in parti-coloured fields.
Old Abram took my son away to kill him, mumbling again,

taking his mutterings as gospel; I grovelled, this is bone, I
said,
of my bone, blood of my blood. When they came home,
chastened,

I knew I was to be (God help me!) mother of the faithful.

for Siobhán Dowling and Fiachra Long

Dream of a Fair Field

for Fr Ronan Drury

Ireland, in the early part of this the twenty-first century, has become an island of greed and sorrow; we have become a nation where the gathering of wealth, no matter what is damaged or who is downtrodden along the way, takes precedence over traditional generosity and Christian belief. We are a county where violence, the thrust for power, collaboration with the US weaponry of war, torture and untruth, the sufferings of the poor, the ill and infirm, oh all of the conditions associated with a 'third world' country ... dominate; and all of this has thrown a distress into the soul that is not easy to deal with. As an aspiring poet, I have found that it has become more and more difficult to write. There is needed a tranquillity of spirit to allow the circumstances of our living to acquire resonance, depth and understanding, but the immediacy and speed of developments are inimical to that tranquillity of spirit. Furthermore, it has become (and there is no other way of saying this) fashionable to deny the validity of religion and religious practices.

The ground of all my living and writing has been an attempt to fashion a language and imagery suitable to the translation of Christian faith in these modern times, and for this I have suffered ridicule and rejection, as a matter of course. How can a poem stand against the United Sates/Israel military machine? How can it bring a sense of integrity and morality to a political system in our own country that works by subterfuge, aiming at perpetuation of power rather than the good of the citizens, when political life has become shameful and overtly dismissive of the deeper values by which Christianity ought to flourish. A poet may be noisily praised and lauded in public but is ignored and dismissed as having nothing 'real' to offer to the 'real' world. I speak of this as the censorship of indifference and this country is rife with it.

I have re-read Isaiah, that great prophet and poet and, (even if 'he' is a gathering of several writers), find the work challenging and uplifting. He spoke out, against his own will, to emphasise the truth of his vision of God to a people suffering their own ills. In the book there is a series of pieces, 'Songs of the Suffering Servant', where the author complains of the indifference of the people to his message. If my faith in the beauty and worth of the Christian heritage to which I owe all hope, urges me to write in order to do what I can to redeem that heritage, then I feel an obligation so to do. I do not compare myself to Isaiah, but one is allowed to echo the work, to recapture its spirit for one's own times:

On scatter-days my words are anger, sometimes
resentful silence; I complain the inadequacy
of words as instruments of peace –
as it has been, and now, and may
all a life-time, be.

The words shift before me, blown sand, blown ash –
chill April days, rooks squabbling in the naked trees –
and I sieve words, to piece together what the Lord God lays
cruelly on my tongue. I have seen morning upon morning
      weariness
on an island without meaning. And I am weak, rebellious,

weak again; I wait, listening. I have hid for shame,
have ducked my head before the dryly critical.
Here, at the roots of trees, the lost twigs of the rookery.
Invisibly the God helps, I will not be confounded;
He who justifies is near me, touches me, the way

the first warm breeze of spring
touches. I, too, grow old
like a much-used overcoat, ripped
raw like a gardener's
glove.

I was brought up to believe in a Christ who is the spoken name (the Word) and nature of the Creator, our Source and Sustenance. That name and nature have always signified, for me, love and service. It is a love that works its way through the very flesh and bones of the earth, through all things, all creatures. From the wild and wonderful beauty of Achill Island, I learned to associate rock and ocean, tree and insect, to the destiny of humanity and find that reading justified in St Paul, in the overwhelming beauty of Romans chapter eight. And it is the blood of the Christ that suffuses this earth, as it suffuses our beings in communion. The Christ bleeds still: and I find it my great need to try and speak out, in the only way I know how:

Unclean Lips
A slow mist fistles across the alder leaves;
rushes stand, still as rust-haired soldiers
waiting; sheep, trailing wool and brambles, shift
lethargically in the fields; morning, and I know –
because I have not spoken – I have unclean lips
and the roof of my mouth is turf-grit dry. Fuchsia
blossoms hang in their scarlet miracles
and rhododendron woods swell in their extravagance;
burn my tongue, I pray, with a live coal
that words on fire and unexpected might yet
flame across the darkening spaces. Too soon
evening sunlight on the mountain slopes will cast
shadow-clouds – spirit-thunderers, truth-falls –
its maps of the difficult boroughs of the sky.

It is a question, too, of language. Of course I miss the great poetry of the psalms, the Song of Songs, the Book of Revelation. I find the dreary forced 'modernity' of music at Mass now wholly wearying, after the glories of Bach and Palestrina. I find that the Christian message is being couched today in a language that is lowered in intensity and seriousness to accommodate a lethargic faith. I know that the use of words like 'immaculate conception', 'transubstantiation', 'pyx', even commoner words like 'sacrament' and 'mercy', are almost meaningless to a younger generation. Christmas has become a time (now months long) for spending and buying, for overeating and over drinking; Easter has become a time for Chocolate eggs and bunnies, and the notion of Lent has become an opportunity to try, once again, to ease back (for the sake of one's health) on smoking or alcohol. I know I exaggerate a little, but only, I think, a little. And all of the ills to which our society is subject, relate back to a lack of structure in life, to a failure of purpose. If motivation gives energy to act, then lack of motivation leads to lethargy, depression and even suicide. Christ back, then, upon Irish souls!

Rarely does one get an opportunity to confront the politicians, those to whom we once looked for leadership and now look on with wholly jaundiced eyes. But when an election comes upon us, so do the politicians, creeping from door to door, begging. I have taken this moment as the urgency of a poem that attempts an overview of our time. It begins with a calling to my door one Sunday morning; I was, in fact, about to head out to Mass, after a walk in the local park; smitten, as I so often am, by the beauty and variety of the physical universe as well as by its violence and indifference, I was in no mood to stand quietly and receptively before the blandishments and hollow promises of a politician.

Sunday Morning
I
I have been walking amongst weeds and wilderness
over by ponds in the suburban park; eye
of the goldeneye, claw of the water rail, a rat
gone dunking down the hollowed heart
of a tree; a heron, rakish-thin, stands above me
as Donne the preacher might have stood
admonishing. The rowan tree by the front door
has loosed its berries and the cowering earth
is rich with knowledge of the ways of God. Soon
he who is beggar, who would be governor,
will stand at the door, and knock; suave and discrete
in his light blue shirt, pink tie, his golfer cufflinks,
he will be braced with promises, with gorgeous lies
bristling like nostril-hairs, like down-tufts in his ears.
The ministerial car parked around the corner, its engine running.

I find it my task to point out, in so far as I am able, through poetry just such a contradiction, that this 'cowering' earth is exemplar to how humankind should stand in relation to unquestioning obedience to the will of God. The man at my door, I was well aware, was typical politician, and the words above are an attempt to convey my feelings without actually 'preaching'. If

poetry is to work, then it needs that distance that takes it away
from rhetoric and controversy and it is precisely that distance
that is difficult to find when emotions are actually running high.
I had been reading Isaiah's terrifying prophecies:

II
I had been taken by the last things, end-days
when the mountains would come keeling over, burying
the villages that had forgotten God; I saw
nations flow like torrents into a broiling sea,
who had turned their metals into gold, their minerals
into smart bombs. Is it a small thing, I will ask him,
that on your watch the bones of children
lie bleaching in the sun? He'll say: there will be
lavender and roses, the hair-fluff on his manly wrists
shivering. I will be nervous but will say, you
are government, the spoils of the poor are in your home;
they sit on plastic seats in supermarket doors while you
slip by in your Mercedes-Benz S-Class, not knowing God
will be standing out at the street crossing, waiting.
You will want to run him down and grind his bones into the
    tar.

Oh dear, these, of course, are the words I wanted to speak to
him, but would they come out in the fervour of moments standing at the door? Of course not; how many of us remember exactly
what we wanted to say, and how to say it, long after the opportunity has passed us by! We look to our politicians to bring order
and harmony to our society, or at least we used to; nowadays, as
it has always been, poetry looks more to the order and harmony
of the physical world about us.

III
That we – even in the labyrinthine dustways
of the suburbs – are formed of, and are one with
ocean, that our names are written on the hill slopes
in white sea-stones, that the cries we hear at night
are the cries of the drowned that go drifting by
in clean bone-constructs or in the guts of shoals –
a high uninterrupted crying that must be part
of the loud hosanna, biddable, like the chough

in acrobatic flight where scream echoes to blood
against the cliffs, or like the cock-eyed sparrow
bathing himself in dust by the back door, eyed
by the tomcat arrogantly spraying car-wheel
and shrub in manicured pathway – does all this
make you say there is no order to the winds? Nor
therefore, order in the labyrinthine dustways of our lives.

The deepest order and harmony that we can be aware of is that which Christ, the breathed-out nature of our God, has shown us, and it is that same Christ that we have put to death, and put to death again, over and over. In Ireland, our awareness too that the Mother of Christ suffered along with her son and touches our hearts most closely, has also seemed to be hidden away in embarrassed confusion. To a poet attempting to touch on these subjects once again, there arises an awareness of personal unworthiness, of one's own ongoing need for forgiveness. And yet the urge to cry out, in the face of the overwhelming violence of our times, takes precedence over such diffidence.

IV
There was a violent death – exquisite pain –
foreshadowed, many times rehearsed, the mother's hands
raised in a gesture of anguish, questioning
how can this be, and why? The ocean's sound
falling against the beach could be the sound he heard
birthing on that hill out of that womb, could be
the sound that is a restless and shifting
violence in the blood. Times were when I could weep
for him, weep for myself and for my children,
weep for betrayal, for forgiveness that I need
seventy times seven and every day. Childmother sits,
innocent, hands stretched wide as the bay's embrace,
though querulous; the son lies dead between her knees,
eyes closed and head lolling in heaviness. Violence
gaining dominion, the bullying human, the hectoring.

Having vented such thoughts, interiorly, and long after the event, and having failed once again to stammer them in actuality to the ears that would, no doubt, be closed against them, I accepted his piece of publicity, he smiled and went on his way, unperturbed. But later the poem comes, much later and now it can take years before a collection of poetry will appear and the rare poetry journals do not like to take on longer pieces of work, so one feels as if the cries are truly those of one mewling in the wilderness. But one mewls on, dropping the words like individual drops of water into a salt ocean.

V

Because you are ashamed of God, when the cities
of your hands crumble in unimaginable heat
you will bow down your heads, your mountains
will blow in dust before the winds; you have turned
your face from the facts of war, you have been paid in cash;
you will thrive, for yet a while, a little while, for yet
a very little while. It is said Isaiah was a small man
insignificant and balding – fist knuckled against his head
to hide embarrassment – but of the people, a fire
blazed unquenchably in his heart; one lazy eye could see
down the corridor of centuries, how the child, uncouth
and cradled in a crib, would start to burn all flesh
to the purest nib, and blow the ash of all that lived
into everlasting dust. I will close the door, softly; he
will turn, walk down the drive and knock, smiling, at the
   next door.

The prophet Jonah was also unwilling to go and speak God's word. Religious poetry, though the tradition of such work in English is truly a magnificent one (Donne, Herbert, Milton, Hopkins, Eliot ...) is often summarily rejected, not for its form, language or worth, but because there are many who presume that once the subject touches on religion, then the poetry does not exist. It is a blindingly foolish approach; one might as well reject out of hand all poetry that touches on swans, or that deals with shipwrecks, or touches on the dejecta of a city's alleyways. Yet a Christian holds that the justice of God is tempered always with love, a fact that annoyed Jonah when his prophecies ultimately were overturned by such a love. Kill me, the prophet Jonah said to a demanding God, because your steadfast love undermines all justice. Your gift, God said, has been mine to give, and yours simply to accept. And so, before the crazy building of the new and grasping Ireland, where so much of our countryside lies like lopped limbs in a war zone, while men in daffodil-yellow hard hats move about like robots carrying wooden planks, it is easy to lose heart; I have been figuring, in a place apart, if this is stitching or unstitching of the world. I would host the bones requiem these days, over ocean juggernauts, mosquito jets masterful in their economies, their deconstructions; in our economic victories such spiritual defeat!

Contemporary society is amused, perhaps even a little bemused, by poetry and generally mocking of religious poetry. And yet I dream on, and attempt to turn my dream of a newly Christian Ireland into some reality, at least a reality in language.

The Dream
And in the dream thousands of young
women and men were wading slowly out
into the lake while the oozing bottom-mud sucked them
further and further until they disappeared with that
   soundless yowl
possible only in dreams though audible
day by day around us, here, in this country, and now, at this
   time.
Can a poem touch on the heart of politics? Can it tell
how the blood-sheen on claw and bill of the chough
is beautiful beyond their machinations? Do they know
how good it is to sleep by an uncurtained window
while the dark side of the mountain looms as guardian
and a high star shades from gold to turquoise-white?
Can they tell how the skylark fills its own lake full
high above the sand-dunes with water-fire music,
can they bring the scent of cotton, of heather and the
   warming bog
into their chambers where they hurl lies and accusations
across our hurting space? The Christ, the poem says,
waltzed across lake water, he is alive, in light, and stone, and
   bone
and do you hear Him? You the anointed of the people,
the disappointed, the disappointing.

'Hierusalem, My Happy Home'

This beautiful poem exists in several versions, some longer, several shorter. It appears to have been written in the late sixteenth century, between 1590-1600, and one version is headed 'A song Made by I.B.P. to the tune of Diana'. This suggests that it is modelled on an older ballad and the initials may stand for somebody with the name of J. B. Priest. The author must have read the monastic Latin hymn by Peter Damien, an eleventh century Italian monk and philosopher: *Ad perennis vitae fontem* ... a hymn urging the human soul to aspire to drinking from the fountain of everlasting life. Perhaps the popular song 'Jerusalem: the Holy City' derives from the same impulse. The original work is based on the Book of Revelation and the author may also have had St Augustine's phrase in mind: 'Thou hast made us for Thyself, O God and our hearts are restless until they rest in Thee.' There is a delightful simplicity and directness to the poem and I set it towards the fountainhead of these essays, as echo, ongoing, and urgent.

Hierusalem, my happy home,
  When shall I come to thee?
When shall my sorrows have an end,
  Thy joys when shall I see?

O happy harbour of the Saints!
  O sweet and pleasant soil!
In thee no sorrow may be found,
  No grief, no care, no toil.

There lust and lucre cannot dwell,
  There envy bears no sway;
There is no hunger, heat, nor cold,
  But pleasure every way.
Thy walls are made of precious stones,

Thy bulwarks diamonds square;
Thy gates are of right orient pearl,
  Exceeding rich and rare.

Thy turrets and thy pinnacles
  With carbuncles do shine;
Thy very streets are paved with gold,
  Surpassing clear and fine.

Ah, my sweet home, Hierusalem,
  Would God I were in thee!
Would God my woes were at an end,
  Thy joys that I might see!

Thy gardens and thy gallant walks
  Continually are green;
There grows such sweet and pleasant flowers
  As nowhere else are seen.

Quite through the streets, with silver sound,
  The flood of Life doth flow;
Upon whose banks on every side
  The wood of Life doth grow.

There trees for evermore bear fruit,
  And evermore do spring;
There evermore the angels sit,
  And evermore do sing.

Our Lady sings Magnificat
  With tones surpassing sweet;
And all the virgins bear their part,
  Sitting about her feet.

Hierusalem, my happy home,
  Would God I were in thee!
Would God my woes were at an end,
  Thy joys that I might see!

Poet as Outlaw
Robert Southwell, Jesuit

Robert Southwell was born in Norfolk in 1561 and was hanged at Tyburn 34 years later. His grandfather, Sir Richard Southwell, had been a wealthy man and a courtier in the reign of Henry VIII, and had helped bring about the Earl of Surrey's execution. On his mother's side Robert was descended from a Shelley family and a remote connection may be traced forward to Percy Bysshe Shelley. In his very early years he was once stolen by gypsies but was found and recovered by his nurse; later he wrote: 'What, had I remained with the gipsy? How abject, how void of all knowledge and reverence of God! In what shameful vices, in how great danger of infamy, in how certain danger of an unhappy death and eternal punishment!'

Robert was brought up a Catholic and sent to Douai to be educated by the Jesuits. This, of course, was the most difficult period in history to be a Catholic in England. He spent some time in Paris and asked to be admitted to the Jesuit order. He was only seventeen at that time and, being refused at first, wrote some passionate laments. In 1578, still only seventeen, he was admitted to the order in Rome and took vows in 1580. He did his noviceship at Tournai and was ordained priest in Rome in 1584, when he was barely twenty-three years old. He spent a short time in the English College in Rome, as prefect of studies. He was sent, as per his earnest request, in 1586, to England with a Fr Henry Garnett and took the secret name of Cotton.

Southwell was worried that many who had been faithful Catholics were now drifting into the Church of England to avoid the fine for every church service from which they absented themselves. Many families held out until they were financially ruined; then they would attempt to make their way to the continent and live on alms. Southwell was made chaplain to the

Countess of Arundel for whom his 'Hundred Meditations on the love of God' were addressed. He worked zealously for some six years on his missionary work, hiding in various places and under various disguises, pretending an interest in the pursuits of country gentlemen to distract pursuers. He appears to have remained aloof from controversy, and carried on his missionary work with gentleness and courage. Most of the remaining Catholics were to be found in the countryside. They longed for better days, the most they hoped for being that a priest might be smuggled into their homes to help them in their last hours.

There was a strong, though permanently watchful, cohesion among the Catholics, recalling in ways the early days of the primitive church. Small groups came together in the semi-darkness to celebrate Mass, always wondering if there might be a traitor amongst them. Eventually, through the treachery of a girl, Anne Bellamy, daughter of a house in which he was staying, he was arrested in 1592 and was subjected to very many cruelties and tortures. He was kept in a dungeon swarming with vermin. He was repeatedly tortured, brought almost to the point of death, revived, and tortured again. He was prodded to inform on the presence of other priests but his steadfastness was remarkable, impressing even his tormentors. After three years in prison he was tried and executed in 1595. Standing in the cart, he began: 'Whether we live, we live unto the Lord: or whether we die, we die unto the Lord. Therefore, whether we live or whether we die, we are the Lord's … I am brought hither to perform the last act of this miserable life, and … I do most humbly desire at the hands of Almighty God for our Saviour Jesus' sake, that he would vouchsafe to pardon and forgive all my sins …'. He had been sentenced to hanging and quartering but was dead before he was cut down and quartered. A remarkable man, and a remarkable poet.

Southwell's writings were popular among his contemporaries and circulated in manuscript form; this was a method of preaching the deepest reaches of his Catholicism to his flock. It has sometimes been suggested that his poems touched the work of Shakespeare. He was, of necessity, a man of action and adventure, in his efforts to remain free among those whom he served but his deepest instincts were towards the mystical life. His poetry was copied by hand and passed around. He wrote in Latin as well as in English, the Latin poems demonstrating a fine and wide literary awareness. His poems in English, given the context of their writing, incorporate the underworld life of risk and danger that he translated into a Catholic tenet. The Catholic Church remembers him as a martyr every year on 21 February.

The poems focus on the person of Christ, and on his sufferings for the benefit of humanity. In this he is a startling contrast to the somewhat later Thomas Traherne whose work focuses on the hope and beauty of the next world. Southwell contemplates, too, the innocence and perseverance that Christ displayed in earthly life, in spite of persecution and death. The outlaw Christ is close to the outlaw poet and as long as this is maintained Southwell feels content. Though there was little physical 'delight' in the world in which the poet priest moved, yet that mystical delight in the alignment with Christ remains strong. The key word is 'true': if the Christ remains true to men then surely it is men's duty to remain true to the Christ, no matter the odds.

A Child My Choice

Let folly praise that fancy loves, I praise and love that Child
Whose heart no thought, whose tongue no word, whose
    hand no deed defiled.

I praise Him most, I love Him best, all praise and love is His;
While Him I love, in Him I live, and cannot live amiss.

Love's sweetest mark, laud's highest theme, man's most
    desired light,
To love Him life, to leave Him death, to live in Him delight.

He mine by gift, I His by debt, thus each to other due;
First friend He was, best friend He is, all times will try Him
    true.

Though young, yet wise; though small, yet strong; though
    man, yet God He is:
As wise, He knows; as strong, He can; as God, He loves to
    bless.

His knowledge rules, His strength defends, His love doth
  cherish all;
His birth our joy, His life our light, His death our end of
  thrall.

Alas! He weeps, He sighs, He pants, yet do His angels sing;
Out of His tears, His sighs and throbs, doth bud a joyful
  spring.

The poem erupts out of personal feeling, personal suffering, personal longing; the broken phrases of the lines combine with the full rhymes to create a strange effect, the inherent contradictions between the Christ as Man and the Christ as God, allied to the need men have to imitate those contradictions. The ending is dramatically powerful, the last couplets moving with an easier movement, 'His love doth cherish all: His death our end of thrall: yet do His angels sing: doth bud a joyful spring.' It is God's selfless love for humankind that Southwell wants to preach; it is the Counter-Reformation doctrines of service in spite of suffering and persecution in the response to that love; it is a preaching that works because the poetry in which it is housed issues from personal commitment and subtle rhyming, careful mimicry in the movement of the verses, an appeal to the common Christian through the best-known and most important movements in Christ's life. And what could be better known and loved among Christians than Christmas day and the very birth of that Saviour, that loving yet demanding Child come to rescue humanity from suffering by undergoing an even more frightful suffering himself?

The Burning Babe
As I in hoary winter's night stood shivering in the snow,
Surprised I was with sudden heat which made my heart to
  glow;
And lifting up a fearful eye to view what fire was near,
A pretty babe all burning bright did in the air appear;
Who, scorchèd with excessive heat, such floods of tears did
  shed
As though his floods should quench his flames which with
  his tears were fed.

Alas, quoth he, but newly born in fiery heats I fry,
Yet none approach to warm their hearts or feel my fire but I!
My faultless breast the furnace is, the fuel wounding thorns,
Love is the fire, and sighs the smoke, the ashes shame and
   scorns;
The fuel justice layeth on, and mercy blows the coals,
The metal in this furnace wrought are men's defilèd souls,
For which, as now on fire I am to work them to their good,
So will I melt into a bath to wash them in my blood.
With this he vanished out of sight and swiftly shrunk away,
And straight I callèd unto mind that it was Christmas day.
Almighty Babe, whose tender arms can force all foes to fly,
Correct my faults, protect my life, direct me when I die!

Fire is the immediately strange but gradually clarifying image in this, perhaps the best-known of Southwell's poems. It is an image that allows no compromise, that offers a total immersion in suffering leading inevitably to purification and death.

By no means all of the poems of Robert Southwell SJ are of this calibre; several of them fail utterly to find, in his need for preaching and exhortation, the reach of imagery and the touch of poetry that lift language from the mud of everyday speech; too often the poems remain on the level of preachery!

Crush the serpent in the head,
Break ill eggs ere they be hatched;
Kill bad chickens in the tread,
Fledged, they hardly can be catched.
In the rising stifle ill,
Lest it grow against thy will.
(*'Loss in Delay'*)

Some of the poems reflect his sense of himself as an outlaw on earth, and this both in the literal and in the metaphysical sense of the word; the work bristles with his death-wish, and martyrdom becomes a boon to be desired:

By force I live, in will I wish to die.
In plaint I pass the length of lingering days.
Free would my soul from mortal body fly,
And tread the track of death's desired ways!

Life is but loss where death is deemed gain,
And loathed pleasures breed displeasing pain.
(*'Life is but Loss'*)

Not the most joyous of poems, but it certainly signals at least
a will to go on suffering in the name of the Lord. And yet perhaps this was the kind of work that encouraged the Catholics
amongst whom he worked to go on in their faith. This approach
to living touches, of course, on the deepest urges of genuine
mysticism, where love is the inspiration behind every taken
breath, and communication with the beloved is the greatest joy.
In Southwell's case, the difficult pleasures of mystical contemplation were unattainable, but love and the ultimate coming into
the presence of the beloved were not. One poem typifies this,
leading on from the last piece where death is called for:

I Die Alive
O Life! what lets thee from a quick decease?
O Death! what draws thee from a present prey?
My feast is done, my soul would be at ease,
My grace is said: O Death! come take away.

I live, but such a life as ever dies;
I die, but such a death as never ends;
My death, to end my dying, life denies,
And life, my living death no whit amends.

Thus still I die, yet still I do revive:
My living death by dying life is fed.
Grace, more than nature, keeps my heart alive,
Whose idle hopes and vain desires are dead.

Not where I breathe, but where I love, I live;
Not where I love, but where I am, I die;
The life I wish must future glory give,
The deaths I feel in present dangers lie.

Apart from the sheer delight in the use of paradox evident in
this piece, it is interesting to speculate that John Donne may well
have come across poems like this which were circulating
amongst Catholics while Donne himself was struggling with his
own conscience. Donne's work, of course, bristles with the plea-

sures of paradox and the self-awareness of the work chimes well with Southwell's verses. Yet I feel there is also a glance backwards in this poem, and in others of Southwell's work, where the use of alliterative words advanced the rhythms of the whole piece. Many of the lines above have fully absorbed that Anglo-Saxon verve and adapted it musically and drawn it with delight into the paradoxes. Even in the first two lines the use of the words 'lets' and 'draw' suggest at least an unconscious, and more than likely a fully conscious awareness of the power of such alliterative rhythmic devices. Southwell's work, then, frequently moves well beyond the uses of catechism and preachery and takes his religious urges deep into the realms of poetry.

Here are four lines from a poem called 'Man to the Wound in Christ's Side', an otherwise not very distinguished poem, though here the influence of the Anglo-Saxon alliterative tradition is very obvious:

Here is the spring of trickling tears,
The mirror of all mourning wights,
With doleful tunes for dumpish ears,
And solemn shows for sorrowed sights.

Another fall-back to earlier centuries occurs in those poems Southwell wrote that retell in verse form the story of the New Testament; the titles themselves, in this series, give the game away: 'The Visitation', 'The Nativity of Christ', 'The Flight into Egypt', and many more. As in the middle ages the method of getting across the story of Christ in memorable form was a worthy one but in Southwell's case, the staid and serious plodding along of the verses, without personal intervention and surely without humour, leaves the reader dry. There is one poem among these that stands out, however, where the impulse for deeper movement and understanding through the techniques of poetry takes over from the preaching impulse.

Christ's Bloody Sweat
Fat soil, full spring, sweet olive, grape of blisse,
That yields, that streams, that pours, that dost distill,
Untilled, undrawn, unstamped, untouched of press,
Dear fruit, clear brooks, fair oil, sweet wine at will!

Thus Christ unforced prevents, in shedding blood,
The whips, the thorns, the nails, the spear, and rood.

He pelican's, He phoenix' fate doth prove,
Whom flames consume, whom streams enforce to die:
How burneth blood, how bleedeth burning love,
Can one in flame and stream both bathe and fry?
How could He join a phoenix' fiery pains
In fainting pelican's still bleeding veins?

Elias once, to prove God's sovereign power,
By prayer procured a fire of wondrous force
That blood and wood and water did devour,
Yea, stones and dust beyond all Nature's course:
Such fire is love, that, fed with gory blood,
Doth burn no less than in the driest wood.

O sacred fire! come show thy force on me,
That sacrifice to Christ I may return.
If withered wood for fuel fittest be,
If stones and dust, if flesh and blood will burn,
I withered am, and stony to all good:
A sack of dust, a mass of flesh and blood.

The movement of this poem is from within the poet outwards, not a simple retelling of the gospel narrative. The poet is
involved, and deeply so, and the many images and sources of
faith in the poem are already familiar from the earlier poems. It
is also hugely tempting to wonder if George Herbert read this
poem and drew from it some awareness of a poetry charged
with a personal God and an awareness of man as dust. Here
again is the commitment to self-sacrifice that this poet-priest-
outlaw laid out for himself; here, too, that imagery of fire so fre-
quent in Southwell's view of suffering, and its contrast with
images of streams and blood. The opening lines offer a sense of
generous giving, and the broken sentences stress the awe of the
poet aware of this extravagance. The movement to the Christ
and his free giving of himself for love of the Father, crowns this
first stanza beautifully.

The second stanza offers strange yet effective imagery and
contrast, the pelican giving her blood for her young, the phoenix

being destroyed by fire but glorying in resurrection. The extravagance of the lines is wonderful: 'How burneth blood, how bleedeth burning love,/ Can one in flame and stream both bathe and fry?' The delight in language and paradox moves side by side with a deeply religious sentiment and the phrases are put in the form of questions to make the reader (or the author himself) probe the truth more deeply. Then he kindly, as preacher cum teacher cum poet, answers his own questions, urging the reader to see how Elias, through prayer, could call down a saving fire from heaven and Elias, we know, was taken up to heaven in a chariot of fire. Southwell equates this fire with love, the power of Divine love answering to the sufferings of mankind. We have moved far and wonderfully and yet gently from the awed and hesitant opening of this poem to the final stanza that stands back in glad amazement from what the poem itself has revealed: 'O sacred fire!' The poem shifts directly into prayer, thus mirroring the poem's movement and drawing both poet and reader into immediate contact with what the poem talks of, the demands of love that result in a loving fire to consume the soul and turn all that is noxious and transitory into ash.

W. B. Yeats wrote: 'Too long a sacrifice can make a stone of the heart. O when may it suffice?' In the case of Robert Southwell the question may be answered, 'only at death'. It was essential for Southwell to lie low, to be an outlaw in his own country, for his faith's sake. It was important, he felt, that his gift for poetry be used to forward his vocation as a missionary and that he use his talents to teach his frightened flock. But his aim always appears to have been martyrdom and it is this desire for self-sacrifice that dominates his work and that, too often, draws the poetry into avenues where it becomes verse only, though even the verse is well-achieved. He held up before his own eyes, and before the eyes of his flock, the examples of martyrs; but he also holds up Mary Stuart, Queen of Scots, as a saint and a martyr. He speaks of her troubles and, of course, he is thinking of his own, and how they are transfigured only in the afterlife. We are back to the Christian paradox of death bringing life, of life being death. If Queen Mary did not dread death because it would bring her closer to Christ, then, Southwell reasons, English

Catholics should not fear death either, mortal life being little more than restricting their contact with the Lord. Here, finally, is the glory of suffering, here is the ultimate example of purification being no more than the method by which one leaves this life and is welcomed into God's life.

Decease Release

Dum morior orior

The pounded spice both taste and scent doth please,
In fading smoke the force doth incense show,
The perished kernel springeth with increase,
The lopped tree doth best and soonest grow.

God's spice I was and pounding was my due,
In fading breath my incense savoured best,
Death was the mean, my kernel to renew,
By lopping shot I up to heavenly rest.

Some things more perfect are in their decay,
Like spark that going out gives clearest light,
Such was my hap, whose doleful dying day
Began my joy and termed fortune's spite.

Alive a Queen, now dead I am a Saint,
Once Mary called, my name now Martyr is,
From earthly reign debarred by restraint,
In lieu whereof I reign in heavenly bliss.

My life my grief, my death hath wrought my joy,
My friends my foil, my foes my weal procured,
My speedy death hath shortened long annoy,
And loss of life an endless life assured.

My scaffold was the bed where ease I found,
The block a pillow of Eternal rest,
My headman cast me in a blissful swound,
His axe cut off my cares from combered breast.

Rue not my death, rejoice at my repose,
It was no death to me but to my woe,
The bud was opened to let out the Rose,
The chains unloosed to let the captive go.

A prince by birth, a prisoner by mishap,
From Crown to cross, from throne to thrall I fell,
My right my ruth, my titles wrought my trap,
My weal my woe, my worldly heaven my hell.

By death from prisoner to a prince enhanced,
From Cross to Crown, from thrall to throne again,
My ruth my right, my trap my style advanced,
From woe to weal, from hell to heavenly reign.

This Glow-worm Faith
William Alabaster (1567-1640)

The strange name comes from the word 'arbalester' which meant a crossbow-man. The name is appropriate in a strange way, reminding readers that Alabaster's life of faith was a battle, and a battle that shifted away from and back to victory over himself with regularity.

William Alabaster was born at Hadleigh, Suffolk in 1567. He was educated at Hadleigh grammar school and Trinity College, Cambridge, which he entered as a scholar in 1584. He took his BA in 1587, and MA in 1591.

Samuel Johnson, in his *Lives of the Poets*, speaking of 'Latin verses with classic elegance', writes: 'If we produced anything worthy of notice before the elegies of Milton, it was perhaps Alabaster's *Roxana*.' This was a Senecan tragedy written in Latin in 1592 and quite successful in its time. He wrote an epic poem in Latin glorifying Elizabeth but it was not published during his lifetime. At this time, his prospects for a grand career looked very bright indeed. Then, in 1596, Alabaster took part, as chaplain, on the expedition to Cadiz, certain that the Earl would find him a position suited to his status and prospects. He was learned, pious and, at this stage, wholly orthodox in his views. It is unclear what actually urged him to convert to Catholicism but one explanation may have been his discovery of Catholic mysticism and its great attraction to his mind. He converted to Catholicism and tried to urge the Earl of Essex to convert, too. He is supposed to have written a pamphlet explaining his conversion, which seems to have been genuine. When he returned to England, Alabaster was imprisoned in a prison in Southwark; there followed a period of imprisonments, exile, escapes, drama! It was 1611 before he recanted, renouncing Catholicism and returning to Anglicanism. This was the period when John Donne was working away from Catholicism towards Anglicanism; it was a hugely difficult time and dangerous for Catholics.

The move by Alabaster gained him much favour and he was made Doctor of Divinity at Cambridge in 1614, made a prebendary of St Paul's and given a living in Hertfordshire. In 1618 he was made chaplain to King James. He wrote several mystical and cabbalistic works during this time and was regarded with some admiration by many. Robert Herrick addressed lines to him:

> To Doctor Alabaster
> Nor art thou less esteemed that I have placed
> Amongst mine honoured, thee almost the last:
> In great processions many lead the way
> To him who is the triumph of the day,
> As these have done to thee who art the one,
> One only glory of a million:
> In whom the spirit of the gods does dwell,
> Firing thy soul, by which thou dost foretell
> When this or that vast dynasty must fall
> Down to a fillet more imperial;
> When this or that horn shall be broke, and when
> Others shall spring up in their place again;
> When times and seasons and all years must lie
> Drowned in the sea of wild eternity;
> When the black books, as yet unsealed,
> Shall by the mighty angel be revealed;
> And when the trumpet which thou late hast found
> Shall call to judgment. Tell us when the sound
> Of this or that great April day shall be,
> And next the Gospel we will credit thee.
> Meantime like earth-worms we will crawl below,
> And wonder at those things that thou dost know.

This is a homage to the learning of Alabaster, to his wisdom and leadership qualities as they then appeared. He published many scholarly works alongside metaphysical and devotional poems in Latin and in English, very few of which survive as they were not printed in his lifetime. He died in 1640, aged 74. He is best remembered for a series of sonnets that he wrote. From these it is clear that his problem with faith remained central to his life. 'The light of faith', like an old-fashioned lamp, needs continual topping up with oil. Life offers a mountain which must be climbed, but Christ having already climbed it, great precedents may be followed. There is the temptation of a 'new-found balk', some new obstacle placed in the way of faith that will test the will of many. Presumably this is the temptation to convert to Catholicism and to remain in that faith, a temptation into which our hero fell but quickly recovered. So he must have seen his own faith as a 'glow-worm faith', or a failure in love, and that 'all that rout' had left a great many people undone.

Here is an exhortation to his own soul, but also a way of gleaning the favours of the leaders of that faith to which he has returned. It is a sonnet that meanders through the maze of human willing and evasion and lacks the exact and self-probing integrity of a Donne or Herbert, yet its focus on the difficulties of faith gives it value, and its somewhat rhetorical immediacy, its rhythmic flow, make it memorable.

Up to Mount Olivet ...
Up to Mount Olivet my soul ascend
The mount spiritual, and there supply
Thy fainting lamp with oil of charity
To make the light of faith the more extend.
Go by this tract which thither right doth tend,
Which Christ did first beat forth to walk thereby,
And sixteen ages of posterity
Have gone it over since from end to end.
But strike not down to any new-found balk,
Which hunters have begun of late to chalk:
For whether 'twere the glow-worm faith went out,
Or want of love did pine them in the way,
Or else the cruel devils rob or slay,
No news comes back of one of all that rout.

In another piece, *'The night, the starless night ...'* Alabaster takes Christ himself as he made haste to come on earth, knowing that ahead of him would be his crucifixion, and all the pain and grief and torments that that would entail. Alabaster sees Christ's preparation for this life of service as a 'martial' approach, the composition of a hymn that would help the hero rush upon his enemies and overcome them. He sees him, too, as making himself aware of all the love and joy that his life would be in contact with and this awareness would be needed to buoy up his soul with strength to face the enormous task of redeeming mankind. Alabaster applies all of this to himself and to his taking of solemn holy vows. This taking of orders is a taking upon oneself, he says, of the very image, the 'portrait' of Christ's death and the poet wills himself to write a book of sonnets that would, as Christ did, contemplate love and give him hymns to face what the priest will have to face. It is a willing of himself forward; it is a push and an urge to his own soul to come to terms with whatever pain and suffering he may have to endure in that life of service.

The poem is not, in itself, very convincing but the sense of a soul not quite sure of itself is extended by the sonnet. This central image of Christ bracing himself by contemplation and the sounding of a sacred hymn to urge him on, is forced and the application of this image to the poet is therefore less than satisfying. If the sonnet runs in plain English from start to finish, it yet ends with a more striking metaphor: 'the coldest ice of fire', that of a faith that is a little scared of what lies ahead and a somewhat frostily-linked call-back to the first line of 'the starless night'. If the dark night that is so common to mystical writing here is intended, and applied to Christ himself, then it is a daring, though none-the-less unconvincing, application of the metaphor. And did Christ set out on the incarnation by bracing himself 'upon his foes to run'? As they say in the west of Ireland: 'I doubt so.'

The night, the starless night …
The night, the starless night of passion
From heaven began, on heaven beneath to fall,
When Christ did sound the onset martial,
A sacred hymn, upon his foes to run;
That with the fiery contemplation
Of love and joy, his soul and senses all
Surcharged might not dread the bitter thrall
Of pain and grief and torments all in one.
Then since my holy vows have undertook

To take the portrait of Christ's death in me,
Then let my love with sonnets fill this book,
With hymns to give the onset as did he;
That thoughts inflamèd with such heavenly muse
The coldest ice of fire may not refuse.

This coldest ice of fire, this love of Christ which is so demanding, this service to his faith, continues always to worry
Alabaster. Man is a bundle of contradictions, spirit and flesh,
heaven and earth; he rarely achieves rest of mind or body, reason struggling with faith, desire fighting with will. The conceit
in the next poem, *O Wretched man ...* is a fairly common one, developed more powerfully by John Donne, yet in the context of
the struggle with faith that was Alabaster's, the honesty and
truthful self-awareness of this sonnet succeeds to a fine extent.
In it he admits that the demanding love of Christ is continually
being undermined by reason, the way the movement of the sun
works on melting ice. Prayer, he concludes, is the only answer to
the contradictions inherent in his sensibility, and a submission
of his own will to the will of God. If individually each of these
sonnets remains commonplace, it is the run of them, taking several of them together to form a meditative sequence, that works
in Alabaster's, the poet's, favour.

O wretched man ...
O wretched man, the knot of contraries,
In whom both heaven and earth doth move and rest,
Heaven of my mind, which with Christ's love is blest,
Death of my heart, which in dull languor lies!
Yet doth my moving will still circulize
My heaven about my earth with thoughts' unrest,
Where reason as a sun from east to west
Darteth his shining beams to melt this ice.
And now with fear it southward doth descend,
Now between both is equinoctial,
And now to joys it higher doth ascend,
And yet continues my sea glacial.
What shall I do, but pray to Christ the Son?
In earth as heaven, Lord, let thy will be done.
Alabaster, in another sonnet, takes this notion of 'contraries'

and develops it in a slightly different direction, keeping, however, the basic image of ice and heat, bringing them on to tears and blushing. The temptations of lust 'scorch' him, and languor 'freezes' him, and both of these are sins; oppose these with 'fear of blame' and 'love of Christ', the heat of the latter will melt languor, and chill of the former will bring reproach, and here there come those fateful lines: 'That shame with heat may cool my looser thought, And tears with cold heat my heart's sluggish deep'. This is a focal point for the poetry of that age, the delight taken in contraries, in paradox and language games, all of which reached their high point in John Donne but here form a central, though not quite fruitful, apex to the imagery of Alabaster. The sonnet moves without the ease and pleasing grace of Donne but its slow seriousness is something of a blessing here, giving the conceits of the poem a touch of genuine grief and a sense of tension that images the querulous soul:

> *With heat and cold ...*
> With heat and cold I feel the spiteful fiend
> To work one mischief by two contraries,
> With lust he doth me scorch, with languor freeze,
> But lust and languor both one Christ offend.
> Let contraries with contraries contend,
> Let fear of blame and love of Christ arise,
> Hot love of Christ to melt in tears mine eyes,
> Cold fear of just reproach my shame to extend,
> That shame with heat may cool my looser thought,
> And tears with cold heat my heart's sluggish deep.
> O happy I if that such grace were wrought!
> Till then, shame blush because tears cannot weep,
> And tears weep you because shame cannot blush,
> Till shame from tears, and tears from shame do flush.

The interesting and focal point about Alabaster's work is, of course, exactly this vacillation, this 'glow-worm', this firefly, this will-o'-the-wisp that is faith. The probing of the sonnets into his failures, his doubts, his weaknesses in regard to faith, offers those of us who experience in our own time the great demands that believing makes on us, will appreciate the integrity of Alabaster's approach. There are times when he makes a statement of will: I will stay faithful, I will be true; faith becomes a question of accepting doubt and difficulty and still carrying on because the decision is made on the side of faith: chaining the will to the will of the Lord. The delight in the following poem is the beginning where he equates his approach to that of Peter who said something similar and went on to deny the Lord, and then repent and become a true apostle. How often in this piece is the word 'will' used: and the honest self-awareness that even though the will is there, the living might not stay true.

Though all forsake thee ...
Though all forsake thee, Lord, yet I will die;
For I have chainèd so my will to thine
That I have no will left my will to untwine,
But will abide with thee most willingly.
Though all forsake thee, Lord, yet cannot I;
For love hath wrought in me thy form divine
That thou art more my heart than heart is mine:
How can I then from myself, thyself, fly?
Thus thought Saint Peter, and thus thinking, fell;
And by his fall did warn us not to swell.
Yet still in love I say I would not fall,
And say in hope, I trust I never shall;
But cannot say in faith what might I do
To learn to say it, by hearing Christ say so.

If the faith outlined in the sonnets of William Alabaster is hard won and even harder kept, yet there is consolation for the reader in knowing and sharing the vacillations the poems betray, and no sonnet of his shows forth this hesitation and its source so much as the following, where the particulars of that faith are faced:

Jesus is risen ...
Jesus is risen from the infernal mire:
But who art thou that say'st Jesus arose?
Such holy words are only fit for those
Whose souls with Christ above the heavens aspire.
But if thou hast not raisèd thy desire

From earth to heaven, but in the world dost close
Thy love which unto heaven thou shouldst dispose,
Say not that Christ is yet ascended higher,
But yet within thy heart he lieth dead,
And by the devil is impoisonèd.
Rejoice not then in vain of his ascent;
For as his glorious rise doth much augment
All good men's hopes, so unto those that tread
False paths, it is a dreadful argument.

The ultimate premise on which all of Christianity is based is that Christ Jesus rose from the dead after his crucifixion; for Roman Catholics or for Anglicans alike, this tenet is the first and foremost and on it all other faith depends. Alabaster asks himself if he has any right to state that Jesus has risen if his own heart does not wholly aspire to rise to heaven with Jesus. What if his longings, his aims, his ambitions are centred on this earth, on the court, perhaps (or on political vantage, in our time!) on wealth and position and honour, then he has no right to link himself with that risen Christ. Oh poor man, thrusting his faith forward, arguing with his own soul, and arguing with direct honesty that shifts the poem from his writing into our hearing, if we, too, face ourselves honestly. Faith, Alabaster knows, lies within the heart and will of the Christian and if that aspiration that is faith is dead to heaven and to Christ, what hope is there? Of all those poems of the late sixteenth century grappling with faith and aware of the goods to be gotten by clinging to advancement and intrigue, perhaps this touches most closely on the essence of the problem. 'It is a dreadful argument.' Alabaster's life and work, then, offer something of unique worth to our time. 'One only glory of a million', as Robert Herrick addressed him; this is flattery beyond the actual truth, as Herrick was responding mainly to the work in Latin, but he knew that Alabaster was touching on real truths

When times and seasons and all years must lie
Drowned in the sea of wild eternity;

with Alabaster's concentration on things of the next life in view of this one, (oh this glow-worm faith, to us who crawl the earth!) Herrick concludes:

FROM THE MARROW-BONE

Meantime like earth-worms we will crawl below,
And wonder at those things that thou dost know.

The Nativity Ode
John Milton (1608-1674)

Milton is one of the heavy-weight professional wrestlers in the area of religious poetry. He was born in London and encouraged by his father in music and literature. He steeped himself in a study of the classics, working in Cambridge where he became as fluent in Latin as he was in English. His poetry, from the very beginning, was already alight with the Puritan fire, that fiercely dogmatic certainty that drove many out of England to find outlets for their faith in virgin territory. Milton took his MA in 1632, then retired for six years to his father's estate to bury himself in acquiring as much knowledge of the world as he possibly could, though out of books, not from the actual lives of real people.

In his work the great heroes of myth become dull and pompous, his God, his Christ, his Sampson, whereas it is clear that the antagonists are real and admirable characters. His stressing of goodness and virtue does not make for easy or complete characterisation. 1638 brought him to Italy and he returned at the outbreak of the Civil War, soon engaging himself with politics and pamphleteering in his desire to see the Reformation through. He married in 1642, strangely enough to a Catholic girl who was merely sixteen years of age; the marriage was a disaster and he began to write a treatise on divorce; when this was censored he wrote a treatise against censorship; later he became, under the rule of Cromwell, a censor himself.

He married again, in 1652, happily this time, although his wife Katharine died in 1658. By now Milton was going blind, though he was still working on his major poems, *Paradise Lost, Paradise Regained* and *Samson Agonistes*. He died in 1674.

The 'major poems' tend towards a monotony of approach, doctrine and language and the style tends to keep both poet and reader at a safe distance from the actual moral urgencies of the work. Without doubt the work is great, filled with passages of lyrical intensity, alert with an imagination that digs and delves into areas of biblical story that are fantastic and yet realistically portrayed. Apart from moments of bombast and throat-gripping antagonism, there are yet many delicate moments and a richness of language which, if it is remote from actual speech, touches areas that are astonishingly moving. In these poems the Christian context is obtrusive, naturally so because of the chosen themes and Milton's own sense of his avocation as poet. However, in Milton one finds the statement of a general and dogmatically held belief, not an individual response to questions of individual faith.

Yet the 'Nativity Ode' is somewhat different; it begins with a sense of awe and innocence, alongside a delight in paradox which characterised an earlier poetry, that of Donne, Herbert, Marvel and others. He sets out to offer a gift to the Child, the gift of himself as one of the ministering angels come to offer the homage of song and praise. From there the poem moves out into an overview of the history of the universe, no less, before returning to that simple nativity scene where we find the poet once more determined to take his place in the choir of angels. The temptation to write in the 'high mode' of rhetorical and admonishing intent, the 'sacred vein' of the Muse that later removes the Paradise poems from immediate contact with us, appears several times in this poem though it begins with that realistic view of the manger and of nature's presence. Perhaps this poem, together with some of the sonnets, brings this magisterial and awe-inspiring poet more close to present-day readers and touches on a genuinely personal statement of faith, a faith that is complicated by Milton's self-allocated role of poet laureate to the Divine.

The poem was written in 1629 when Milton was a mere twenty-one years of age. It is a poem of immense ambition as is, perhaps, to be expected from a very bright young man. He sees himself as offering a fresh start to human beings, both in terms of setting out a definitive religious worldview and thereby bringing an end to the mixum-getherum of previous pagan philosophies and uncertain dogmatic theodicies. Milton anticipates, in the birth of Christ, just such a purification and rejuvenation of the human condition. This, alongside a poetic endeavour that touches on the same purification and rejuvenation of earlier poetics, and that sets out to establish the writer as one of the chosen.

Ode on the Morning of Christ's Nativity

I

This is the Month, and this the happy morn
Wherein the Son of Heav'ns eternal King,
Of wedded Maid, and Virgin Mother born,
Our great redemption from above did bring;
For so the holy sages once did sing,
That he our deadly forfeit should release,
And with his Father work us a perpetual peace.

II

That glorious Form, that Light unsufferable,
And that far-beaming blaze of Majesty,
Wherwith he wont at Heav'ns high Council-Table,
To sit the midst of Trinal Unity,
He laid aside; and here with us to be,
Forsook the Courts of everlasting Day,
And chose with us a darksome House of mortal Clay.

III

Say Heav'nly Muse, shall not thy sacred vein
Afford a present to the Infant God?
Hast thou no verse, no hymn, or solemn strain,
To welcome him to this his new abode,
Now while the Heav'n by the Sun's team untrod,
Hath took no print of the approaching light,
And all the spangled host keep watch in squadrons bright?

IV

See how from far upon the Eastern rode
The Star-led Wizards haste with odours sweet:
O run, prevent them with thy humble ode,
And lay it lowly at his blessed feet;
Have thou the honour first, thy Lord to greet,
And join thy voice unto the Angel Choir,
From out his secret Altar touched with hallow'd fire.

Milton sees the Godhead as utterly remote and above human living: 'That glorious Form, that Light unsufferable,/ And that far-beaming blaze of Majesty': this is not a God to encourage personal relationships! However, this Majesty, of himself and his own willing, forsook such distance to be as close as possible to our human living; in contrast to the Light, there is our 'dark-some' house, in contrast to Majesty there is our 'mortal clay'. The theme of alteration, for our benefit, pervades the poem. In this introductory section there is also evidence of Milton's sense of his own powers and his own worth; this is not a young man to be easily ignored! He is in contact with a 'Heavenly Muse' and he is hopeful that the darkness of ordinary night persisting, the Muse might offer him a verse or 'solemn strain' that might even anticipate the arrival of the Magi. Alongside that he wishes to join his voice to the choir of angels as this extraordinary 'inspir-ation' comes touched with holy fire. This, of course, brings us back to the prophet Isaiah who, conscious of his sinfulness, was unwilling to speak before the people until Yahweh sent an angel to touch his lips with a burning coal. The Magi, the Choir of Angels, the prophet Isaiah: no shallow ambition this!

The great difficulty with Milton's work is just that sense of poetry as something far beyond ordinary human activity, every-day living. The poetry begins with his religious sensibility which is doctrinaire, fully formed and hugely intellectual. There is a feeling, when reading John Milton, that he is well aware of the powerlessness that is part of our human condition, yet that powerlessness remains, for him, a question of theory and does not issue in actual everyday experience and living. This, too, may be a fundamental difficulty with the Puritan ethic, an inher-ent contradiction between knowledge and practice, leading to a pride that is based on a feeling of being chosen, of being active in the meriting of God's grace. If this vitiates the poetry of Milton to some extent, it must yet not distract wholly from the power of the versifying, the musical quality of the rhymes and language, the rhythmic flow that catches up the reader in a breathless surge before leaving him or her, awe smitten, on a deserted shore.

The Hymn

I

It was the Winter wild,
While the Heav'n-born-child,
All meanly wrapped in the rude manger lies;
Nature in awe to him
Had doffed her gaudy trim,
With her great Master so to sympathize.
It was no season then for her
To wanton with the Sun her lusty Paramour.

II

Only with speeches fair
She woos the gentle Air
To hide her guilty front with innocent Snow,
And on her naked shame,
Pollute with sinful blame,
The Saintly Veil of Maiden white to throw,
Confounded, that her Maker's eyes
Should look so near upon her foul deformities

The first stanza of the actual poem begins that sense of alteration in Nature that the incarnation was to bring about. The first verb is interestingly in the past tense: 'It was the Winter ...' while the rest of the stanza moves into the present tense: 'in the rude manger lies'. The Christ, then, is ever-present amongst us, after the initial event of the birth, and Nature herself must avoid the old ways in which the classical authors described her, the 'wantoning', the Paramour. We are, of course, still in the early part of the seventeenth century; between that era and now a sea-change occurred in the poets' view of 'Nature', accepting, at long last, the world in which we live as part of our very being, as opposed to that time when things of the world were merely useful, or to be avoided as distracting or dangerous. Milton's insistence on Nature being 'guilty' was a common one, as if the 'deformities' of Nature were things of shame. If the world in which we live is so viewed, then we who live in that world must share that shame, that deformity, that guilt.

III
But he her fears to cease,
Sent down the meek-eyed Peace,
She crowned with Olive green, came softly sliding
Down through the turning sphere,
His ready Harbinger,
With Turtle wing the amorous clouds dividing,
And waving wide her myrtle wand,
She strikes a universal Peace through Sea and Land.

IV
No War, or Battle's sound
Was heard the World around:
The idle spear and shield were high uphung;
The hooked Chariot stood
Unstained with hostile blood,
The Trumpet spake not to the armed throng,
And Kings sat still with awful eye,
As if they surely knew their sovereign Lord was by.

V
But peaceful was the night
Wherein the Prince of light
His reign of peace upon the earth began:
The Winds, with wonder whist,
Smoothly the waters kissed,
Whispering new joys to the mild Ocean,
Who now hath quite forgot to rave,
While Birds of Calm sit brooding on the charmed wave.

The third stanza moves us back into the past tense; the events of that sacred night are over, but the incarnation continues. An ideal mood is offered in the poem, one which, we fear, is scarcely imaginable, it is mere wishful thinking that even for that night all strife on earth was suspended. Would that it could be so! This imaginative flight rests in the poem and does not transfer itself into the real world and this is where a great deal of Milton leaves us admiring but cold and distant from the work. The talk of chariot and trumpet, of kings and princes, of the 'birds of calm', those imagined sea birds which lay their eggs in the midst of winter during a period of calm on the seas, the 'halcyon days'; these birds make their nests a week before the shortest day of the year and lay their eggs a week after. So we remain still in the realm of classical allusion and imagination and the whole sense of involvement with the actual incarnation of the Christ is placed at a stern remove.

VI

The Stars with deep amaze
Stand fixed in steadfast gaze,
Bending one way their precious influence,
And will not take their flight,
For all the morning light,
Or *Lucifer* that often warned them thence;
But in their glimmering Orbs did glow,
Until their Lord himself bespake, and bid them go.

VII

And though the shady gloom
Had given day her room,
The Sun himself with-held his wonted speed,
And hid his head for shame,
As his inferior flame,
The new-enlightened world no more should need;
He saw a greater Sun appear
Than his bright Throne, or burning Axletree could bear.

VIII

The Shepherds on the Lawn,
Or ere the point of dawn,
Sate simply chatting in a rustic row;
Full little thought they than,
That the mighty Pan
Was kindly come to live with them below;
Perhaps their loves, or else their sheep,
Was all that did their silly thoughts so busy keep.

The poem continues with the young and confident poet allowing himself free rein to display his powers and the ongoing impetus of his verse form. The 'Lucifer' is the morning star at whose appearance daylight must quench the light of the stars.

All so beautiful, all so distant, all so cool and lovely. We move into the realms of the skies from that of the peace on earth, talk of stars and sun before moving on to the shepherds, those classical shapes (rather than real working men and women) who are simple, silly, busy and rustic. The cleverness of words like 'enlightened' serve to redeem, but only on an intellectual basis, the whole thrust of the work so far. The shepherds are portrayed as pagans deeply involved with the ancient polytheistic beliefs and we note words like 'lawn', 'simply chatting', their 'silly' (simple) thoughts and are aware we are in a very unreal world indeed, a world beloved of the poets of the late fifteenth century who saw their swains sporting in the glade, rather than the uneducated farmers mucking about in the cow byre.

IX
When such music sweet
Their hearts and ears did greet,
As never was by mortal finger struck,
Divinely-warbled voice
Answering the stringed noise,
As all their souls in blissful rapture took:
The Air such pleasure loath to lose,
With thousand echoes still prolongs each heavenly close.

X
Nature that heard such sound
Beneath the hollow round
Of Cynthia's seat, the Airy region thrilling,
Now was almost won
To think her part was done,
And that her reign had here its last fulfilling;
She knew such harmony alone
Could hold all Heav'n and Earth in happier union.

From the shepherds we move into the world of music, from the heavenly choirs to the medieval notion of the music of the spheres. The 'hollow round …' is the moon, now aware that all the ancient beliefs and harmonies are being surpassed by the incarnation. The whole concept of the poem rests in this translation from the old world to the world of the God taking flesh; it is

the unchecked self-indulgence of the classically-learned poet
that greys the whole notion for contemporary readers. Milton's
attempt to justify God's ways to mankind, taken to its extreme in
Paradise Lost, urges reason to take control and lays aside the
great tradition of myth and mystery that had served human beings so well for so long. The Puritan view of religion was based
on John Calvin's theories, on a God who seemed to offer neither
happiness nor compassion. Predestination became a thorn in the
Puritan minds, and this led to terrors of being flung forever into
hell in spite of their best efforts. An utter dependence on God became central to their living, along with a strict adherence to rule
and law, such complete following of the literal tenets drawn
from the Bible being a sign of possible predestination. In
Cromwell's violent working out of these notions, it was believed
that God was about to establish his kingdom on England's soil.
A vision of this kingdom, created and maintained by the sword,
crept into human consciousness.

XI
At last surrounds their sight
A Globe of circular light,
That with long beams the shame-faced night arrayed,
The helmed Cherubim
And sworded Seraphim
Are seen in glittering ranks with wings displayed,
Harping in loud and solemn quire,
With unexpressive notes to Heaven's new-born Heir.

XII
Such Music (as 'tis said)
Before was never made,
But when of old the sons of morning sung,
While the Creator Great
His constellations set,
And the well-balanced world on hinges hung,
And cast the dark foundations deep,
And bid the weltering waves their oozy channel keep.

XIII
Ring out ye Crystal spheres,
Once bless our human ears,

(If ye have power to touch our senses so)
And let your silver chime
Move in melodious time;
And let the Base of Heaven's deep Organ blow,
And with your ninefold harmony
Make up full consort to th' Angelic symphony.

The dream was a return to that close presence of the Great God, before the Fall of Man, a dream of recreating the conditions of the Garden of Eden, when all of creation along with human beings, were instinct with the rules of God's reign. All of this appears to bypass St Paul's Epistle to the Galatians, chapter three: 'Let me ask you this: Have you received the Spirit by works of the law, or by hearing with faith? Are you quite so foolish? Having begun in the Spirit are you now ending in the flesh? Does he who offers you the Spirit and works miracles amongst you do this by words of the law, or by hearing with faith?' Paul is urging love, love that opens up the soul to walking in the ways of Christ in faith, in trust and in care for others, a love that leads to joy and freedom: 'And because you are sons, God has sent the Spirit of his Son into your hearts, crying Abba! Father!' It is rather hopeless and self-defeating to try and run the clock back, take up again the conditions along with the rules and laws that were once relied upon, in the hope of freshening the human view of the world. The need, according to Paul, is to work in the world with the freedom and love that Christ himself urged and to view the bones of this earth as the bones of the Christian Body, an openness and hopefulness that lead to freedom and truth.

XIV
For if such holy Song
Enwrap our fancy long,
Time will run back, and fetch the age of gold,
And speckled vanity
Will sicken soon and die,
And leprous sin will melt from earthly mould,
And Hell itself will pass away,
And leave her dolorous mansions to the peering day.

XV

Yea Truth, and Justice then
Will down return to men,
Th' enameled Arras of the Rainbow wearing,
And Mercy set between,
Throned in Celestial sheen,
With radiant feet the tissued clouds down steering,
And Heav'n as at some festival,
Will open wide the Gates of her high Palace Hall.

XVI

But wisest Fate says no,
This must not yet be so,
The Babe lies yet in smiling Infancy,
That on the bitter cross
Must redeem our loss;
So both himself and us to glorify:
Yet first to those ychained in sleep,
The wakeful trump of doom must thunder through the deep,

XVII

With such a horrid clang
As on mount Sinai rang
While the red fire, and smouldering clouds out brake:
The aged Earth aghast
With terror of that blast,
Shall from the surface to the centre shake,
When at the worlds last session,
The dreadful Judge in middle Air shall spread his throne.

Milton is fully aware that a great deal has yet to happen before the final day of judgement and man's entrance into bliss. The Christ, now an infant, has to suffer and die, descend into Sheol and release the souls held there; the world itself has to suffer the dreadful arrival of the Judge amongst us, to see whether we have obeyed the laws or not. In the following stanza Milton displays the delight in writing about Satan that he will develop in *Paradise Lost*; the last line of this stanza is physical, startling, imaginatively vibrant, one of the best lines in the whole poem!

XVIII
And then at last our bliss
Full and perfect is,
But now begins; for from this happy day
Th' old Dragon under ground,
In straiter limits bound,
Not half so far casts his usurped sway,
And wrath to see his Kingdom fail,
Swindges the scaly Horror of his folded tail.

XIX
The Oracles are dumb,
No voice or hideous hum
Runs through the arched roof in words deceiving.
Apollo from his shrine
Can no more divine,
With hollow shriek the steep of Delphos leaving.
No nightly trance, or breathed spell,
Inspires the pale-eyed Priest from the prophetic cell.

XX
The lonely mountains o'er,
And the resounding shore,
A voice of weeping heard, and loud lament;
From haunted spring and dale
Edged with poplar pale,
The parting Genius is with sighing sent,
With flower inwoven tresses torn
The Nymphs in twilight shade of tangled thickets mourn.

Milton views the coming of Christ as the event that brought an end to the pagan notions of pantheism; the One true God displacing all the gods that had gone before. The fact that the whole of classical literature circles around these gods is yet a worry to the poet and he takes great delight in outlining them and displaying his knowledge of them. Perhaps one of the things that helps take this great poet more close to us his readers, is this contradiction in his own nature, this enjoyable battle between mind and imagination. Too often, however, the mind wins out.

XXI

In consecrated Earth,
And on the holy Hearth,
The *Lars*, and *Lemurs* moan with midnight plaint,
In Urns, and Altars round,
A drear, and dying sound
Affrights the *Flamins* at their service quaint;
And the chill Marble seems to sweat,
While each peculiar power forgoes his wonted seat.

XXII

Peor, and *Baalim*,
Forsake their Temples dim,
With that twice-batter'd god of *Palestine*,
And mooned *Ashtaroth*,
Heaven's Queen and Mother both,
Now sits not girt with Tapers holy shine,
The Libyc *Hammon* shrinks his horn,
In vain the *Tyrian* Maids their wounded *Thamuz* mourn.

XXIII

And sullen *Moloch* fled,
Hath left in shadows dread.
His burning Idol all of blackest hue,
In vain with Cymbals ring,
They call the grisly king,
In dismal dance about the furnace blue;
The brutish gods of *Nile* as fast,
Isis and *Orus*, and the Dog *Anubis* hast.

XXIV

Nor is *Osiris* seen
In *Memphian* Grove, or Green,
Trampling the unshowered Grass with lowings loud:
Nor can he be at rest
Within his sacred chest,
Naught but profoundest Hell can be his shroud:
In vain with Timbreled Anthems dark
The sable-stoled Sorcerers bear his worshipped Ark.

XXV
He feels from *Juda*'s land
The dreaded Infants hand,
The rays of *Bethlehem* blind his dusky eyn;
Nor all the gods beside,
Longer dare abide,
Nor *Typhon* huge ending in snaky twine:
Our Babe, to show his Godhead true,
Can in his swaddling bands control the damned crew.

We are brought back, at last, into the stable at Bethlehem. The length and scope of Milton's numbering of the old gods and the ancient myths become a little tedious and the reader grows a little impatient, the focus turned towards the poet's learning rather than towards the moment of the poem.

XXVI
So when the Sun in bed,
Curtained with cloudy red,
Pillows his chin upon an Orient wave.
The flocking shadows pale
Troop to th' infernal jail,
Each fettered Ghost slips to his several grave,
And the yellow-skirted *Fayes*
Fly after the Night-steeds, leaving their Moon-loved maze.

XXVII
But see the Virgin blest,
Hath laid her Babe to rest.
Time is our tedious Song should here have ending,
Heaven's youngest-teemed Star
Hath fixed her polished Car,
Her sleeping Lord with Handmaid Lamp attending.
And all about the Courtly Stable,
Bright-harnessed Angels sit in order serviceable.

I do not feel that Milton is serious about 'our tedious Song' ... His notion of the vocation of the poet was a serious one, a dedication of life and morals to the task; as he wrote in *Paradise Lost*:

what in me is dark

Illumine, what is low raise and support;
That to the height of this great argument
I may assert eternal providence,
And justify the ways of God to men.

The writing of poetry he saw as a gift from God, and it must be developed by industry, by study, work, and by an immersion in the great good works of the past. 'For who', he asks in Prolusion 7, 'can worthily gaze upon and contemplate the Ideas of things human or divine, unless he possesses a mind trained and ennobled by Learning and study, without which he can know practically nothing of them?' The Nativity Ode is a result of this awareness and determination, the first sustained attempt to achieve the great goals he set for himself. He is, henceforth, a poet dedicated to the service of God, a thoroughly Christian poet. By writing the Ode then, he sees himself as one of God's angels: 'And join thy voice unto the angel quire/ From out his secret altar touched with hallowed fire.' Having ranged through Creation and the 'pagan' pantheon, Milton ends his song by joining with the angels in the stable, by being one of those who 'sit in order serviceable'. Having got all of this out of the way, and in undeniably powerful style, Milton sees himself as prepared for future great tasks in his 'justifying' of the works of God.

We have moved a desperate distance from this view of poetry, from its sense of high calling and service to a Christian outlook, to a notion of poetry workshops, public readings hardly attended, and booklets of gathered lyric offerings of a very passing nature. If we see the 'Nativity Ode' of John Milton as a preface to the rest of his work, then it stands as something extraordinary, something worthwhile, but very much beyond our petty century's material concerns

Andrew Marvell
My Fruits are Only Flowers

Born in Yorkshire in 1621, Andrew Marvell's family moved to Hull where his father, Rev Andrew Marvell, was made a lecturer in Holy Trinity Church. He studied in Trinity College, Cambridge, where he wrote poems in Latin and Greek. He received his BA in 1638 and shortly after that his mother died. In 1640 his father was drowned and Andrew left Cambridge. He travelled in Europe for several years and in 1650 became tutor to Mary Fairfax, daughter of the retired Lord General of the parliamentary forces. He appears to have done a great deal of writing at the Fairfax family home, Nun Appleton House, examining, in a poem titled 'Upon Appleton House', the claims of public versus private life. By 1653 he had become a friend of John Milton who recommended him for the post of Assistant Latin Secretary to the Council of State. Marvell joined the Cromwellian side and tutored Cromwell's nephew at Eton.

After the Restoration, Marvell seems to have returned to favour and was instrumental in saving Milton from an extended jail sentence, and perhaps even from execution. In 1659 Marvell was elected MP for Hull. Each step Marvell took along his road seems to have been taken with careful deliberation, not merely for safety's sake. He was a very brief convert to Roman Catholicism and, like John Donne, he thought long and hard about his faith. His work embodies the classical virtues of poise and elegance, though his overuse of 'does' and 'do' etc. to fill out lines, somewhat detracts from their power. He remained an MP until his death and was deeply engaged in political activities. His poise was a European poise, the simplicity of his work being a studied effect, particularly in poems like 'Bermudas'. Poetry as artifice keeps the ego and poetry separate from one another and Marvell's religious poems move outside and around his own being. Later generations have largely forgotten his political activities while remaining smitten by the grace of his finest lyrics. His range is wide, his sophistication notable; his imagination, from being highly introspective, turned later to satire and commentary on the foibles of his fellow humans. With Marvell, poetry in England moves into a more sophisticated stage, more highly wrought verse forms and a polished, intellectual awareness of the world. He died suddenly of a fever in 1678.

On a Drop of Dew
See, how the orient dew,
Shed from the bosom of the morn
   Into the blowing roses,
  (Yet careless of its mansion new,
For the clear region where 'twas born,)
   Round in itself incloses;
   And, in its little globe's extent,
Frames, as it can, its native element.
   How it the purple flower does slight,
    Scarce touching where it lies;
   But gazing back upon the skies,
    Shines with a mournful light,
     Like its own tear,
Because so long divided from the sphere.
   Restless it rolls, and unsecure,
    Trembling, lest it grow impure;
  Till the warm sun pity its pain,
And to the skies exhale it back again.
    So the soul, that drop, that ray
Of the clear fountain of eternal day,
(Could it within the human flower be seen,)
   Remembering still its former height,
   Shuns the sweet leaves, and blossoms green,
   And, recollecting its own light,
Does, in its pure and circling thoughts, express
The greater heaven in an heaven less.
   In how coy a figure wound,
   Every way it turns away;
   So the world-excluding round,

Yet receiving in the day;
    Dark beneath, but bright above,
    Here disdaining, there in love.
How loose and easy hence to go;
How girt and ready to ascend;
    Moving but on a point below,
    It all about does upwards bend.
Such did the manna's sacred dew distil;
White and entire, though congealed and chill;
Congealed on earth; but does, dissolving, run
Into the glories of the almighty sun.

'On a Drop of Dew' is a fair example of Marvell's method, of setting up a scene or argument and developing it in a carefully pre-planned way. The poem begins on something of the same level as the work of Herbert Vaughan, the soul remembering its glory in Paradise before it was sent on earth. The drop of dew does not give much to the rose on which it falls, instead remembering the region it came from. While it is on the flower it tries to reconstruct within itself the world of glory from which it has come. If you gaze on such a drop of dew you will see a world figured there; Marvell extends this image to say that the dew ignores the beauty of the flower and gazes back up to the sky from which it fell. It looks, indeed, like its own tear, in its sorrow at being sent away from the heavens. It dreads the loss of its purity, and waits until the heat of the sun causes it to evaporate and rise back up to its source. Now the soul is 'that drop, that ray / Of the clear fountain of eternal day' and remembering this, despises the world where it finds itself. The soul, like the dew, will find itself 'loose' and it will be 'easy hence to go'. The last four lines refer to the manna in the desert, offered to the fleeing Israelites to keep them on their way.

The poem is finely wrought, imaging the dewdrop that reflects within itself the whole wonder of the sky and earth, and the beauty of its surroundings. The conceit is simple and perfectly handled, with sophistication, without undue emphasis. However, the reader is constantly aware of how the imagery is being manipulated, almost like a sermon whose ending we foresee, but not how that ending will be achieved. The notion, of course, is that this physical earth on which we move and roll about, is a transitory thing, not to be relied on; the soul and its salvation is wrought by a turning from this world towards the next. We are roughly mid-seventeenth century; the work of Thomas Traherne was not known, work that had begun to turn from the enmity to the earth towards a more all-embracing awareness.

The Coronet
When for the thorns with which I long, too long,
With many a piercing wound,
My Saviour's head have crowned,
I seek with garlands to redress that wrong —
Through every garden, every mead,
I gather flowers (my fruits are only flowers),
Dismantling all the fragrant towers
That once adorned my shepherdess's head:
And now, when I have summed up all my store,
Thinking (so I my self deceive)
So rich a chaplet thence to weave
As never yet the King of Glory wore,
Alas! I find the Serpent old,
That, twining in his speckled breast,
About the flowers disguised, does fold
With wreaths of fame and interest.
Ah, foolish man, that wouldst debase with them,
And mortal glory, Heaven's diadem!
But thou who only couldst the Serpent tame,
Either his slippery knots at once untie,
And disentangle all his winding snare,
Or shatter too with him my curious frame,
And let these wither – so that he may die –
Though set with skill, and chosen out with care;
That they, while thou on both their spoils dost tread,
May crown Thy feet, that could not crown Thy head.

This is a more personal poem, a poem that gazes inwards at the poet's own soul, instead of making a general statement on his view of faith as in 'A Drop of Dew'. Has he longed, indeed, to suffer the thorns that Christ suffered? There is an echo of the more gentle, questioning voice of George Herbert here. And is there a touch of Milton's wish to join the angelic choir in Marvell's wish to 'redress that wrong'? Searching for such thorns he finds only flowers (lucky man!). Though this seems difficult to credit, yet the meaning and intention are clear, a turning away from secular love affairs (as John Donne kept promising he would do, but thankfully did not) and moving away, too, from the shepherd/ shepherdess imagery so prevalent at the end of the sixteenth and beginning of the seventeenth centuries. We come to the honest heart of the poem when he faces the truth, that the flowers he has gathered to offer to Christ are spoiled by the poet's urge towards self-interest. To this we can all respond with nods of the head and an acceptance of the truth of our own weaknesses. 'Fame and interest' so quickly push out even the most sincere and genuine will to sanctity and the generosity of faith in the Person of Jesus. Fame and interest, too, will not form part of anything in heaven; the temptation towards such mortal glory was once initiated by the serpent in Eden and it was only Christ himself who destroyed the power of the serpent; Marvell now prays that Christ might crush the poet's own desires along with the tempter so that these his flowers, 'though set with skill, and chosen out with care' might wither away. Up to this point the poem reads with personal integrity and honesty; in the mood of the times; however, the final two lines shift into that paradox and punning that, for our age, too easily undermine such truth. In this poem one must allow the propensity for such writing and accept that it is not just intellectual games being played, but that it is a way of offering one's truth to God: by trampling the writer's desires, then Christ's feet will be garlanded with the flowers with which the poet was unable, by his own efforts, to crown Christ's head.

While the poem moves with a central metaphorical force and maintains that force to the end, yet there is a danger that such work skirt the immediacy that we have come to expect from later poets. It is impossible, of course, to gauge the sincerity of the sentiments expressed in the poem, the brilliance of form and imagery tending to suggest a corresponding intellectual and imaginative game, a willed response, but that may well be unfair. The fact that most of Marvell's work was devoted to politics does not help make a decision; indeed, a decision does not have to be made at all; the poem stands, and it is a glorious work.

I turn to a longer piece, a kind of poem that was popular in those times, a 'dialogue' imagined between opposing notions. It is in a form conventional for the time; it sets up, in its alternating stanzas, a kind of dramatic atmosphere, loosely reminiscent of the hugely popular medieval Morality Plays. The word 'Resolved' in the title, already gives the game away, however; we know from the start that Soul will win out. It is the subtlety and new-ness of the answers of the soul that must excite our interest. The following lines come from another poem, 'Eyes and Tears', and I quote them to link the flower imagery with this dialogue.

I have through every garden been,
Amongst the red, the white, the green,
And yet from all the flowers I saw,
No honey, but these tears could draw.

The 'Dialogue' opens with an encouragement to the self to put on the armour of grace and truth, again a conventional set of metaphors often used around that time. Life is a continuous struggle between man's willingness to serve his Maker and the flesh's constant urging for supremacy; in Marvell the final two lines of this opening are quite disconcerting to us in our time. If it has taken us centuries to allow the worth of God's creation its place in our living, then Marvell was yet quite far from that thought, if he truly holds that it is 'Nature' that works to over-throw the 'resolved heart'. Nature, in this context, must rather mean the lower impulses of the human soul, rather than, we should hope, the great wonders of the natural world which are celebrated by Marvell in his poem on the Bermudas. The urge, however, of 'Pleasure' to the soul to make 'the souls of fruits and flowers' an aid to heighten the soul of man, is summarily rejected in the dialogue. And again, in our time, it is tempting to dismiss the answers of the soul as too pithy, too prissy, too cocky. It is es-sential all the time to remember the conventions out of which Marvell is writing. The dialogue is intent on setting up moments when the concise couplet gains mastery over the more rambling four-line temptations.

A Dialogue Between the Resolved Soul and Created Pleasure
Courage my Soul, now learn to wield
The weight of thine immortal shield.
Close on thy head thy helmet bright.
Balance thy sword against the fight.
See where an army, strong as fair,
With silken banners spreads the air.
Now, if thou bee'st that thing Divine,
In this day's combat let it shine:
And show that Nature wants an art
To conquer one resolved heart.

Pleasure
Welcome the creation's guest,
    Lord of earth, and heaven's heir.
Lay aside that Warlike crest,
    And of Nature's banquet share:
Where the souls of fruits and flowers
    Stand prepared to heighten yours.

Soul
I sup above, and cannot stay
To bait so long upon the way.   (take pleasure)

Pleasure
On these downy pillows lie,
    Whose soft plumes will thither fly:
On these roses strewed so plain
    Lest one leaf thy side should strain.

Soul
My gentler rest is on a thought,
Conscious of doing what I ought.

Pleasure
If thou bee'st with perfumes pleased,
    Such as oft the Gods appeased,
Thou in fragrant clouds shalt show
    Like another God below.

Soul
A Soul that knows not to presume
Is heaven's and its own perfume.

Pleasure
Every thing does seem to vie
  Which should first attract thine eye:
But since none deserves that grace,
  In this crystal view thy face.

Soul
When the Creator's skill is prized,
The rest is all but earth disguised.

Pleasure
Hark how music then prepares
  For thy stay these charming airs;
Which the posting winds recall,
  And suspend the river's fall.

Soul
Had I but any time to lose,
On this I would it all dispose.
Cease tempter. None can chain a mind
Whom this sweet cordage cannot bind.

Chorus
Earth cannot show so brave a sight
As when a single soul does fence
The batteries of alluring sense,
And Heaven views it with delight.
Then persevere: for still new charges sound:
And if thou overcom'st thou shalt be crown'd.

Pleasure
All this fair, and cost, and sweet,
  Which scatteringly doth shine,
Shall within one beauty meet,
  And she be only thine.

Soul
If things of sight such Heavens be,
What Heavens are those we cannot see?

Pleasure
Where so e're thy foot shall go
  The minted gold shall lie;

Till thou purchase all below,
  And want new worlds to buy.

Soul
Wer't not a price who'd value gold?
And that's worth naught that can be sold.

Pleasure
Wilt thou all the glory have
  That war or peace commend?
Half the world shall be thy slave
  The other half thy friend.

Soul
What friends, if to myself untrue?
What slaves, unless I captive you?

Pleasure
Thou shalt know each hidden cause;
  And see the future time:
Try what depth the centre draws;
  And then to Heaven climb.

Soul
None thither mounts by the degree
Of knowledge, but humility.

Chorus
Triumph, triumph, victorious Soul;
The world has not one pleasure more:
The rest does lie beyond the pole,
And is thine everlasting Store.

How convincing all of this is depends on two things: firstly, one's own awareness of the loveliness of the earth on which we live and move, and whether or not we believe that loveliness to be a snare or a help to bring us to awareness of the Creator; and secondly, on the smooth and quick-running rhythms, the perfect rhymes, the contrast of the quick response and the challenging music of the temptations. There is no contest in the poem; the winner is announced before the battle begins. The often pithy and memorable couplets of the responding soul leave a sense of certainty and righteousness that is admirable and, if we are honest, slightly pompous and self-regarding; yet their truth as to faith and practice at that difficult time in the history of belief, are undeniable. It is, ultimately, the consummate skill of the craftsman in verse that makes the poem a success.

There is another poem in the same vein; perhaps the battle is more clearly enunciated here, the body being the enemy that imprisons and enslaves the soul, invading and disturbing eye and ear, nerves, arteries and veins, as well as the head and heart, splitting the latter into two: love for the flesh and longed-for love of higher things. The body, too, claims imprisonment, never being allowed to rest under the tyranny of the demands of the soul. Sickness appears to the soul to be a good that leads (echoes of John Donne here) to a turning of the body towards higher things; this is disrupted by the body's wish to be cured and to continue living on this earth. Body complains there is no cure for what the soul urges to body to attempt in terms of mortification and self-denial; body suffers the drag and pull of contradictory impulses that the soul infuses.

A Dialogue between the Soul and Body
Soul
O, who shall from this dungeon raise
A soul enslaved so many ways?
With bolts of bones, that fettered stands
In feet, and manacled in hands;
Here blinded with an eye, and there
Deaf with the drumming of an ear;
A soul hung up, as 'twere, in chains
Of nerves, and arteries, and veins;
Tortured, besides each other part,
In a vain head, and double heart?

Body
O, who shall me deliver whole,
From bonds of this tyrannic soul?
Which, stretched upright, impales me so
That mine own precipice I go;
And warms and moves this needless frame,
(A fever could but do the same),
And, wanting where its spite to try,

Has made me live to let me die
A body that could never rest,
Since this ill spirit it possessed.

Soul
What magic could me thus confine
Within another's grief to pine?
Where, whatsoever it complain,
I feel, that cannot feel, the pain;
And all my care itself employs,
That to preserve which me destroys;
Constrained not only to endure
Diseases, but, what's worse, the cure;
And, ready oft the port to gain,
Am shipwrecked into health again.

Body
But Physic yet could never reach
The maladies thou me dost teach;
Whom first the cramp of hope does tear,
And then the palsy shakes of fear;
The pestilence of love does heat,
Or hatred's hidden ulcer eat;
Joy's cheerful madness does perplex,
Or sorrow's other madness vex;
Which knowledge forces me to know,
And memory will not forego;
What but a soul could have the wit
To build me up for sin so fit?
So architects do square and hew
Green trees that in the forest grew.

Sharper and more inclined towards the body, this poem yet remains somewhat flat on the page, redeemed somewhat by the last stanza and its delight in paradox so typical of that age. Marvell is deeply aware of the inherent problems in being forced to live in a greatly demanding physical world while at the same time being urged to keep one's mind fixed on heavenly things. This latter poem remains more in the realm of earthly ambitions but, placed with the first Dialogue, points to the tur-

moil in the lives of thinking spirits in a difficult age. 'Bermudas'
is quite something else:

Bermudas
Where the remote Bermudas ride
In th'ocean's bosom unespied,
From a small boat, that rowed along,
The listening winds received this song.
     'What should we do but sing his praise
That led us through the watery maze,
Unto an isle so long unknown,
And yet far kinder than our own?
Where he the huge sea-monsters wracks,
That lift the deep upon their backs,
He lands us on a grassy stage,
Safe from the storms, and prelate's rage.
He gave us this eternal spring,
Which here enamels everything,
And sends the fowl to us in care,
On daily visits through the air.
He hangs in shades the orange bright,
Like golden lamps in a green night,
And does in the pom'grantes close
Jewels more rich than Ormus shows.
He makes the figs our mouths to meet,
And throws the melons at our feet,
But apples plants of such a price,
No tree could ever bear them twice.
With cedars, chosen by his hand,
From Lebanon, he stores the land,
And makes the hollow seas, that roar,
Proclaim the ambergris on shore.
He cast (of which we rather boast)
The Gospel's pearl upon our coast,
And in these rocks for us did frame
A temple where to sound His name.
Oh ! let our voice His praise exalt,
Till it arrive at Heaven's vault,
Which, thence (perhaps) rebounding, may
Echo beyond the Mexique Bay.'

Thus sung they, in the English boat,
An holy and a cheerful note;
And all the way, to guide their chime,
With falling oars they kept the time.

On the surface everything seems plain: a group of English sailors has left the storms of religious controversy to find somewhere they may practise their puritan beliefs without persecution; they find a sort of Paradise, a new island 'far kinder than our own'. The sailors sing a song of praise to God for leading them here. Firstly, it is not easy to believe that ordinary English sailors would have chanted such a song; nevertheless, the sense of what's going on is clear enough, folks driven from England by religious intolerance find, not only a place of peace where they can practise their own faith, but that God has been even more generous in presenting them with a kind of Eden. It is a song 'overheard', not a personal response, therefore, but more a longing and therefore the ideal conditions can be seen to be more credible. Have they found Utopia? Is it a song of praise, a psalm of thanks, a celebration of the physical world (against the thrust of the other works), is it a sea shanty? There are many questions to be asked and this, of course, is not accidental in such an accomplished poet as Marvell. What, then, is his purpose?

Firstly the poem begins in the present tense with 'ride', then goes into the past with 'rowed'. Apart from the strange association of sound between those two words, there ought not to be a sense of the past tense of 'ride'. The Bermudas are remote and 'unespied', yet the details offered in the poem make it seem that they have been long 'espied'. Further, the boat is still on the ocean, rowing along; and indeed the sailors seem at first to be a little grudging of their singing task: 'What should we do but …?' Marvell has clearly found some references to the Bermudas and uses his rich imagination to fill out the concept of a new Jerusalem, a place of beauty and peace, overflowing with the generosity of the Creator. In the years 1613 and 1624 books appeared reporting on the Bermudas and Marvell must have perused them; these were works hoping to persuade other English Puritans to come and join the growing commonwealth in the islands. However, Marvell's vision omits the problems and some of the more ugly details suggested in these works. His notion of an eternal spring was not mentioned, nor is it actual. The islands had been discovered long before by a Spaniard, Juan Bermudez, and an attempt to change the name to The Summer Islands, for the English, when Captain Summers was shipwrecked there in 1609, did not succeed. From all of which it becomes more obvious that Marvell is simply writing about the longing for movement, for escape from English turmoil, for journeying, for 'rowing along' and if the hoped-for Paradise is not reached, yet the going towards it is what matters. For this reason songs of praise must be raised; reaching back to the earlier poems, one realises that here again, though wonderfully disguised, is the notion that 'we have here no lasting city' and that we must keep journeying onwards to find the perfect place. We may never actually come ashore to relish this abundance of God's generosity, save in the next life. It is the journeying that matters, the seeking, and the singing of God's praises. Hence the several somewhat disturbing notes in the poem; jewels and ambergris and pineapples of great price suggest trade already and even piracy; the praise they sing may well, but only maybe, perhaps, touch other coasts as well. And through it all is the sense of time, the rowing, the rhythms of the seasons, the tides, time, time, time. Marvell's language creates a wonderful Edenic view, particularly those magic lines: 'He hangs in shades the orange bright, Like golden lamps in a green night'; but underneath the magic is the strong realism, even the negative view of the physical world that has always captured Marvell's mind.

Such Great Felicity
Thomas Traherne (1637-1674)

Thomas Traherne was born in Herefordshire. His father was a
shoe-maker who died when Thomas was still quite young. The
boy was brought up by an uncle amidst a poverty which always
remained vivid in his mind. He won an MA in arts and divinity
in Brasenose College, Oxford, and in 1657 was given the rectory
of Credenhill, near Hereford where he served as parish priest for
ten years. In 1667 he was appointed private chaplain to the Lord
Keeper of the Seals under Charles II but still appears to have
spent most of his life in humble parish duties. He was described
as 'a good and Godly man, well learned, a good preacher, a very
devout liver'. He died in his patron's house at Teddington,
Hampton, and was buried in the church there.

Traherne is seen as one of the last of the so-called metaphysical poets, though very little of his work was published in his lifetime. It took until 1896 for someone to discover a manuscript of
his poems at a bookstall in London, and the publication of his
poems began in 1903. Even then some of the poems were
thought to be the work of Henry Vaughan. If Vaughan's emphasis
is on looking back to a time of innocence, Traherne prefers to
look to the present and to take delight in the works of the
Creator. This would be a better homage to him, Traherne holds,
than the continual nostalgia for better times. Yet he shares, with
Vaughan, the wish that mankind should remain childlike, holding on to as much of the innocence in which he was born as possible. Traherne did not marry; he devoted himself to prayer and
good works and left after him some houses devoted to the help
of the poor in Hereford. A good man, then and, if not one of the
greatest of poets, yet a good poet and a dedicated and serious
Christian.

Traherne lived through an era of terrifying religious controversies; the Puritan movement was gathering force; the Civil War brought terror and death, and the restoration of Charles II brought a great deal of corruption back into high places. At a moment when he was struggling with agnosticism the following occurred: (Traherne has written it in *Centuries of Meditation*) 'Another time, in a lowering and sad evening, being alone in the field, when all things were dead and quiet, a certain want and horror fell upon me, beyond imagination. The unprofitableness and silence of the place dissatisfied me, its wideness terrified me, from the utmost ends of the earth fears surrounded me. How did I know but dangers might suddenly arise from the east, and invade me from the unknown regions beyond the seas? I was a weak and little child, and had forgotten there was a man alive in the earth. Yet something also of hope and expectation comforted me from every border. This taught me that I was concerned in all the world, and that in the remotest borders the causes of peace delight me; and the beauties of the earth when seen were made to entertain me; that I was made to hold a communion with the secrets of divine providence in all the world … The comfort of houses and friends, and the clear assurance of treasures everywhere, God's care and love, his goodness, wisdom and power, his presence and watchfulness in all the ends of the earth were my strength and assurance forever.' It is a moment of extraordinary epiphany, yet we need read nothing unique into the experience, such epiphanies being common to young men of intellect and integrity everywhere. What may be remarkable is that it affected Traherne's life and work so deeply from that day on. His giving of himself, in his life and in his poetry, to the interior conviction he discovered at that time, was quite exemplary, matched perhaps only by the unswerving devotion of a George Herbert.

Many claims have been made on Traherne's behalf, efforts to draw him into all sorts of esoteric sects and movements, using a phrase like 'Teach me, O Lord, these mysterious ascensions. By descending into Hell for the sake of others, let me ascend into the glory of the Highest Heavens', again from 'Centuries'. This is little more than a prayer that, through suffering, he might rise to the love of God. The fact that he was familiar with Platonic thought and the work of thinkers like Plotinus, does not move him beyond a mild Christian mysticism into secret societies of any kind. Traherne was a searcher for truth, and he was a poet, expressing his deepest emotional life through the medium of rhyme, rhythm and metaphor. None of this makes him a crank. However, it is important to understand aright his notion of joy and light in his concept of happiness on earth and in relation to God; otherwise he can be seen as a rather naïve innocent in this harsh world.

Traherne willed to have no nonsense in his work, wishing to show 'the naked truth', to use 'A simple light, transparent words ...' And the object of the exercise was to allow the soul to see its 'great felicity' and know the bliss to which it is heir. He will, then, avoid all 'curling metaphors' and 'painted eloquence'. His will be 'An easy style drawn from a native vein' in an effort to make us wise. His simple metaphor is that of a man richly dressed in 'woven silks and well-made suits', with gems and polished flesh; how men notice such but are not aware of God's work, nor the soul where God abides:

> Even thus do idle fancies, toys and words,
> (Like gilded scabbards hiding rusty swords)
> Take vulgar souls, who gaze on rich attire
> But God's diviner works do ne'er admire.

The link, in the poetry, with Henry Vaughan, is obvious and has often been remarked, but I find Traherne's work moves a great distance away from Vaughan. An early poem expresses the wonder of being born, a notion common to us all, that we are alive in this place at this time, but here well expressed in the sense of amazement at the gift of living:

> Long time before
>   I in my mother's womb was born,
> A God preparing did this glorious store,
>   The world, for me adorn.
> Into this Eden so divine and fair,
> So wide and bright, I come His son and heir.
> *(The Salutation)*

Traherne, then, rather than being a simpleton drunk on unfounded joy, sees this world as a prelude to another where everything is filled with light and joy, and because we are already heirs to this wonderful existence, what is needed is to maintain awareness of that world and exult in our awareness of it. This awareness is best expressed, according to Traherne, through the eyes of a child that is still unconscious of wickedness. There are multitudes who might not see this world as an 'Eden so divine and fair' but that is not the point here, the emphasis is on the free gift of God's creating. And this is one of the first statements of such a notion, the world up to this time being regarded as a source of sin, to be avoided in favour of purely spiritual notions. If Vaughan sees our arrival on earth as a loss and our growth as a gradually diminishing memory of great times into a miserably sinful living, Traherne prefers to concentrate on the actual moment:

Wonder
How like an Angel came I down!
  How bright are all things here!
When first among His works I did appear
  O how their glory me did crown!
The world resembled His Eternity,
  In which my soul did walk;
And every thing that I did see
  Did with me talk.

The skies in their magnificence,
  The lively, lovely air,
Oh how divine, how soft, how sweet, how fair!
  The stars did entertain my sense,
And all the works of God, so bright and pure,
  So rich and great did seem,
  As if they ever must endure
  In my esteem.

A native health and innocence
  Within my bones did grow,
And while my God did all his Glories show,
  I felt a vigour in my sense
That was all Spirit. I within did flow
  With seas of life, like wine;

I nothing in the world did know
    But 'twas divine.

Harsh ragged objects were concealed,
    Oppressions, tears and cries,
Sins, griefs, complaints, dissensions, weeping eyes
    Were hid, and only things revealed
Which heavenly Spirits and the Angels prize.
    The state of Innocence
And bliss, not trades and poverties,
    Did fill my sense.

The streets were paved with golden stones,
    The boys and girls were mine,
Oh how did all their lovely faces shine!
    The sons of men were holy ones,
In joy and beauty they appeared to me,
    And every thing which here I found,
    While like an Angel I did see,
    Adorned the ground.

Rich diamond and pearl and gold
    In every place was seen;
Rare splendours, yellow, blue, red, white and green,
    Mine eyes did everywhere behold.
Great wonders clothed with glory did appear,
    Amazement was my bliss,
    That and my wealth was everywhere;
    No joy to this!

Cursed and devised proprieties,
    With envy, avarice
And fraud, those fiends that spoil even Paradise,
    Flew from the splendour of mine eyes,
And so did hedges, ditches, limits, bounds,
    I dreamed not aught of those,
    But wandered over all men's grounds,
    And found repose.

Proprieties themselves were mine,
    And hedges ornaments;

Walls, boxes, coffers, and their rich contents
  Did not divide my joys, but all combine.
Clothes, ribbons, jewels, laces, I esteemed
    My joys by others worn:
    For me they all to wear them seemed
    When I was born.

Traherne wished to know no limits, no borders, no boxes that might contain and divide the glory of the world in which we live. We come from the realm of angels and, as Vaughan insists, we remember that realm although it gradually fades from memory; Traherne is aware of a 'native health and innocence' and, as the poem progresses through its delicately modulated rhymes, its steady rhythmic flow, one keeps expecting a 'but' ... There is none, at least, not in this poem. And therefore it is a uniquely refreshing work, one of the very first in the great cannon of poetry in English, to betray such pleasure in things of earth. Of course the poem was not read until many years later and hence it had no influence on those who came after him, but it is still good to know that Traherne was writing such poetry at such a time.

There is the word 'mystic', a word often mis-used, employed without much distinction as to a mere sense of the wonders of nature or an actual and direct contact with 'the divine'. The latter is, of course, the Christian definition and the word needs to be used carefully. Whether or not Traherne was a mystic in this Christian sense is debatable, and we will never know. A writer like D. H. Lawrence exemplifies the first type of 'nature-mystic' and it is clear that this is not Traherne's bent. It would seem best simply to say that Traherne's sense of wonder in the things of the world drew him to a more sustained attempt to know and love the Creator of the world that moved him deeply.

Traherne's individual poems are linked to one another so that his work reads as one long sequence of poems. He is, then, better read as a whole rather than in individual pieces.

... Whether it be that nature is so pure
And custom only vicious, or that sure
God did by miracle the guilt remove

And make my soul to feel his love
So early; or that 'twas one day
Where in this happiness I found,
Whose strength and brightness so do ray
That still it seemeth to surround:

What e'er it is, it is a light
So endless unto me
That I a world of true delight
Did then and to this day do see.

The imagery of light permeates the poetry along with that of being an Adam in Eden before any sense of sin entered the souls of mortals. Before awareness – 'I was an inward sphere of light'. In a poem called 'The Preparative', he is close to echoing Vaughan:

Unbodied and devoid of care,
Just as in heaven the holy angels are.
    For simple sense
Is lord of all created excellence.

Man is born 'as free/ As if there were nor sin, nor misery'. And all happiness on earth is bound up with vision, with light, with an awareness of that great life to which we are heir: 'Felicity/ Appears to none but them that purely see'. Traherne spent his life seeking that felicity, that vision of the Divine permeating all of creation, that awareness of 'the Jesus body, the Jesus bones' that St Paul outlined as the mystical body of the universe, where God wills the happiness of all creation. The light of a man's living is to be trained towards this vision, this awareness; and the poetry reflects and highlights the progress towards felicity.

Traherne was not so naïve and foolish that he would not admit the darkness of the world, and the forces that continually work to destroy that felicity. But, he states, that awareness will not shake the deepest roots of his vision:

The first impressions are immortal all;
And let mine enemies hoop, cry, roar, call,
Yet these will whisper if I will but hear,
And penetrate the heart if not the ear.

It is the heart, then, that matters to the work of Traherne, and in his life he exemplified the true Christian sense of charity and service. At times the poetry tends to labour this theme of innocence and complicity with the world, and the rhymes and rhythms tend to remain rather repetitive and dull. But the ongoing work examines the self, for understanding of the human place in the grand scheme of things. 'Nature teacheth nothing but the truth', and by an awareness of nature man comes to a knowledge of God: 'The world's fair beauty set my soul on fire'.

A secret self I had enclosed within
That was not bounded with my clothes or skin
Or terminated with my sight, the sphere
Of which was bounded with the heavens here:
But that did rather, like the subtle light,
Secured from rough and raging storms by night,
Break through the lantern's sides, and freely ray
Dispersing and dilating every way;
Whose steady beams, too subtle for the wind,
Are such that we their bounds can scarcely find.
It did encompass and possess rare things,
But yet felt more, and on its angel wings
Pierced through the skies immediately and sought
For all that could beyond all worlds be thought.
(*from 'Nature'*)

This inward exploration, starting from a love of outward things, brings Traherne to a sense of joy and belonging, to a sense, too, that there is more than all this outward show: 'All which were made that I might ever be/ With some great workman, some great Deity'. And if all that he saw, by the light of the universe, appeared good: 'Which fountain of delights must needs be love/ As all the goodness of the things did prove'. None of this, it is clear, is new or strange to a modern mind but it must be remembered that Traherne wrote during a period when the things of this world were to be despised in favour of the things of the next, when the beauty of the world was seen as a distraction from the right path, when what was required was a life lived in the darkness of blind faith, rather than in the brightness of God's created day. He lived, too, at a time when there was desperate Civil War in England, leading to the beheading of King Charles I, followed by a cruel reign presided over by Oliver Cromwell and the Puritan excesses where anything to do with the physical world was to be wholly despised; then came the restoration of King Charles II and a long period of frivolity and foolishness. The Christian churches, too, were at one another's throats. Yet in the midst of all of this Traherne found a way of harnessing his soul to the other world, of allowing the desire for peace and love and fulfilment to take control of his living. He touched on the purity of childhood and to that he returned, for strength.

> *The Return*
> To infancy, O Lord, again I come,
>   That I my manhood may improve;
> My early tutor is the womb,
>   I still my cradle love.
> 'Tis strange that I should wisest be
> When least I could an error see.
>
> Till I gain strength against temptation I
>   Perceive it safest to abide
> An infant still, and therefore fly
>   (A lowly state may hide
> A man from danger) to the womb,
> That I may yet new-born become.
>
> My God, thy bounty then did ravish me!
>   Before I learnèd to be poor,
> I always did thy riches see
>   And thankfully adore:
> Thy glory and thy goodness were
> My sweet companions all the year.

This rediscovery of innocence in childhood is perhaps the closest Traherne comes to the poetry of Vaughan yet it is clear from the rest of the work that Traherne is following his own course and that this view of childhood, of man's initial innocence, is his own and part of his overall concerns. Men, he writes, are 'More fools at twenty years than ten'. Out of all of this his vision of a perfect world to which we may aspire forms the heart of Traherne's work. A poem called 'Christendom' outlines his vision of a perfectly attuned city, in harmony with itself and with each inhabitant:

> Beneath the lofty trees
>   I saw, of all degrees,
> Folk calmly sitting in their doors, while some
>   Did standing with them kindly talk,
>   Some smile, some sing, or what was done
>   Observe, while others by did walk;
>   They viewed the boys
>   And girls, their joys,
> The streets adorning with their angel-faces,
> Themselves diverting in those pleasant places.

This is a more down-to-earth vision of the Heavenly City than is offered in the Book of Revelation; it is the town next door uplifted to an ideal place. The people who dwell in this town are perfected, they are innocent like children, they are 'incarnate cherubin':

> In fresh and cooler rooms
>   Retired they dine; perfumes
> They wanted not, having the pleasant shade
>   And peace to bless their house within,
>   By sprinkled waters cooler made
>   For those incarnate cherubin.
>   This happy place
>   With all the grace,
> The joy and beauty which it did beseem,
> Did ravish me and heighten my esteem.

Traherne's quiet vision of Utopia differs in several ways from that of other writers, of his own time and of previous generations. Setting aside the awkward syntax, the repetition of his images and the often simplistic view he elaborated of innocence, Traherne sets his theme firmly on the real world and outlines it in direct language that offers conviction and emphasis on an unswerving faith. He offers no great intellectual debate, unlike the poets who flourished before him, such as Donne, Crashaw, Marvell. Still, it does appear that Traherne's poetry was not unaffected by the enthusiasm of such thinking, and by the scientific examination of the universe that was then beginning to unfold. People like Galileo were opening up the universe and thrusting new questions on the peoples of Europe. In a seemingly expanding universe, human potential appeared to be opening up to vast, unthought-of growth. Oxford, while Traherne was there, became a centre for the study of science. Francis Bacon (1561-1626) had popularised in England his own scientific method, and though this had been born in an era of hermetic studies and alchemical research, Bacon demanded an approach to knowledge that was planned and carefully deductive. Research and science, in other words, begin in actual experience and proceed from there. In his *Centuries of Meditations* Traherne writes: 'Our Saviour's meaning when He said, "He must be born again and become a little child that will enter into the kingdom of heaven" is deeper far than is generally believed. It is not only in a careless reliance upon divine providence that we are to become little children, or in the feebleness and shortness of our anger and simplicity of our passions; but in the peace and purity of all our soul. Which purity also is a deeper thing than is commonly apprehended, for we must disrobe ourselves of all false colours, and unclothe our souls of evil habits; all our thoughts must be infant-like and clear, the powers of our soul free from the leaven of this world, and disentangled from men's conceits and customs. Grit in the eye or the yellow jaundice will not let a man see those objects truly that are before it.' Innocence and childlike viewing of our world, then, is not the mere absence of sin and egotism that poets like Vaughan desired; innocence is the conscious stripping away of that egotism that blinds the mind to objective truth. Sin and wrong desires result, Traherne says, from falling away from that clear approach to the world.

One of the strangest poems in Traherne's output, one that joins itself most obviously to the age in which he was writing, that famous 'metaphysical' age, is:

On Leaping Over the Moon
I saw new worlds beneath the water lie,
  New people; yea, another sky
    And sun, which seen by day

Might things more clear display.
　　Just such another
　　Of late my brother
Did in his travel see, and saw by night,
　A much more strange and wondrous sight:
Nor could the world exhibit such another,
　So great a sight, but in a brother.

Adventure strange! No such in story we,
　New or old, true or feigned, see.
　　On earth he seemed to move
　　Yet heaven went above;
　　　Up in the skies
　　　His body flies
In open, visible, yet magic, sort:
　As he along the way did sport,
Like Icarus over the flood he soars
　Without the help of wings or oars.

As he went tripping o'er the king's high-way,
　A little pearly river lay
　　O'er which, without a wing
　　Or oar, he dared to swim,
　　　Swim through the air
　　　On body fair;
He would not use or trust Icarian wings
　Lest they should prove deceitful things;
For had he fallen, it had been wondrous high,
　Not from, but from above, the sky:

He might have dropt through that thin element
　Into a fathomless descent;
　　Unto the nether sky
　　That did beneath him lie,
　　　And there might tell
　　　What wonders dwell

On earth above. Yet doth he briskly run,
  And bold the danger overcome;
Who, as he leapt, with joy related soon
  How happy he o'er-leapt the moon.

What wondrous things upon the earth are done
  Beneath, and yet above the sun?
    Deeds all appear again
    In higher spheres; remain
      In clouds as yet:
      But there they get
Another light, and in another way
  Themselves to us above display.
The skies themselves this earthly globe surround;
  We are even here within them found.

On heavenly ground within the skies we walk,
  And in this middle centre talk:
    Did we but wisely move,
    On earth in heaven above,
      Then soon should we
      Exalted be
Above the sky: from whence whoever falls,
  Through the long dismal precipice,
Sinks to the deep abyss where Satan crawls
  Where horrid death and despair lies.

As much as others thought themselves to lie
  Beneath the moon, so much more high
    Himself and thought to fly
    Above the starry sky,
      As that he spied
      Below the tide.
Thus did he yield me in the shady night
  A wondrous and instructive light,
Which taught me that under our feet there is
  As o'er our heads, a place of bliss.

* * *

To the same purpose; he, not long before
  Brought home from nurse, going to the door
    To do some little thing
    He must not do within,
      With wonder cries,
      As in the skies
He saw the moon, 'O yonder is the moon
  Newly come after me to town,
That shined at Lugwardin but yesternight,
  Where I enjoyed the self-same light.'

As if it had even twenty thousand faces,
  It shined at once in many places;
    To all the earth so wide
    God doth the stars divide
      With so much art
      The moon impart,
They serve us all; serve wholly every one
  As if they served him alone.
While every single person hath such store,
  'Tis want of sense that makes us poor.

The poem is quite carefully constructed, beginning with the poet's vision of day, followed by his brother's vision of the moon, back to the poet's wisdom and ending once more with the brother and the moon. We start with an experience of sunlight in which the poet sees beyond what mere sunlight on the earth will display; his brother, then, in leaping over the moon reflected in a stream of water, gets another view of creation. The image of Icarus is cleverly used and developed for it is the sunlight that destroyed the wings in the original myth and the fall of Icarus was a disaster. If the poet's brother had fallen into the water he would have fallen through, as far as the moon itself; a beautiful 'conceit', the fall being down and up at the same time, painful and revealing, a vision and a hurt. And always it is the existence of another view of the world that is in question. If he had fallen through into the reflected sky, he could have described to the inhabitants what it was like on the earth above them, thus once again turning our physical world on its head. There are echoes of phrases from the Bible, 'What wondrous things upon the earth are done ... on earth as it is in heaven ...' There are worlds held within worlds. While we are on earth we are in heaven and while in heaven we are on earth and how rightly does the first conclusion come: 'Did we but wisely move, On earth in heaven above, We then should be Exalted high Above the sky'. The lovely word 'tripping' along the King's highway, suggests the danger and the joy of moving in the actual world, all of which eventually comes down to the use of neither oar nor wing, but 'swimming', and in this case swimming in the air; the cleverness of this is admirable. All of this 'unreasonable' and highly imaginative work, is yet fully earthed, particularly in the final two stanzas where the brother, after a stint in hospital, 'brought home from nurse', has to go outside to use the toilet: 'To do some little thing He must not do within'; even the name of the village where Thomas and Philip lived is used. Like the moon and the stars, that shine always somewhere in the world, God too is available to everyone and it is our poor minds alone that are unwilling to open up to the wonder and mercy of God's presence.

The special grace of Traherne's poetry is its positive response to the story of Christ's revelation of God and of the human destiny. Reading this poet almost inevitably arouses an answering hope, almost a conviction, in the reader. The surface innocence of the verse, with its often repeated memories of childhood integrity, is still carefully focused on his theme, and the individual poems are constructed with intelligence and purpose.

Joseph Mary Plunkett (1887-1916)

Joseph Mary Plunkett was born the son of a papal count and developed close ties of friendship with the literary world of early twentieth-century Ireland, becoming, most notably, a friend of Thomas MacDonagh with whom he worked as director of the Irish Theatre and co-editor of the *Irish Review*. His home in Dublin was used as one of the clearing stations for a cargo of arms landed at Howth in 1914 for the Irish Volunteers and also as a training camp for men brought by the family to Ireland to avoid conscription during World War One, and expected to fight for an Independent Ireland. For much of his life he suffered from ill health and had to struggle out of bed to partake in the 1916 Rising; his Aide de Camp was one Michael Collins. He married the woman he loved, Grace Gifford, in Kilmainham Gaol, hours before he was executed. The poetry suffers from a somewhat feverish acceptance of the extremes of romantic and mystical imagery but the clarity and lyrical wholeness of the poems included here give at least these works a special power and lasting strength; the rhymes, the rhythms and the semi-mystical imagery all coalesce to offer a view of Christian faith growing into favour in our own time.

I See His Blood upon the Rose
I see his blood upon the rose
And in the stars the glory of his eyes,
His body gleams amid eternal snows,
His tears fall from the skies.

I see his face in every flower;
The thunder and the singing of the birds
Are but his voice – and carven by his power
Rocks are his written words.

All pathways by his feet are worn,
His strong heart stirs the ever-beating sea,
His crown of thorns is twined with every thorn,
His cross is every tree.

The Stars Sang in God's Garden
The stars sang in God's garden;
The stars are the birds of God;
The night-time is God's harvest,
Its fruits are the words of God.

God ploughed His fields at morning,
God sowed His seed at noon,
God reaped and gathered in His corn
With the rising of the moon.

The sun rose up at midnight,
The sun rose red as blood,
It showed the Reaper, the dead Christ,
Upon His cross of wood.

For many live that one may die,
And one must die that many live –
The stars are silent in the sky
Lest my poor songs be fugitive.

I Saw the Sun at Midnight
I saw the Sun at midnight, rising red,
Deep-hued yet glowing, heavy with the stain
Of blood-compassion, and I saw It gain
Swiftly in size and growing till It spread
Over the stars; the heavens bowed their head
As from Its heart slow dripped a crimson rain,
Then a great tremor shook It, as of pain –
The night fell, moaning, as It hung there dead.

O Sun, O Christ, O bleeding Heart of flame!
Thou givest Thine agony as our life's worth,
And makest it infinite, lest we have dearth
Of rights wherewith to call upon Thy Name;
Thou pawnest Heaven as a pledge for Earth
And for our glory sufferest all shame.

The Fly in Marmalade
William Butler Yeats

T. S. Eliot, in his essay *On Poetry and Poets*, marvels at how Yeats 'after becoming unquestionably the master', continued to develop his poetry to the very end. He puts this down to concentration and hard work and indeed it is clear that all of Yeats's energies went into the development of his writing. There is more, too, there is character; Yeats lived the artist's life and, as an artist, he was never content with his achievement. Eliot characterises this as a moral excellence, a quality very rare in contemporary writing where so much that tends to distract and alienate the writer from actually developing the work, can overwhelm. Yeats was able to adapt to the changing experiences of his advancing years; he coped with winning the Nobel Prize, with his growing fame, with the role of public figure and never yielded to writing what he thought his public might expect of him. It comes down to being honest with oneself, with knowing oneself, and with responding to everything with integrity.

Working and writing like this, Yeats was able to see art as a rejuvenating, even an eternalising power. Death is the great beast that tells us life is meaningless unless that life achieve a form which death cannot alter; for Yeats, this was art, the constant remaking of the self in an attempt to escape meaningless recurrence or even pointless extinction. It is a way of turning disorder into order, and chance into power. Yeats grew old and as he aged his poetry grew stronger. What a wonderful and unusual thing! How many writers gloat in the success of their early work and take the reward of promise for the fact, holding fast to the same themes and forms that originally offered excellence. Yeats, in his lament for his ageing body, saw his being as one with a dying civilisation; as in the superb late poem, 'Long-Legged Fly', the poetry of personal crisis slips easily, for the writer whose life and work form a unified whole, into a sense of general apocalypse.

It is well rehearsed that Yeats assumed various poses as he made his way through life, annoying many, winning some admirers yet rarely in the poems did the pose intrude in a way that damaged the work. Indeed the pose became a mask, in due time, and that mask developed into a kind of antithetical self with which Yeats argued, and out of that argument came his greatest works. If a pose, for most of us, is a way of hiding our own inadequacies in private or in public, it must yet be something close to our dreams and our willing in order that we may put it on. It is this battle with himself that Yeats consciously cultivated, the self and the anti-self, the actual circumstances of his living and the image of the ideal world of which he dreamed. In battling with himself consciously Yeats avoided any possibility of self-delusion; by facing the actual world in which he lived and contrasting it with the archetypal world, he found a continuing theme, and a developing one. In his poem from the 1919 collection *The Wild Swans at Coole*, 'Ego Dominus Tuus', this battling harmony is seen at its clearest. The *Hic* of the poem is the rational, the sceptical, the liberal and individualistic man of circumstance and immediate awareness; the *Ille* is the struggling self challenging that immediacy.

> *Ego Dominus Tuus*
> *Hic.* On the grey sand beside the shallow stream
> Under your old wind-beaten tower, where still
> A lamp burns on beside the open book
> That Michael Robartes left, you walk in the moon,
> And, though you have passed the best of life, still trace,
> Enthralled by the unconquerable delusion,
> Magical shapes.
>
> *Ille.*   By the help of an image
> I call to my own opposite, summon all
> That I have handled least, least looked upon.
>
> *Hic.* And I would find myself and not an image.
>
>
> Ille. That is our modern hope, and by its light

We have lit upon the gentle, sensitive mind
And lost the old nonchalance of the hand;
Whether we have chosen chisel, pen or brush,
We are but critics, or but half create,
Timid, entangled, empty and abashed,
Lacking the countenance of our friends.

Hic. And yet
The chief imagination of Christendom,
Dante Alighieri, so utterly found himself
That he has made that hollow face of his
More plain to the mind's eye than any face
But that of Christ.

Ille.   And did he find himself
Or was the hunger that had made it hollow
A hunger for the apple on the bough
Most out of reach? and is that spectral image
The man that Lapo and that Guido knew?
I think he fashioned from his opposite
An image that might have been a stony face
Staring upon a Bedouin's horse-hair roof
From doored and windowed cliff, or half upturned
Among the coarse grass and the camel-dung.
He set his chisel to the hardest stone.
Being mocked by Guido for his lecherous life,
Derided and deriding, driven out
To climb that stair and eat that bitter bread,
He found the unpersuadable justice, he found
The most exalted lady loved by a man.

Hic. Yet surely there are men who have made their art
Out of no tragic war, lovers of life,
Impulsive men that look for happiness
And sing when they have found it.

Ille.   No, not sing,
For those that love the world serve it in action,
Grow rich, popular and full of influence,
And should they paint or write, still it is action:
The struggle of the fly in marmalade.

The rhetorician would deceive his neighbours,
The sentimentalist himself; while art
Is but a vision of reality.
What portion in the world can the artist have
Who has awakened from the common dream
But dissipation and despair?

Hic.   And yet
No one denies to Keats love of the world;
Remember his deliberate happiness.

Ille. His art is happy, but who knows his mind?
I see a schoolboy when I think of him,
With face and nose pressed to a sweet-shop window,
For certainly he sank into his grave
His senses and his heart unsatisfied,
And made – being poor, ailing and ignorant,
Shut out from all the luxury of the world,
The coarse-bred son of a livery-stable keeper –
Luxuriant song.

Hic. Why should you leave the lamp
Burning alone beside an open book,
And trace these characters upon the sands?
A style is found by sedentary toil
And by the imitation of great masters.

Ille. Because I seek an image, not a book.
Those men that in their writings are most wise,
Own nothing but their blind, stupefied hearts.
I call to the mysterious one who yet
Shall walk the wet sands by the edge of the stream
And look most like me, being indeed my double,
And prove of all imaginable things
The most unlike, being my anti-self,
And, standing by these characters, disclose
All that I seek; and whisper it as though
He were afraid the birds, who cry aloud
Their momentary cries before it is dawn,
Would carry it away to blasphemous men.

Around the time he wrote this poem, 1915, Yeats was a member of the Order of the Golden Dawn and was a postulant of another order; he was frequenting mediums. In a diary begun in 1908 he wrote: 'I think all happiness depends on the energy to assume the mask of some other life, on a re-birth as something not one's self ... If we cannot imagine ourselves as different from what we are, and try to assume that second self, we cannot impose a discipline on ourselves though we may accept one from others.' This is also the period when he was working on Noh plays where the mask is the key; it was all part of his effort to write an 'impersonal' poetry to distract from the bitterness and anger that were left in him from his practical efforts in life.

He begins by examining the idea of symbolism, arcane studies, artistic inspiration, using the personae of Michael Robartes and Owen Aherne from his early fiction. Loosely, *Hic* is body, and *Ille* soul, the latter working to discover its true nature. Yeats was looking forward to a life of seclusion and inspiration in his Tower at Ballylee. The danger would be the loss of inspiration in favour of criticism and this leads to a study of creativity in the modern age, an argument about the relationship of personality to reality in the work of Dante and Keats. Yet the weight of argument suggests the value of inspiration instead of immersion in reality: the choice appears to be between action and vision, the artist being the one who wakens from 'the common dream' and thus, stepping outside the ordinary and acceptable activities of dailikind, lends himself to dissipation and despair. The robust pragmatism of *Hic* opposes the dedicated supernaturalism of *Ille*. His own 'guide', one Leo Africanus, clarifies Yeats's commitment to search for something outside of the self. Opposites struggle and bring forth a real answer.

The text of *Per Amica Silentia Lunae*, 1917, has this passage: 'Nor has any poet I have read of or heard of or met with been a sentimentalist. The other self, the anti-self or the antithetical self, as one may choose to name it, comes but to those who are no longer deceived, whose passion is reality. The sentimentalists are practical men who believe in money, in position, in a marriage bell, and whose understanding of happiness is to be so busy whether at work or at play that all is forgotten but the momentary aim. They find their pleasure in a cup that is filled from

Lethe's wharf, and for the awakening, for the vision, for the revelation of reality, tradition offers us a different word – ecstasy.'

Yeats saw, at that time, *Hic* and people of that sort in the ascendancy, artists out of style. The *Ille* in us all still hopes for a creative flowering in our own time! Hope keeps sending out its little blood-red shoots. Maud Gonne reported that a priest in Paris 'said, pointing to Mr Yeats, "Tell him our Lord says he must write for Him. He must become an Apostle of the Sacred Heart. He will have special help for doing this" ' – and the message reminded Yeats that he had been working out a scheme for a poem, 'praying that somewhere upon some seashore or upon some mountain I should meet face to face with the divine image of myself. I tried to understand what it would be if the heart of that image lived completely within my heart, and the poetry full of instinct full of tenderness for all life it would enable me to write'. This was to become part of 'Ego Dominus Tuus', this searching of art and personality. So: does it come down to a choice between action and contemplation? 'Those that love the world serve it in action': Yeats succeeded, up to a point, in the active life, both in helping found a national theatre, and in the senate; his letters to the newspapers also show a man intent on ordering the world about him. Yet the poem sees active men as inadequate artists, their purpose being the accomplishment of mundane and immediate effects, not lasting ones. The true artist, Yeats holds, builds a cool and impersonal work that holds within itself a lasting vision of reality. The antithetical self urges the ego to break free from the self and dive into objective wisdom, thus providing the world with something vastly more valuable than frantic activity.

One of Yeats's most haunting and memorable refrains comes in the following poem:

Long-legged Fly
That civilisation may not sink,
Its great battle lost,
Quiet the dog, tether the pony
To a distant post;
Our master Caesar is in the tent
Where the maps are spread,

His eyes fixed upon nothing,
A hand upon his head.
Like a long-legged fly upon the stream
His mind moves upon silence.

That the topless towers be burnt
And men recall that face,   •
Move most gently if move you must
In this lonely place.
She thinks, part woman, three parts a child,
That nobody looks; her feet
Practise a tinker shuffle
Picked up on a street.
Like a long-legged fly upon the stream
Her mind moves upon silence.

That girls at puberty may find
The first Adam in their thought,
Shut the door of the Pope's chapel,
Keep those children out.
There on that scaffolding resides
Michael Angelo.
With no more sound than the mice make
His hand moves to and fro.
Like a long-legged fly upon the stream
His mind moves upon silence.

In these three tableaux Yeats points out his awareness of people who have discovered, through the indwelling power of their own unity of being, how to move others. Caesar's mind is fixed upon nothing in order to allow the force of the universe without, space to dwell in his mind; Helen of Troy, with echoes of Maud or Iseult Gonne, allows that power to take her over, and Michelangelo, the artist, becomes a medium where that unity of created being simply flows through his body onto the ceiling of the chapel. Each of the three is portrayed in a moment of achieved transcendence, the unity of self and anti-self outlined in *Ego Dominus Tuus*. The military genius springs from within the moment of perfect contemplation, silence being achieved; even grace and beauty develop only in achieved silence, turning the ordinary things into beautiful things; and Michelangelo, creating paintings on the Sistine chapel ceiling that are so perfect they stir the longings of young girls, will only do so if he, too, allows the power of supernatural force to work through him. And that refrain: its beauty rests on many facets, not least the accuracy and strangeness of the image, but also on the open vowels that create an almost mesmeric music that lulls the very rhythms towards peace, and therefore wholeness; the long-legged fly rests perfectly on the surface of a calm water, and without the calmness the fly would be overwhelmed; in the poem the fly is merely 'upon' the stream, suggesting rest without movement, yet being carried along by the momentum of the stream beneath.

The link to *Ego Dominus Tuus* is clear but this is, perhaps, in its clarity and mystery, one of the finest lyrics Yeats ever wrote, capturing as it does a great deal of the thinking and research that are more expositional in other works. Michelangelo, of course, is the greatest painter and sculptor of religious works expressed in the perfection of naked flesh; all three instances delineate instinctive genius brought to fruition by perfect contemplation.

Let me move to a slighter poem:

The Mother of God
The threefold terror of love; a fallen flare
Through the hollow of an ear;
Wings beating about the room;
The terror of all terrors that I bore
The Heavens in my womb.

Had I not found content among the shows
Every common woman knows,
Chimney corner, garden walk,
Or rocky cistern where we tread the clothes
And gather all the talk?

What is this flesh I purchased with my pains,
This fallen star my milk sustains,
This love that makes my heart's blood stop
Or strikes a sudden chill into my bones
And bids my hair stand up?

Yeats wrote of the first stanza: 'I had in my memory

Byzantine mosaic pictures of the Annunciation, which show a line drawn from a star to the ear of the Virgin.' Whether or not this star is the star 'that stood over the place where the Child was' in Bethlehem, the point seems to be that in the poem Yeats sees Mary as laying herself open to the forces of the universe and thus, like the three geniuses in the long-legged fly poem, bringing forth something of immense worth. If Yeats's fascination with Christianity still brought him to reject it as inimical to artistic individuality, yet its images and language found their way into his work. Being open to love is a terrifying thing, the laying bare of the soul to the possibility of immense suffering, yet also to immense joy. The bringing forth of anything of special genius is also seen as the result of huge self-discipline and labour; the line 'wings beating about the room' bring to mind the *Leda and the Swan* poem though here the result is the bearing of something far more wonderful and terrifying. The rest of the poem moves through a series of questions where Mary wonders how, even amongst the most banal everyday activities of a woman, she had achieved such unity of being. The final stanza remains in the realm of questioning; the star that had sent its power into her is now being nourished at her womb and all the terror she had left herself open to has produced its physical effects of fear and commitment in her.

So to one of Yeats's later poems:

The Circus Animals' Desertion
I
I sought a theme and sought for it in vain,
I sought it daily for six weeks or so.
Maybe at last, being but a broken man,
I must be satisfied with my heart, although
Winter and summer till old age began
My circus animals were all on show,
Those stilted boys, that burnished chariot,
Lion and woman and the Lord knows what.

II
What can I but enumerate old themes?
First that sea-rider Oisin led by the nose

Through three enchanted islands, allegorical dreams,
Vain gaiety, vain battle, vain repose,
Themes of the embittered heart, or so it seems,
That might adorn old songs or courtly shows;
But what cared I that set him on to ride,
I, starved for the bosom of his faery bride?

And then a counter-truth filled out its play,
'The Countess Cathleen' was the name I gave it;
She, pity-crazed, had given her soul away,
But masterful Heaven had intervened to save it.
I thought my dear must her own soul destroy,
So did fanaticism and hate enslave it,
And this brought forth a dream and soon enough
This dream itself had all my thought and love.

And when the Fool and Blind Man stole the bread
Cuchulain fought the ungovernable sea;
Heart-mysteries there, and yet when all is said
It was the dream itself enchanted me:
Character isolated by a deed
To engross the present and dominate memory.
Players and painted stage took all my love,
And not those things that they were emblems of.

III
Those masterful images because complete
Grew in pure mind, but out of what began?
A mound of refuse or the sweepings of a street,
Old kettles, old bottles, and a broken can,
Old iron, old bones, old rags, that raving slut
Who keeps the till. Now that my ladder's gone,
I must lie down where all the ladders start
In the foul rag and bone shop of the heart.

The older poet looks back on his earlier works to see if he can
refresh his waning inspiration; old age leaves him 'a broken
man' who now sees his earlier poems as circus animals and
therefore not touching on what life is really all about. The 'stilted

boys', the young loves of his early life, the mythologies: they are touched on with a sense of dismissal. The 'maybe' of this first stanza is also somewhat of a throwaway: is he reduced to his own heart as theme? The circus animals are part of that fantasy world Yeats always worked to get away from so that he could rest in the present, as the characters of Long-Legged Fly rested, and thereby effect something real. Oisin he dismisses now as 'led by the nose', and everything is vain; he knows he opposed the life of activity with the life of dreams. There is a fine and intimate self-revelation here, an awareness that he has taken the masks he used for his earlier works and put them, 'players and painted stage', in place of reality. The poem ends with another twist, an admission that the dreams, the masks, all came from an awareness of actual, sordid reality, and while being aware of that reality he used the 'ladder' of his dreams and masks to climb up out of that actuality. The ladder being gone, old age forcing him into awareness, he admits that he must lie down now at the base of that ladder, among the sordid things of life.

Yeats completed this poem late in 1938. In a rejected stanza he had written 'A dab of black enhances every white', the notion that his approaching death was giving an added but lurid light to what he had written. The last stanza, as the poem stands, is one of his most memorable, most illustrative and profound insights into his own life, and not only that: it can provide a framework for any thought about the writing of great literature.

Some years earlier Yeats had put a sequence together which he called 'Supernatural Songs'; I want to take these pieces one at a time though the sequence should be read at one go, slowly, allowing each to stitch and restitch itself into the others:

Supernatural Songs

1 Ribh at the Tomb of Baile and Ailinn
Because you have found me in the pitch-dark night
With open book you ask me what I do.
Mark and digest my tale, carry it afar
To those that never saw this tonsured head
Nor heard this voice that ninety years have cracked.
Of Baile and Ailinn you need not speak,
All know their tale, all know what leaf and twig,

What juncture of the apple and the yew,
Surmount their bones; but speak what none have heard:
The miracle that gave them such a death
Transfigured to pure substance what had once
Been bone and sinew; when such bodies join
There is no touching here, nor touching there,
Nor straining joy, but whole is joined to whole;
For the intercourse of angels is a light
Where for its moment both seem lost, consumed.

Here in the pitch-dark atmosphere above
The trembling of the apple and the yew,
Here on the anniversary of their death,
The anniversary of their first embrace,
These lovers, purified by tragedy,
Hurry into each other's arms; these eyes,
By water, herb and solitary prayer
Made aquiline, are open to that light.
Though somewhat broken by the leaves, that light
Lies in a circle on the grass; therein
I turn the pages of my holy book.

The sequence as a whole is a microcosm of all that Yeats felt, thought and ruminated on. *Ribh* is one of his 'circus animals', one of his masks, a hermit living in the early times of Christianity, thus close to the origins of Christian teaching and understanding. And yet Yeats sees in him a holy man more immersed in pre-Christian awareness, thus creating a character that straddles the natural and supernatural, a position Yeats found fruitful for his poetry. By now Ribh is ninety, he is speaking out of the darkness of night where he sits reading. The 'you' of the first line is a vague person used simply to start Ribh speaking. The hermit reads by the light of the intercourse of angels, by the light of the love of two beings, Baile and Ailinn who represent the perfection of human loving. They are seen to have achieved that same wholeness that Caesar, Helen and Michelangelo had achieved in their moments of perfect silence and concentration, allowing the unity of the universe to penetrate their souls and bodies. Yeats, through his reading of

Swedenborg, had developed the idea that spirits, when they meet, become a single conflagration and that humans, at moments of sexual completion, find the same unity. At the instant of speaking, 'the anniversary of their first embrace', that light of perfect oneness lights up the spot where the hermit reads his book.

Yeats had told the story of Baile and Ailinn in a poem written in 1903, one of his narrative pieces; the epigraph says 'Baile and Ailinn were lovers, but Aengus, the Master of Love, wishing them to be happy in his own land among the dead, told to each a story of the other's death, so that their hearts were broken and they died.' The hermit is placed in a position where Christianity and Irish legends mingle, as the apple of Genesis and the yew of myth are also intertwined. The ideal set up is 'whole joined to whole', the complete embrace between angels creating light, the human achievement of wholeness brought about by suffering, or in the case of the legendary lovers, by 'tragedy', is an admixture of natural and supernatural. The consummation here is a sexual one and Yeats's probing into Celtic Christianity has begun.

2. Ribh denounces Patrick
An abstract Greek absurdity has crazed the man –
Recall that masculine Trinity. Man, woman, child (a
    daughter or a son),
That's how all natural or supernatural stories run.

Natural and supernatural with the self-same ring are wed.
As man, as beast, as an ephemeral fly begets, Godhead begets
    Godhead,
For things below are copies, the Great Smaragdine Tablet
    said.

Yet all must copy copies, all increase their kind;
When the conflagration of their passion sinks, damped by
    the body or the mind,
That juggling nature mounts, her coil in their embraces
    twined.

The mirror-scalèd serpent is multiplicity,
But all that run in couples, on earth, in flood or air, share God
    that is but three,

And could beget or bear themselves could they but love as
  He.

The world below, our world, is a copy of the world above. So
earthen lovers create, in their passion, something of the light the
angels shape even though, while they are still on earth, that
light, that creation, is incomplete. The darkness of both flesh and
mind dim that light; the serpent that undid Adam and Eve is
hidden in the embrace of lovers; and though human love imi-
tates the love between Godhead and Godhead, it is incapable of
self-consuming fire and leads on to 'multiplicity', the begetting
of children. There is a denunciation of Christianity in its viewing
of this Godhead love for Godhead as producing male offspring
from a male union; all begetting must include male and female.
Again we are back to the Yeatsian ideal of the consuming of the
self in complete fulfilment, that of Caesar or Helen or Michelangelo, though in this poem the consummation is seen as sexual,
and the fault lies in the impossibility of perfect consummation.
Christianity, in the person of Patrick, is built on an 'abstract
Greek absurdity', that of the all-male Trinity. Human beings are
destined to go on loving in the hopeless attempt to imitate the
loving of a god.

3 *Ribh in Ecstasy*
What matter that you understood no word!
Doubtless I spoke or sang what I had heard
In broken sentences. My soul had found
All happiness in its own cause or ground.
Godhead on Godhead in sexual spasm begot
Godhead. Some shadow fell. My soul forgot
Those amorous cries that out of quiet come
And must the common round of day resume.

We are reminded of the scene of the poem, Ribh speaking to
this unknown 'you', who clearly has not understood all this
about Godhead begetting Godhead. The sentences are 'broken',
the moment of the Godhead's sexual spasm being something incapable of being caught in purely grammatical exactness. It is
perhaps the shadow of the listener that falls across the speak-
er/writer and brings him back to the common round, to reality.

The next short piece tells of that place 'there', where all mythological circles come together, into a design of complete coherence, there where Godhead begets Godhead, where all is organic unity, where everything comes together in one, as opposed to this our common round where multiplicity rules and things fall apart. Only when the circle is closed is there unbroken perfection, and this is not to be found in everyday bits and pieces of our living.

IV There
There all the barrel-hoops are knit,
There all the serpent-tails are bit,
There all the gyres converge in one,
There all the planets drop in the Sun.

V Ribh considers Christian Love insufficient
Why should I seek for love or study it?
It is of God and passes human wit.
I study hatred with great diligence,
For that's a passion in my own control,
A sort of besom that can clear the soul
Of everything that is not mind or sense.

Why do I hate man, woman or event?
That is a light my jealous soul has sent.
From terror and deception freed it can
Discover impurities, can show at last
How soul may walk when all such things are past,
How soul could walk before such things began.

Then my delivered soul herself shall learn
A darker knowledge and in hatred turn
From every thought of God mankind has had.
Thought is a garment and the soul's a bride
That cannot in that trash and tinsel hide:
Hatred of God may bring the soul to God.

At stroke of midnight soul cannot endure
A bodily or mental furniture.
What can she take until her Master give!
Where can she look until He make the show!

What can she know until He bid her know!
How can she live till in her blood He live!

We are come to the central point of the sequence. If pure love is incapable of being found by us below, hatred may well be the way to come to a knowledge of God. Such hatred is a way to 'clear the soul', the way Swift, or Pope may have cleared their souls; by making known the impurities inherent in mankind, hatred may figure out how humans without such impurities (before or after their time on earth) may exist. Figuring things out in this way the soul discovers a 'darker knowledge', freed from the corrupt knowledge that flesh can discover; any sense of God being born of human ingenuity is dismissed, human thought being no more than 'trash and tinsel'. Hatred of what we have already, in our flesh, conceived of God, and hatred of the things of flesh, may well then bring the soul to that moment of complete openness, a mystical moment when the movement is made by the Master and God himself takes over human living. This is the negative way of the mystical union with God, when all things of flesh and human thinking are set aside and the soul lies clear and naked to be taken over by God; 'hatred' may be an extreme way of putting it, but the word is effective and the position clear. The unifying force that brings the soul into harmony with its God is called 'decreation' by the philosopher Simone Weil: the undoing of the self, to allow that self to be taken over by its Creator.

VI He and She
As the moon sidles up
Must she sidle up,
As trips the sacred moon
Away she must trip:
'His light had struck me blind
Dared I stop'.

She sings as the moon sings:
'I am I, am I;
The greater grows my light
The further that I fly'.
All creation shivers
With that sweet cry.

The 'she' of this poem is the soul purified of flesh and seeking the 'sacred moon', her partner, 'he'. This is the 'sweet dancer', the sacred dance, when both find themselves purified and therefore perfect, finding in such purification their true selves. Like the angels sacred in their lovemaking, like Godhead begetting Godhead, these two have found that moment of union when the Master has taken them over and in that condition their love can 'shiver' all creation. This is the moment of intense and mystical ecstasy, the wholeness and unity of the soul having at last been brought about.

VII What Magic Drum?
He holds him from desire, all but stops his breathing lest
Primordial Motherhood forsake his limbs, the child no
    longer rest,
Drinking joy as it were milk upon his breast.

Through light-obliterating garden foliage what magic drum?
Down limb and breast or down that glimmering belly
    move his mouth and sinewy tongue.
What from the forest came? What beast has licked its young?

Yeats has been talking about the moment of sexual ecstasy when unification of beings occurs; what of those human mothers who have been forced to form alliances with a beast, such as Leda and the Swan, or the Sphinx of 'The Second Coming'? Here such a father has come to visit his offspring, though we are not given any kind of clarity as to which beast or God is intended; it is the conjunction of the natural and supernatural. The ambiguity and vagueness here are, of course, intentional, and we can broaden the references as we will: back to Patrick who sees the Trinity as merely masculine; back to Blake and his forest tiger, and on into the gyres and movements of history so favoured by Yeats. The fourth line brings us back to Ribh as he is in the first poem where there is the light the lovers have known 'though somewhat broken by the leaves ...' The poem moves at once into the next movement:

VIII Whence had they come?
Eternity is passion, girl or boy

Cry at the onset of their sexual joy
'For ever and for ever'; then awake
Ignorant what Dramatis Personae spake;
A passion-driven exultant man sings out
Sentences that he has never thought;
The Flagellant lashes those submissive loins
Ignorant what that dramatist enjoins,
What master made the lash. Whence had they come,
The hand and lash that beat down frigid Rome?
What sacred drama through her body heaved
When world-transforming Charlemagne was conceived?

The first line again touches on Blake and the 'Dramatis Personae' leads us back to that magic drum. The poem has broadened hugely into the changes that bring about new eras and new civilisations. The birth of someone powerful as Charlemagne is seen as one of those moments of supernatural ecstasy when Godhead begets Godhead, the great world-transforming heroes being born of such unions. Human love at first appears to be, in the wonder of union, a thing of eternity, but quickly fades into some vague memory. When driven by passion a man will sing out 'Sentences he has never thought' and the passionate pilgrim or penitent suffers willingly though ignorant of 'What master made the lash'. The mob, too, can be driven by passions of which it does not know the origins. The last two lines can once more be linked to the Leda myth, even to the Mother of God. As if in slow meditation, Yeats, in this sequence, is teasing out his own thoughts and though the forms and language vary greatly from piece to piece, yet the linking together by image and thought is firm and undoubted.

IX *The Four Ages of Man*
He with body waged a fight,
But body won; it walks upright.

Then he struggled with the heart;
Innocence and peace depart.

Then he struggled with the mind;
His proud heart he left behind.

Now his wars on God begin;
At stroke of midnight God shall win.

Throughout a lifetime we suffer many defeats and in the final one, when death takes us, God is the victor. Yeats saw these four ages, body – the physical awareness; heart – love and ambition and hope; the mind – intellectual endeavour; finally, religion – death; he saw them also as the four ages through which the whole of civilisation passes. They correspond to earth or vegetative functions: water, or blood and sex; air, or breath and intellect and finally, fire, the soul, God. All the time through the sequence the protagonist, Ribh, is exploring the relationship between love, the human and God; at this stage the poems have almost dismissed body, unless it find perfect unity with another, and unless that unity leads to a more passionate living.

X *Conjunctions*
If Jupiter and Saturn meet,
What a crop of mummy wheat!

The sword's a cross; thereon He died:
On breast of Mars the goddess sighed.

XI *A Needle's Eye*
All the stream that's roaring by
Came out of a needle's eye;
Things unborn, things that are gone,
From needle's eye still goad it on.

It is impossible that Jupiter and Saturn should meet; only in heaven will opposites meet and be reconciled: like love and violence, like Mars and Venus. In the 'Conjunctions', Mars and Venus are seen as two copulating gods. 'A Needle's Eye' takes us back to an earlier poem of Yeats, 'Veronica's Napkin' that contrasts two kinds of religion, one focusing on transcendence, the other on actual living; the napkin Veronica used to wipe Jesus' face is symbol of religion being lived, the constellations represent transcendence; Yeats saw the possibility of representing infinity by something especially tiny, as well as by something vastly beyond our ken. That poem also used the notion of opposites, contradictions, conjunctions, a preliminary exploration of the theme of 'Supernatural Songs.' The final poem in the sequence, 'Meru', is a binding together of the whole work, the whole sequence:

XII Meru
Civilisation is hooped together, brought
Under a rule, under the semblance of peace
By manifold illusion; but man's life is thought,
And he, despite his terror, cannot cease
Ravening through century after century,
Ravening, raging, and uprooting that he may come
Into the desolation of reality:
Egypt and Greece, good-bye, and good-bye, Rome!
Hermits upon Mount Meru or Everest,
Caverned in night under the drifted snow,
Or where that snow and winter's dreadful blast
Beat down upon their naked bodies, know
That day brings round the night, that before dawn
His glory and his monuments are gone.

Ribh has already made clear that humankind is doomed to error and that all the machinations of civilisation with its urge towards peace and rules that bring about peace are 'manifold illusion'. And yet, because of human reason, despite the terror man faces before the rolling out of history and the overshadowing of the gods, he is continually doomed also to search and seek, to discover 'the desolation of reality'. The sequence has already spoken about the impossibility of discovering that reality in the things of the world. Ribh then turns from Greek abstraction, from Egyptian and Roman wisdom, for Western thought has been moving in the wrong direction. It is only the utter surrender of the naked hermit, in remote and inhospitable places, under the severest of natural conditions, that will bring about the only knowledge that is viable, the awareness of the circling of time and the failure of everything man has worked towards.

This bleak conclusion (roundly executed in sonnet form, appropriately) leads Yeats to dismiss even logical thinking and the systems such thought has created. What remains is the wisdom gained by the mystic, a minimal wisdom, summing all up in an almost Beckettian nihilism, yet a nihilism faced with the awareness of the superiority of the 'gods'. 'Meru', as bleak as Everest, is that Indian mountain where every human achievement is greeted with derision.

This is a poem where Yeats has been stripping away all masks; and, masks being abandoned, the human is left alone to start afresh and find some meaning. Yeats set himself this task very late in life. The fact that this final sonnet is spoken by Ribh, the Christian hermit, suggests that this final moment of awareness may not mean that man is faced with mere blankness, mere nothingness, but that the achievement of such wisdom prepares the soul for that unity of being he has described the gods achieve in their ecstasy, such quiet and openness that allows the mind 'like a long-legged fly' to 'move upon silence'. The sequence as a whole is coloured a rich purple by the erotic and sexual imagery everywhere deployed: that coiling of limbs, that deeply engaged togetherness that almost melds one body into another. And 'Meru' itself is a distinctly musical and resonant poem, in its imagery, its sensual boast of the snows and nudity, its rhythmic regularity and the perfection of its rhymes, a perfection that leaves a huge vibration in the reader with that word 'gone'.

Yeats, the poet, the man, the exemplar; even though this sequence (and indeed a great many of Yeats's poems) has sections and stanzas that read as intellectual background to the strong poems, yet it builds to a climax that is irresistible. And it is a poem that stands exemplary of the way a poet must lay himself or herself open to the universe, to that complete unity of body and soul with the movement of the creation so that the writer becomes the medium for the expression of the great power, or god, or gods, or God.

The Sails are blowing Southward
Austin Clarke (1896-1974)

William Butler Yeats cast a long shadow and it almost over-whelmed Austin Clarke. Yeats omitted Clarke from his 1936 *Oxford Book of Modern Verse*. It seems a petty thing to have done, the elder poet already perfectly established, the younger man just published and needing support. Clarke also began his career under the shadow of the movement towards a recapture of Irish mythology, writing on old Irish legends that were the romance of pre-Christian Ireland. Perhaps Yeats was not happy with this intrusion into his own territory but Clarke soon moved from this area into another, linked and closer to his own concerns. He had hoped, in probing pre-Christian legends, to point to an Ireland where sexual freedom and romantic love were the norm; by shifting forward into monastic Ireland, still holding close to Gaelic traditions, he hoped to show how early Christian Ireland still held to individual responsibility against Catholic aversion to sexuality and freedom.

The ascetic lives of the medieval monks presented something of worth, while refusing the demands of the body and here Clarke found something his own mind could grapple with: the trouble between man seen as sinful and needing to repress his sexuality, and man seen as inherently good. His exploration of this area of Irish history offered him perhaps his greatest work and it is on this period of his life I want to focus my attention. His disappointment with Irish society and with its reaction to his poetry forced him to leave Ireland for some time. There is a gap of some twenty years in his work before he returns with a Swiftian note of satire, blaming the Catholic Church for its denial of freedom and social welfare. He had moved from excited and exciting exploration into the world of blame and anger. And his later poems moved into a more overt and challenging explor-ation of the erotic.

Austin Clarke was born in 1896, and began writing poetry that explored the myths and legends of ancient Ireland. These poems were, for the most part, long narrative pieces that were successful in the climate of the time but are now seen as longwinded and dated. He differed from Yeats, however, and others of that Celtic Twilight movement, by being and remaining a Catholic. Catholicism, and particularly its brand of repressive Irish Catholicism, was deeply ingrained on his spirit and gradually he began to explore how this negative and stultifying influence might be countered. It was when he discovered the wealth of medieval monastic Ireland, with its contradictions and its glories, that he discovered his own voice in poetry. He wrote verse plays for some time, leaving Ireland in 1922 and spending many years in London in a form of self-imposed exile; on his return to Ireland and the publication of his collection, *Ancient Lights*, Clarke's reputation grew steadily. He settled in Templeogue in Dublin and worked as journalist, critic and presenter of a weekly radio programme that was quite influential. He died in Dublin in 1974.

The early poetry suffered under the overwhelming influence of Yeats. His first book, *The Vengeance of Fionn*, was a long narrative poem retelling an Ossianic legend. It met with critical acclaim and, unusually for a first book of poetry, went to a second edition. Between this and the 1938 collection *Night and Morning*, Clarke published a number of collections, all of which, to one extent or another, can be seen as being written in the shadow of Yeats. Already, however, themes of guilt and repentance appear here and there through this early work.

Clarke experienced Irish Catholicism, in its repressive and contradictory elements, as close to English Puritan ethics. In his own spirit, and as the twentieth century began to move into a new awareness of human potential, Clarke hoped to develop his own sense of secular humanism, though in the context of Ireland and under the aegis of Irish history and myth. His work benefited wonderfully from his knowledge of Gaelic poetical techniques, assonance, half-rhymes, the complex musical patterns of old verse, all of which enabled him to retain a sense of Gaelic antiquity that fructified his most seriously personal poetry. This is most evident in two major collections, *Pilgrimage* of 1929 and *Night and Morning* of 1938.

Clarke saw the flourishing of monastic life in medieval Ireland as in many ways a golden age in Ireland with its love and concern for art in all its forms, for the value it placed on study and learning, and Clarke contrasted this with the repression evident in his own Ireland. He was also aware, however, of the extreme asceticism which he saw as repressive in its own way, during that flowering of monastic culture. So that period in Irish history became metaphor for Clarke, for his awareness of the contradictions visible in Catholic belief. He knew what great discipline and rigour was needed for human sanctity and he saw how this all undermined humanity's need for learning and art. He turned inwards in his verse, exploring his own reactions in the light of these contradictions, focusing the medieval torch-light onto his contemporary Irish mores, and did this to wonderful effect. Not only do the poems sing with the music of ancient Gaelic poetic techniques, they also bristle with the contradictions inherent in religious extremism, and with the tensions that leave the human spirit thrilling and thrumming.

Pilgrimage
When the far south glittered
Behind the grey beaded plains,
And cloudier ships were bitted
Among the pale waves,
The showery breeze – that plies
A mile from Ara – stood
And took our boats on sand:
There by dim wells the women tied
A wish on thorn, while rainfall
Was quiet as the turning of books
In the holy schools at dawn.

Grey holdings of rain
Had grown less with the fields,
As we came to that blessed place
Where hail and honey meet.
O Clonmacnoise was crossed
With light: those cloistered scholars,
Whose knowledge of the gospel
Is cast as metal in pure voices,

Were all rejoicing daily,
And cunning hands with cold and jewels
Brought chalices to flame.

Loud above the grassland,
In Cashel of the towers,
We heard with the yellow candles
The chanting of the hours,
White clergy saying High Mass,
A fasting crowd at prayer,
A choir that sang before them;
And in stained glass the holy day
Was sainted as we passed
Beyond that chancel where the dragons
Are carved upon the arch.

Treasured with chasuble,
Sun-braided, rich cloak'd wine-cup,
We saw, there, iron handbells,
Great annals in the shrine
A high-king bore to battle:
Where, from the branch of Adam,
The noble forms of language –
Brighter than green or blue enamels
Burned in white bronze – embodied
The wings and fiery animals
Which veil the chair of God.

Beyond a rocky townland
And that last tower where ocean
Is dim as haze, a sound
Of wild confession rose:
Black congregations moved
Around the booths of prayer
To hear a saint reprove them;
And from his boat he raised a blessing
To souls that had come down
The holy mountain of the west
Or wailed still in the cloud.

Light in the tide of Shannon
May ride at anchor half
The day and, high in spar-top
Or leather sails of their craft,
Wine merchants will have sleep;
But on a barren isle,
Where Paradise is praised
At daycome, smaller than the sea-gulls,
We heard white Culdees pray
Until our hollow ship was kneeling
Over the longer waves.

'Pilgrimage' is a poem rich and rare in sound and meaning. Whole chapters could be written outlining the techniques Clarke used; suffice it here to point out some of the effects, and suggest the value of their use. Firstly, the poem outlines a pilgrimage made to several centres of Christian culture in Ireland. Yet everywhere, traces of an older 'pagan' culture are found. Clarke thus suggests how much of value Christian Ireland destroyed in terms of artistic and scholarly achievements and wills that such values may yet continue in the hidden pulse of contemporary Irish living. The 'wish on thorn' of the first stanza is a form of fertility rite yet immediately the sense of beauty, peace and wealth of learning is suggested so wonderfully by the final musical lines of that stanza:

rainfall
Was quiet as the turning of books
In the holy schools at dawn.

Pagan and Christian encounter each other right through the poem. Any trip around Ireland will still be able to find old high crosses on which are carved, alongside biblical and New Testament stories, dragons and other creatures associated with pagan myths. The third stanza in Clarke's poem adds dragons to the stained glass of Clonmacnoise, the fourth has 'the wings and fiery animals' about God's throne. The poem outlines the art and learning that were a feature of those monasteries yet the later stanzas of the poem suggest the darkness of the faith, the confession, the black congregations, the booths and there are words

like 'reprove ... wailed ... barren'; there is a distinctly questioning mood in the imagery that closes the poem, a leaving of such
places yet bearing too a sense of ongoing prayer as their hollow
boat is 'kneeling' over the waves.

This sense of a visited richness is carried deep into the reader
not only by the glory of the imagery employed but by the carefully worked Gaelic poetry techniques with which each stanza is
constructed. Take that fifth stanza and its first line with the
word 'townland' and how that 'ow' sound threads its way
through the stanza to the final word, 'cloud'. It is echoed in the
second line, 'tower' and chimes with the third, 'sound'; it mig-
rates into the 'oo' sound of 'booth' and on to 'reprove' before
turning back again through 'souls' to 'down/ The holy mountain' before closing with that word 'cloud'. Such patterns can be
found throughout Clarke's work at this stage of his career, offering the poetry a powerful echo of Gaelic verse and carrying with
that echo a sense of actual and real presence.

This first poem 'Pilgrimage' remains for the most part in the
area of distance, where the poet has not yet related the picture
he paints to his contemporary situation. There is more of a sense
of awe and wonder, of hesitant wistfulness, about the piece. The
poem that follows moves directly into the sexual conflict that
disturbed one of those hermits in his will to sanctity:

Celibacy
On a brown isle of Lough Corrib,
When clouds were bare as branch
And water had been thorned
By colder days, I sank
In torment of her side;
But still that woman stayed,
For eye obeys the mind.

Bedraggled in the briar
And grey fire of the nettle,
Three nights, I fell, I groaned
On the flagstone of help
To pluck her from my body;
For servant ribbed with hunger
May climb his rungs to God.

Eyelid stood back in sleep,
I saw what seemed an Angel:
Dews dripped from those bright feet.
But, O, I knew the stranger
By her deceit and, tired
All night by tempting flesh,
I wrestled her in hair-shirt.

On pale knees in the dawn,
Parting the straw that wrapped me,
She sank until I saw
The bright roots of her scalp.
She pulled me down to sleep,
But I fled as the Baptist
To thistle and to reed.

The dragons of the Gospel
Are cast by bell and crook;
But fiery as the frost
Or bladed light, she drew
The reeds back, when I fought
The arrow-headed airs
That darken on the water.

The sexual conflict was one that dominated Catholic consciousness for a great deal of the twentieth century and was most pronounced when Clarke was writing. One of the most common sermons of the time would take the notion of 'temptation', those beautiful and satanic visitations in the imagination of voluptuous women eager to draw the soul away from God; tales of the lives of the saints were lurid with such work. I spent some years myself in a seminary; there we were given, as young and impressionable novices, a book of such stories, written by one called Rodriguez; mid-morning we were sent out, there were some 45 of us, to walk around a rose-bed reading to ourselves the strangest yarns; what could you do but giggle at it all, and what could Clarke do but mock the notion? This is a poem I wrote later and I offer it, in the shadow of Austin Clarke, merely to suggest that what Clarke struggled with was a very real and ongoing problem:

Matins
We walked round shrubbery, cowled in silence,
somewhere in the long pause of mid-morning;
the fuchsia hung in scarlet, bees drew out
their honey; high trees benignly watched, long
used to circling figures on the gravel; we
read Rodriguez, his tome of huge wonders, deeds
of saints, glories of holiness, miracles
sprouting out of deserts. Secretly, I longed
that those naked whores spirited out of hell
into the monks' cells should tempt me, too;
I fasted, prayed, scaled the cliffs of sanctity
to no avail; always the sudden wren
distracted, a weed's unexpected beauty on a stone,
coolness of peas burning against my palette; I
stayed in my tiny group, going round and round.

Clarke's poem goes straight to the point, mingling once again the pagan, 'the dragons of the Gospel/ Are cast by bell and crook,' with the Christian. The efforts of the monk to overcome what is in fact a very natural and human urge are doomed to failure, being unreal, casting on the individual an impossible task, creating guilt, a focus on what was meant to be avoided, an over-emphasis on asceticism. The poem relates, of course, to the time of the Culdees, mentioned in 'Pilgrimage', but it carries forward to our own time, or at least to Clarke's time.

Not all of the collection *Pilgrimage and Other Poems* is concerned with this fraught struggle. There is a poem that delights in the situation of the scholar who is engaged simply in art and intellectual study. The poem is a translation, a mode in which Clarke excelled, from Gaelic texts; here the poem avoids any notion of sexual difficulties and moves instead into another area that was problematic for Clarke, reason (study, art, intellect) and the demands of faith:

The Scholar
Summer delights the scholar
With knowledge and reason.
Who is happy in hedgerow
Or meadow as he is?

211

Paying no dues to the parish,
He argues in logic
And has no care of cattle
But a satchel and stick.

The showery airs grow softer,
He profits from his ploughland
For the share of the schoolmen
Is a pen in hand.

When midday hides the reaping
He sleeps by a river
Or comes to the stone plain
Where the saints live.

But in winter by the big fires,
The ignorant hear his fiddle,
And he battles on the chessboard,
As the land lords bid him.

Here is Austin Clarke indulging himself in lyrical ease, using his finely honed techniques of rhyme, assonance and variable rhythm to capture an idealised picture of one whose only worry is weather, whose delight is in wisdom and who is free of the world of the 'saints'. The life of knowledge, Clarke suggests, is the higher life; the other poems he worked on contrast that life with the soul-destroying rigours of a harsh faith.

The collection *Night and Morning* appeared in 1938 but such had been the devastating neglect of his recent work that it was published in an edition limited to some 200 copies. Yet it is one of the seminal collections of Irish verse of the twentieth century, holding a basketful of exquisitely wrought poems and offering a mature and reasoned critique of Irish Catholic living at the time. Here the forces of reason and religion battle it out; we move, as well, into a more confessional mode where the conflict between repressive Catholic doctrines and the demands of reason and learning impinge more on the poet's personal experience; the war between mind and soul and body, engaged in by the Catholic Church, becomes a war that matters in daily living.

Tenebrae

This is the hour that we must mourn
With tallows on the black triangle,
Night has a napkin deep in fold
To keep the cup; yet who dare pray
If all in reason should be lost,
The agony of man betrayed
At every station of the cross?

O when the forehead is too young,
Those centuries of mortal anguish,
Dabbed by a consecrated thumb
That crumbles into dust, will bring
Despair with all that we can know;
And there is nothing left to sing,
Remembering our innocence.

I hammer on that common door,
Too frantic in my superstition,
Transfix with nails that I have broken,
The angry notice of the mind.
Close as the thought that suffers him,
The habit every man in time
Must wear beneath his ironed shirt.

An open mind disturbs the soul,
And in disdain I turn my back
Upon the sun that makes a show
Of half the world, yet still deny
The pain that lives within the past,
The flame sinking upon the spike,
Darkness that man must dread at last.

In this poem the perfectly flowing rhythms and the erotically charged language of earlier work have given place to a colder, more austere language and form. Clarke berates the heartache men suffer because reason has been held up as dangerous to faith; the poem is more than a diatribe, however, the awareness Clarke always had of the need for balance in human activity agreeing here that the spiritual must always be allowed; Clarke's work is not moving in a brash dismissal of one side of the argument against the other. Notice how the construction of the poem hinges on that little word 'yet', just four lines from the end. The Holy Week ritual of 'tenebrae' touches on the betrayal of the Christ by the apostles, this happening in the darkness of the evening and night of Christ's being taken by the soldiers. So the imagery of darkness besets the poem, and the same word 'yet' turns the first stanza towards the problem Clarke faced head on, the conflict perceived and actual then between religious faith and human reasoning. There is a duty on believers, 'we must', the need to mourn our sinfulness that brought about Christ's death and yet, if we do allow this betrayal to be our individual guilt, then reason itself is negated. The thumb that consecrates us in faith is itself destined to corruption and all we can hope to do is remember our innocence. The third stanza mingles wonderfully the notion of 'nails' suggesting the Cross, and Luther's hammering onto the door of 'the angry notice of the mind', opposing the neglect of reasonable approaches to living. Death itself, that 'habit', that shroud we all wear under our shirts, the death that is in store for us, urges still the call of faith.

All the time, however, 'an open mind disturbs the soul'; this is the great dilemma; do we have to close off our reasoning to accept faith? And if we leave our minds open, does that mean that our faith is unreasonable? This has become part of a great debate in our own time though in Clarke's era there was no debate, there was dogma, and there was defiance; these did not come together. In this final stanza the poet turns his back on reason that illuminates only 'half the world', yet faith itself is none too sure, save for the final dread, that darkness that surrounds and envelops any religious belief. The poem succeeds brilliantly in its intellectually urged development, and in its transitions and twists and turns, echoed superbly in the language and music, but it remains perhaps too much in the realm of conscious deliberation, without the rise and roll of emotional upheaval.

The poem 'Martha Blake' makes the poetry more real, moving on from the blank anger of statement of many of the other poems. Because of Clarke's taking on of a persona he is able to demonstrate rather than argue both sides of the conflict. This slight but meaningful distancing of the self, allows Clarke a bolder and more physically grounded analysis, and the freedom granted also eases the verse form into magic. The choice of persona, this Martha Blake, is also richly inspired; the name sounds true as any Dublin woman's name might be at that time. And yet the Blake surname suggests the soar and urge of the great visionary poet and believer, William Blake, while the Martha name suggests that careful and domestic personage we meet alongside her more spiritually inclined sister, Mary, when the Christ comes to visit.

Martha Blake
Before the day is everywhere
And the timid warmth of sleep
Is delicate on limb, she dares
The silence of the street
Until the double bells are thrown back
For Mass and echoes bound
In the chapel yard, O then her soul
Makes bold in the arms of sound.

But in the shadow of the nave
Her well-taught knees are humble,
She does not see through any saint
That stands in the sun
With veins of lead, with painful crown;
She waits that dreaded coming,
When all the congregation bows
And none may look up.

The word is said, the Word sent down,
The miracle is done
Beneath those hands that have been rounded
Over the embodied cup,
And with a few, she leaves her place
Kept by an east-filled window
And kneels at the communion rail
Starching beneath her chin.

She trembles for the Son of Man,
While the priest is murmuring
What she can scarcely tell, her heart
Is making such a stir;

But when he picks a particle
And she puts out her tongue,
That joy is the glittering of candles
And benediction sung.

Her soul is lying in the Presence
Until her senses, one
By one, desiring to attend her,
Come as for feast and run
So fast to share the sacrament,
Her mouth must mother them:
'Sweet tooth grow wise, lip, gum be gentle,
I touch a purple hem.'

Afflicted by that love she turns
To multiply her praise,
Goes over all the foolish words
And finds they are the same;
But now she feels within her breast
Such calm that she is silent,
For soul can never be immodest
Where body may not listen.

On a holy day of obligation
I saw her first in prayer,
But mortal eye had been too late
For all that thought could dare.
The flame in heart is never grieved
That pride and intellect
Were cast below, when God revealed
A heaven for this earth.

So to begin the common day
She needs a miracle,
Knowing the safety of angels
That see her home again,
Yet ignorant of all the rest,
The hidden grace that people
Hurrying to business
Look after in the street.

The poem shows great skill in taking on a persona and offering a bifurcated view of religious dogma taking over a life and the loss of human freedom. The near-rhymes, the chiming and re-echoing of the words, all of these techniques are quietly present, and in their effect they offer an unsettling sense to the language, thus rehearsing what the poem is actually about. The hesitancy in the woman begins with the word 'dares' and, of course 'the timid warmth of sleep', so that we know here is a woman cowed already and she is scarcely on her way to attend the rituals of morning Mass. It is the reassuring sound of the bell that offers her some boldness, living as she does in an aura of faith, 'in the arms' of the church bell. The pun in the second stanza is brave but, I feel, effective, 'She does not see through any saint' in the stained window. Martha Blake joins the others in waiting for that 'dreaded coming', the transubstantiation of the bread into the Sacred Body, and the life of peccadilloes and greater sins for which the church threatened everlasting punishment on all those who did not follow the rituals exactly, 'none may look up'. She makes her way up to receive that Sacred Body, moving 'with a few', the note of loss and hesitation continuing to echo sadly through the poem.

She receives, in all humility and in all faith, and there is a joy she knows at this moment, in spite of all the compunction, the hesitation, the little shiverings of guilt, though it is a joy that she forces upon herself as she imagines that her pleasure is actually sensual and she mutters prayers to those senses: 'Sweet tooth grow wise, lip, gum be gentle,/ I touch a purple hem.' And so Clarke has succeeded most admirably in being able to use the words 'Afflicted by that love' as she turns back to 'multiply her praise' and only now, as she notices how the words are so often repeated they have lost real meaning and she is forced to try for silence and calm. The ending of the stanza, with the words chiming: 'silent' and 'listen', offers a deeply disruptive feeling to the poem and underpins the struggle between soul and body.

At this point the perspective shifts, the writer's presence is noticed. 'On a holy day of obligation/ I saw her first in prayer'. He is obviously struck by compassion and understanding but finds that thought and intellect, in the context of such strained devotion in Martha Blake, can find no place, God having re-

vealed 'A heaven for this earth'. It strikes the reader as something of an intrusion at this point, almost a pointing out of the
moral and point of view offered by the poet himself. But the
poem closes still from the same perspective, the poet summing
up the human need for 'miracle' and the company of safeguard-
ing angels, and suggesting that the world of business and commerce must not be ignored. We are left bemused: is Martha
Blake's innocence the way to go or is there grace also to be found
in the realities of everyday living? One is forced to reflect that if
Martha Blake had access to a more profound intelligence she
might be able to underpin her faith with a more meaningful
sense of ritual and, perhaps, also partake of the life of the streets.

The poem that brings together, at this point of his career, all
the great skills of technique and craft together with a more subtle use of the persona than the Martha Blake poem, that Austin
Clarke had mastered at this stage, is one of the most memorable
pieces of poetry written in Ireland: 'The Straying Student' offers
wonderfully melodic sound-patterns that do not strike the reader
as forced but that read with an ease and naturalness that show a
wordsmith at his highest powers. The subjects recur, the flesh
versus the spirit, reason versus religion. The internal assonance
is worthy of a Hopkins and the poem moves to a lyrical climax
of extraordinary power. In the final stanza the music winds
down, the way an old gramophone record might slow to a halt,
in a sense of doubt and despair, in the suggestions that 'all life
ends with death and each day dies with sleep' (Hopkins), and
that neither a life of pleasure nor a life of reasoned living will ultimately satisfy.

The Straying Student
On a holy day when sails were blowing southward,
A bishop sang the Mass at Inishmore,
Men took one side, their wives were on the other
But I heard the woman coming from the shore:
And wild in despair my parents cried aloud
For the saw the vision draw me to the doorway.

Long had she lived in Rome when Popes were bad,
The wealth of every age she makes her own,
Yet smiled on me in eager admiration,

And for a summer taught me all I know,
Banishing shame with her great laugh that rang
As if a pillar caught it back alone.

I learned the prouder counsel of her throat,
My mind was growing bold as light in Greece;
And when in sleep her stirring limbs were shown,
I blessed the noonday rock that knew no tree:
And for an hour the mountain was her throne,
Although her eyes were bright with mockery.

They say I was sent back from Salamanca
And failed in logic, but I wrote her praise
Nine times upon a college wall in France.
She laid her hand at darkfall on my page
That I might read the heavens in a glance
And I knew every star the Moors have named.

Awake or in my sleep, I have no peace now,
Before the ball is struck, my breath has gone,
And yet I tremble lest she may deceive me
And leave me in this land, where every woman's son
Must carry his own coffin and believe,
In dread, all that the clergy teach the young.

Take the musical prowess of any stanza and note how finely wrought it is, and yet how it moves with fluency and ease: the last stanza for instance, how the rhymes and chimes of the second, fourth and final line work to leave that summary in the mind: 'gone ... son ... young', ringing almost like a knell. The word 'deceive' is echoed in its opposite, 'believe' and the word 'tremble' finds its chime in 'dread', which itself echoes to the word 'clergy'. In this way the whole patterning of the poem underscores the sense and the music moves deep into the subconscious mind of the reader.

The student is at Mass, dutifully, with his parents. The woman who draws him away is the embodiment of human sexual love, and of intellectual and artistic freedom. If the student is at Mass, yet outside the sails blow southward, towards that world where light and freedom may well be more acceptable. Even the division in the church emphasises the fear of sexuality always (and still) there in the Catholic Church. The poet outlines how the freedom of the woman drew the student ever closer, 'Banishing shame', offering 'her great laugh'; the whole European tradition in learning and culture is evoked, subtly and sensuously, from 'light in Greece' through Salamanca and France, even as far as the esoteric knowledge of 'the Moors'. All of this is offered as being inimical to the whole thrust of Catholic dogma and yet, once again in this poem, Clarke offers the opposite view of things, suggesting that in spite of learning, freedom, culture, the student says 'I have no peace now'; if he has succeeded in spoiling the dogmas of the church, he yet admits doubts as to the lasting power over him of this woman, that she may yet deceive him and leave him struggling back in the land of dread and prohibition.

Poetry, in the work of Austin Clarke, is not a method of discovering answers; it serves its purpose well by posing questions, alternatives, and by suggesting uncertainties and doubts. In this lies its lasting strength. Austin Clarke was the first great Irish poet to propose such doubts, and to do so in a poetry that is rich, musical, memorable and wholly honest. I touch here merely on one aspect of his work, but it is the aspect that concerns this study. It is yet my hope and belief that Ireland, and the rest of the world, will soon accord to Austin Clarke his deserved place in the rich and various tapestry of Irish poetry.

Mayo Theology
a poem for Enda McDonagh

There were high brown candles about the coffin,
the vague gesturing of their light
imaged in the sheen on the wood; I listened, hurt,
to the ongoing jeremiads and could believe
a ganglion of devils cavorted in the air;

I had to stand outside during the services, the valley –
with its dark church rising out of a copse of alders –
being an alien place, inhabited by dark invaders;

we had to wait among the gravestones that leaned,
greening, over against one another, and suffer
the ministry of midges, their almost invisible insistence
not letting us settle, as they bit and bothered
scalp and wrist and nostril.

                                Nanna
on her best days, stood comfortable in her body,
murmuring as she worked, her hands soothed
by flour to the elbows, relishing her skills
with potato-cake, potato-farl, and mash;

when Harriet Graham-Green, a widow, called
to sell black roses made of crepe paper and blue
pipe cleaners, Nanna was gracious; sure, she said,
the Protestants now are down on their luck.
Later she sang, as the butter melted on the hot
potato delicacies:

    Slievemore, Slievemore you are standing there,
    your head so high and your sides so bare
    some day please God you will surely fall
    and bury the Colony Jumpers all.

In the spring a young man's fancy turns
to spiritual heights; Nangle, foreigner,
boasting the weight of his white beard, white hair,
came angling for souls on the western coast;

potatoes failed: but there were sea-foods,
dillisc, carrigeen, periwinkle, crab; the Irish
grew lean and tough as sticks of kelp; Nangle
offered soup, a hospital, a school, and built
an ordered village, set-square-shape, buying

half the side of a hill; the old men twisted caps
in their red hands, the women smiled and tried
the Gaelic tongue; it was God, dragging them
by the arms, now left, now right. They abandoned
their crooked village, straggling away uphill
over stones and bog-pools and wet turf,
carrying the ever-heavier burden of their faith
down, with faint hope, into the next valley.

Lucas Cranach the Younger painted him,
our sombre plump-faced man, with internal troubles,
watching a little upwards, with curious eyes;
dear Eleutherius, shocked at our abject failure
to achieve the perfection of the Christ; Luther –

they called him leper and loathsome fellow
with a brain of brass and a nose of iron;
truculent, the Bible pages open to show
the history of God. Blank walls before him. Anxieties
skittering like marbles across his brain, the Christ
accusing, Hell's maw gaping.

                        Nanna
sat on the steps of the stairs, her head
hidden in her hands, her index fingers
in her ears; she hummed loudly, to drown
the rattling of thunder; the devils, she said,
are playing loose among the skillets and pans.

November, All Souls, souls like a fall of rain, upwards,
the spirits released from pain when we, she said,

go in and out the chapel doors, and say the prayers;
I heard the small-growth-rustling of her rosaries,
the beads clicked softly against the polished
wood of the pew.

                    At last, braving Satan
I hammered on the door of their grey church,
listened to the hollow sound, like the anxious pounding
of the human heart. What, then is faith? a black
stone body, inside structured grey, with plaques
to the titled dead and the lost of many wars?

or an everywhichway Church, loose cannons, a rag-
and-bone and regimented tagglebunch, marshalled
into the corral of Rome? Wittenberg, the theses;
Dugort, the darkened graves waiting
under the drawling western mist. The fall of earth
down on the polished wood was like fingernails
fibulating in my gut; I watched
a ruly goldcrest on the old high yew, its acrobatic
busyness and mastery. Their Christmas cards,

                    Nanna said, are robins
hopping in the snow, or horse-drawn carriages
drawing up to lamp-lit houses; they carol
Good King Wenceslas and talk mulled wine
and boxing day.

The hymns they sing, said Nanna,
are square like chests of tea and go on and on
interminably; and the words they use are square:
abide, vouchsafe, and gladsome. We have cribs,
an adult baby Jesus, shepherds stunned by baroque
organs in the sky; we sing Adeste, have Stephen's Day
and three wise men come offering their gifts.

Cujus regio, eius religio, a mighty fortress is our God; faith
of our fathers – and we settle down to our polite antagonisms.

A Shy Believer
Denise Levertov

Denise Levertov was born in England in 1923 and absorbed a good deal of the English tradition in poetry. Her mother was Welsh and her father was a Hasidic Jew from Russia who had converted to Christianity before his marriage in 1910; he became an Anglican priest and dedicated his work to Jewish-Christian dialogue. In 1948 Denise married Mitchell Goodman and went to live with him in the United States. In those decades North American poetry was becoming conscious of itself, breaking up into movements and working in a rush of excitement, many poets rejecting delightedly the conventions of the 'old' English poetry and its perceived academic formalism. Levertov responded quickly to the work of William Carlos Williams, its accuracy of vision, its incisiveness, its modulations of the speaking voice.

She had a son, Nickolai, with Mitchell Goodman and they lived in New York. In 1955 she became a naturalised US citizen. She later divorced from Goodman. In the sixties and seventies she became quite politically active; she was a feminist, she joined the War Resisters' League. Many of her 'political' poems were written during the Vietnam War and she took part, with poets like Daniel Berrigan SJ, in major anti-war demonstrations. Later she taught in several universities in the United States, spending some eleven years as professor in Stanford University. She died in 1997 from complications arising out of lymphoma. She published many collections of her poetry and read in many countries around the world. She came to Ireland several times and made a great number of friends in this country.

I wish, of course, to concentrate on the religious aspect of Levertov's writings, but want to emphasise at once and always that there are many other themes and interests in her work. From a very young age religion was an influence in her life. In her father she encountered both Christianity and Judaism. She converted finally to Christianity in 1984 though the poems continued to voice hesitations, Levertov often taking to herself the character of Thomas Didymus, the 'doubter', as persona. She sees her life, as many writers do, in terms of a pilgrimage, a spiritual journey. It is a journey through the real, broken and often tragic world and Levertov's respect for and love of natural things remains a constant in her work. It is also a journey out of darkness into the light of faith, beginning, naturally, in doubt and a search for relevance. If both doubt and darkness recur in her work they are yet both accommodated in the later poems in a new and meaningful way. And so absence is a central focus, and the accepted fact of the absence of God sits side by side with the acceptance of the human being's natural tendency to doubt, and to suffer in darkness. It is acceptable not to have answers; it is essential to ask the questions.

Her awareness of the double, the one grounding the two, is an essential strength in her work; paradox yes, but in the sense that unity joins the all. The question of unity and variety surfaces everywhere. She does not labour her Jewish and Christian inheritance. Yet even from early on she celebrates sacramentality, the sacred in the mundane. A developing sense too of how human beings violate this unity in exploiting nature and their fellow human beings leads to a demanding political effort. So, could she write a poetry of moral outrage and still continue a poetry of celebration? Her later poetry gives the centring mystery a name: the Christian incarnation. Can it lead the human being to a position of praise? This finally becomes the source of both her inspiration and her politics; mysticism and liberation theology are the double face of the Word in the world.

Angels dream in and out amongst the lines and poems of Levertov's collections. In a moment of quiet once, in Dublin, she told me of walking by the edge of a wood somewhere and stepping off the road into the wood (a moment reminiscent of Dante) where she relished a short but vivid 'seeing' of angels. She spoke without emphasis or any effort to convince me but whatever she had seen she had interpreted it as an encounter with real spirit beings, a simple statement of her faith, nothing too incredible, nothing too dramatic. It was the gentle telling of the moment that impressed me, and the knowledge that her belief was deep and convinced. Angels negotiate the space between man and God and Levertov's work also negotiates that space. The word 'epiphany' naturally comes to mind, that moment of revelation when the human touches on the divine and God dips down momentarily to receive that touch.

> The Servant Girl at Emmaus
> (a painting by Velásquez)
> She listens, listens, holding
> her breath. Surely that voice
> is his – the one
> who had looked at her, once, across the crowd,
> as no one ever had looked?
> Had seen her? Had spoken as if to her?
>
> Surely those hands were his,
> taking the platter of bread from hers just now?
> Hands he'd laid on the dying and made them well?
>
> Surely that face – ?
>
> The man they'd crucified for sedition and blasphemy.
> The man whose body disappeared from its tomb.
> The man it was rumoured now some women had seen this
>   morning, alive?
>
> Those who had brought this stranger home to their table
> didn't recognize yet with whom they sit.
> But she in the kitchen, absently touching
>   the winejug she's to take in,
> a young Black servant intently listening,
>
> swings round and sees
> the light around him
> and is sure.

What a beautiful moment of epiphany! It is the simply marvellous moment of apprehension of the wonderful amidst the commonplace. The person chosen by Denise to have this sudden awareness is a servant girl, no prince or merchant, and the mode of reception is listening: being attentive and open to whatever message is coming: 'holding her breath'. The message comes by means of his voice, a voice she had heard before while standing amongst a crowd and feeling, by a glance of his, that both his words and gaze were for her. The 'message' of love is for everyone, Denise is saying, and it is delivered in a personal way to each and every human being as if that human were the only one in the world. As if she had served him before at table she believes she recognises the hands as they now take the platter from her, healing hands, hands gentle with love. The coming of the Christ is through ordinary human senses, voice, ear, hand ... The single, hesitating line that is merely an incomplete question, mirrors the girl's wonder and hesitation: 'Surely that face – ?' But she is also deeply aware of the history of this man, of his crucifixion as a criminal, of the disappearance of his dead body, of rumours of recent sightings of his living flesh. Only gradually do we come to realise the difference in this servant girl, how she seems chosen because she had remained totally open, how she is among those not regarded as the holy ones, she is black, she is the one who knows him, and knows for certain it is he because she sees the light about him. This is a poem where the twists and turns of the verse form image beautifully the twists and turns of the servant girl's mind and her growing awareness of what she is witness to. And here is Levertov again, witnessing to the divine, witnessing to the way that God hovers everywhere about us, even in our doubts, even in the moments of darkness.

It is this moment of sudden but gentle awareness, of new perception, of seeing, that Levertov pursues in her poetry. She knows the human being builds a hard shell of egotism around herself against the ravages of the world; she was aware of human depravity, and struggled, in often perilous personal circumstance, to make the world aware of the destructive energies that are fuelled by our wars; she saw the enormous power for destruction in the egotism of rulers but in the everyday world it is a modicum of that same self-focus that she tried so hard to break down in poems. When something occurs to break through that hard outer shell, then wonders may occur.

On the Mystery of the Incarnation
It's when we face for a moment
the worst our kind can do, and shudder to know
the taint in our own selves, that awe

cracks the mind's shell and enters the heart:
not to a flower, not to a dolphin,
to no innocent form
but to this creature vainly sure
it and no other is god-like, God
(out of compassion for our ugly
failure to evolve) entrusts,
as guest, as brother,
the Word.

This is, of course, the greatest wonder, the fact of the incarn-ation, the fact that the Word himself, God the Son, would break through into the physical actuality and the flesh and blood of the earth and of mankind, and that we should thereby learn 'the glory, filled with grace and truth' that is God himself. It is also something that breaks through that shell of our being, when we become aware of how the human can create such terror and suf-fering among his own kind. War, and the savagery of war, are the most obvious depravities of mankind and even in spite of this, in spite of the fact that man considers himself the one and only creature in existence that is god-like, it is out of sheer com-passion for our foolishness that the Word is entrusted to us. This is the fact of grace, kindness done for the sheer sake of kindness, not out of merit of any kind on the part of humanity. This is the stance Levertov took, it is the only truly Christian stance, and it is clearly and meticulously put in her work. This, too, is the rea-son why most of Levertov's work moves in the area of mystery between the temporal and the eternal, the borderland that exists between the everyday and the wonderful, that moves along the edge of that wood where darkness and light mingle to create meaningful shapes. Indeed, in one poem, she overtly speaks of how one comes by grace, that it is not won, not earned, but a gift given:

The Avowal
for Carolyn Kizer and John Woodbridge,
Recalling Our Celebration
of George Herbert's Birthday, 1983

As swimmers dare
to lie face to the sky

and water bears them,
as hawks rest upon air
and air sustains them,
so would I learn to attain
freefall, and float
into Creator Spirit's deep embrace,
knowing no effort earns
that all-surrounding grace.

The recalling of George Herbert touches on the same truth that earlier poet wrote about so well, that unearned though freely given gift of God's love, the gift so often refused until our God cajoles and welcomes, urges and invites, until the soul, acknowledging its weakness, dares to respond fondly to that invitation to love.

The work of Denise Levertov seems, on the surface, simple and immediate if not, at times, even simplistic. We are, however, living in an age of utter doubt and extreme secularism in which any 'vision' beyond the physical seems questionable. She was brought up in an environment of faith, even of mystical faith, in which the surface of the world is exactly that, merely a surface, and life, truth, vision must penetrate beneath that surface. Her approach to poetry was, then, that of visioning, of seeking to capture and extend those moments of epiphany when the bland or the beautiful opens up to a truth beyond itself. And this, of course, leads to praise, to the glorification of what is the source of that visionary approach. If we take the old-fashioned, male-orientated *Gloria Patri* ... for example, 'Glory be to the Father and to the Son and to the Holy Ghost ...' and give it a more modern slant, such as 'Glory to You, Source and Sustenance of our being ...' then Denise's poetry attempts to touch upon that source and sustenance. Her father, rabbi and later Christian, and her devout mother, evidently brought up their daughter to have an imagination open to the mystical and the sacred; for her it was natural and everyday that religious imagery support and enhance the factual. To follow Levertov's poetry is to be born again, into sustaining spirituality, into the poetry of the source. Let me quote a poem from her 1982 collection *Candles in Babylon*:

Rain Spirit Passing
Have you ever heard the rain at night
streaming its flaxen hair against
the walls of your house?

Have you ever heard the rain at night
drifting its black, shiny, seaweed hair
through multi-storeyed arcades of leaves?

And have you risen then
from bed and felt your way
to the window, and raised the blind, and seen

> stillness, unmisted moonlight, the air
> dry? Street and garden
> empty and silent?

You had been lying awake; the rain
was no dream. Yet where is it?
When did that rain descend and descend,
filling your chalices
until their petals loosened

and wafted
down to rest
on grass and the wet ground,

and your roots in their burrows
stretched and sighed?

Vision, in its sense of being fully alert and open to experience, is nourishing and sustaining in poetry like this. Things are sacraments, offering, if we are open to seeing them, ways beyond the mere drab actuality of our days. From here, and with her Jewish and Christian background in our minds, it is easy to see how Levertov made religious inheritance an important force in her work and in her life. As a corollary to this faith and vision, Levertov grew aware of a wholeness of being, of a source and sustaining power that holds all the world in being and in unity. And her work shows how often and how terribly human beings can disturb and destroy this unity. Along with her poetry of celebration of vision there is a poetry of moral outrage; nor are these works separate, the unifying force everywhere is the incarnation; Christ's coming on earth, the manifestation of the Source and Sustenance, gives focus and extension to human living. Back to the *Gloria Patri*: now we may say Glory to You, Source and Sustenance of our being, and to You, Spoken Name and Nature of that Source ... In our age, when every effort is made to 'grow a business', build a fortune, garner as much treasure as possible, it is necessary to read a poet like Levertov so that vision may become a necessary, indeed a vital, ingredient to re-evaluate our aims and ideals. To admit mystery into our urgent labours towards living, to allow wonder to slow down our days, to allow spirit to permeate the physical hardnesses of our environment, this is to respond to the poetry of Denise Levertov.

One of the poems begins: 'Human being – walking/ in doubt from childhood on'; existence remains always for her a mystery and it is this honesty and integrity in the work that has always appealed to me. Faith becomes, and remains, a great gift, a mystery in itself:

Candlemas
With certitude
Simeon opened
ancient arms
to infant light.
Decades
before the cross, the tomb
and the new life,
he knew
new life.
What depth
of faith he drew on,
turning illumined
towards deep night.

We return, with Levertov, always to the notion of vision, of seeing, a vision that ultimately rests on faith, and on a faith that is reasonable, and unreasonable. The delight and wonder in things of nature are ever-present in the work, but it is the seeing past and beyond all of that that matters. It is the search for what is spiritual beyond the materiality of the moment that matters to her and that gives the poetry its bite. Faith, this seeing beyond, is something that must be worked at, something you cannot simply will and then stay motionless with regard to it:

> Faith's a tide, it seems, ebbs and flows responsive
> to action and inaction.
> Remain in stasis, blown sand
> stings your face, anemones
> shrivel in rock pools no wave renews.

A delightful and delicate poem catches the faith that holds even in the moments of deepest doubt:

> *Suspended*
> I had grasped God's garment in the void
> but my hand slipped
> on the rich silk of it.
> The 'everlasting arms' my sister loved to remember
> must have upheld my leaden weight
> from falling, even so,
> for though I claw at empty air and feel
> nothing, no embrace,
> I have not plummeted.

Through her poems, then, Denise Levertov has set up a personal and richly rewarding series of works. These are not a bunch of poems gathered together into an individual collection, but permeate all the work, their radiance illuminating and enriching the poetry gathered around them. The ongoing exploration of human consciousness enriched by a close observation of nature and human behaviour, leads to a wholly honest dealing between faith and doubt, the scales falling towards faith, a faith that has the same almost innocent yet dramatic trust in the sustaining power of God's love, even towards the hesitant and forgetful soul. It is from the intensity of watching, the egotistic self momentarily removed so that this watching is not self-focused but disinterested, it is in allowing the world in all its objectivity into the observing soul that the poem begins. She wrote: 'So – as the poet stands open-mouthed in the temple of life, contemplating his experience, there come to him the first words of the poem, if there is to be a poem. The pressure of the demand and the meditation on its elements culminate in a moment of vision, of crystallisation, in which some inkling of the correspondence between those elements occurs; and it occurs as words.'

In a poem entitled 'Conversion of Brother Lawrence' it is the notice by the young man of a tree in especially beautiful flowering that suddenly alters the man's way of life:

>   Clumsy footman,
> apt to drop the ornate objects handed to you,
> cursed and cuffed by butlers and grooms,
> your inner life unsuspected,
> you heard, that day, a more-than-green
> voice from the stripped branches.
> Wooden lace, a celestial geometry, uttered
> more than familiar rhythms of growth.
> It said *By the Grace of God*.

With acute and attentive vision to the actualities of this world, Levertov senses often a moment of acute revelation; many of the poems present such a moment and hence, naturally, the moment of 'annunciation' to Mary, the young Palestinian woman living up until then a life of dull and everyday inconsequence, takes hold on Levertov's imagination.

> She was free
> to accept or to refuse, choice
> integral to humanness.

> Aren't there annunciations
> of one sort or another
> in most lives?
>   Some unwillingly
> undertake great destinies,
> enact them in sullen pride,
> uncomprehending.
>   More often
> those moments
>   when roads of light and storm
>   open from darkness in a man or woman,
> are turned away from
> in dread, in a wave of weakness, in despair
> and with relief.

Ordinary lives continue.
God does not smite them.
But the gates close, the pathway vanishes.

Vision, then, is not sufficient in itself; nor is faith allied with vision sufficient; what is further needed, and we know this too well, is the courage to live by faith and vision. Here is the kernel of Christian belief, the focal point, here, in fact, is the Cross. Levertov's life was lived in response to this vision and faith, and she did not shirk the responsibilities, she did not avoid the Cross.

One of the final poems in the last collection published while she was alive is called 'The Prayer Plant', and in brackets its Latin name, *Maranta Leuconeura*. This is a small plant native to Brazil, with broad leaves that fold upwards at night into the shape of hands at prayer.

The Prayer Plant
The prayer plant must long
for darkness, that it may fold and raise
its many pairs of green hands
to speak at last, in that gesture;

the way a shy believer,
at last in solitude, at last,
with what relief
kneels down to praise You.

The poem clearly expresses Levertov's hesitations over the years, and her longing to be able to commit herself fully to faith. The second stanza is a masterpiece of sense and sensual sound and expresses beautifully such hesitation and longing. The seeing is over, the seeing to believe; what is left is prayer but it is not the prayer of selfishness, it is praise. The loss of Denise Levertov to poetry in general and to religious poetry in particular, at a stage when she was close, as Simone Weil came close, to complete acceptance of Christianity, is an incalculable loss. She spent evenings at my home, among my family; I have photographs of her with my children; she sits, shy as they, modest and integrate, a gentle familiar and a deeply powerful poet. *Ar dheis Dé go raibh a hanam dilis.*

Look Back in Quietness
The poetry of Gerard Smyth

In issue 86 of *Poetry Ireland Review* and writing of *A New Tenancy*, David Cameron says: 'Smyth's poems are suffused with religious imagery without being statements of belief.' He singles out 'Interlude' as perhaps the only completely successful poem of religious imagery here. The title of Smyth's 1977 collection, *World Without End* (New Writers Press) with its epigraph: 'as it was in the beginning, is now, and ever shall be, world without end,' suggests some engagement with life on a religious level, but the poems eschew any such exploration, remaining in the realms of an attempt to come to terms with everyday living, in city and country, and in particular with the grim darkness hovering over our lives. Many poems touch on graveyards and dying, the dismal sides of modern living, the hungers, poverty, the desolation. Inner city Dublin is a place of darkness, of sadness and some misery, but there is no doubt that the writer measures his place with acuity and affection. The title poem of this early collection is a laying out before the reader of things that are held in a kind of prison, leading inevitably to its final line:

World Without End
Water locked in a frozen pond.
Time stopped in broken clocks.
Blood safe in the healing wound.
A toy forgotten in its box.

The vanished meal during supper.
A dance that ends too soon.
The aftermath of a laughter
Becomes a moment of doom.

A doubt among the certainties.
The child gone from the womb.
The listening silence echoes
the seconds in a ticking room.

The seed waiting for birth.
The dead entering the earth.

The poet keeps a distance from the list of ended things and part of this distancing is in the unusual rhyming, and the end-stopping, both of which give a feeling of a grim funereal progress to the lines. But it is this feeling that, in a way reminiscent of the accuracy of observation of Thomas Kinsella, gives the poem an overall sense of glum obstinacy in the face of the bleaker realities of our living. Death, absence, decay ... all these feature in the early work of this poet, born in Dublin in 1951, who has spent a great deal of his life as a journalist. In this early work, (and the stance is maintained, while evolving, in later work) Smyth appears to honour the Eliot stance of keeping self as far from the poem as possible; this is not confessional poetry, it is a bleak and restrained, lyrical and elegiac, watching poetry; there are no conclusions drawn, easy or difficult, no rhetorical overtones.

In 2002 Smyth published a collection called *Daytime Sleeper* (Dedalus Press), which included several of the earlier poems in revised form. Amongst these was 'World Without End'. The revisions are hugely interesting; the poem is no longer a sonnet, now it is reduced to three four-line stanzas; the third stanza is simply dropped; the couplet that made the end of the sonnet becomes the first two lines of the final stanza:

The seed waiting for birth.
The dead entering the earth.
Opulence bursts in one hand,
another hand is dividing bread.

The word 'opulence' is wonderfully suggestive of hope and generous living, while the image of dividing bread inevitably calls up the Christ figure. The poem then is turned towards a wholly positive view of life, the *Gloria Patri* title is given extra substance by the final line, and the suggested rather than full rhyme at the end of the poem is musically startling and emphatically life-giving. Twenty-five years have shifted their length between first and second versions. While the tense and imagistic accuracy of observation and detail remain, indeed are even more carefully constructed, the emphasis here is clearly towards life and life-giving things. Those extra two lines were originally part of a poem that appeared in the collection *Loss and Gain* (Raven Arts Press, 1981) a piece called 'Reality', not particularly successful in itself and dropped from later selections. In this 1981 book, however, Gerard Smyth takes his religious faith by the wrist and leads it into a section of poems that closes the collection.

This section opens with the lines:

Tense crosses pierce the earth
where mercy most abounds.

The setting is Glendalough and Smyth sees the sacred place as a locale where suffering has taught its lessons of harshness and death, where no miracles are to be sought; yet it is here that mercy most abounds, though as yet the poem does not expatiate on what these lines are to mean. The poem 'This Day's Bread' may give an answer:

This Day's Bread
Bread my solace
and grapes that taste of the covenant
The brimming cup surmounts
all that is unendurable

Ascetic cheeks
kindled by impassive flame
Soul feasts on passion to no avail

O smashed embrace and forsaken citadel
Already the age's requiem is sung.

The reference takes us back to the 'opulence' and the hand dividing bread, of the earlier poem, and takes us into the heart of the sacrament of communion, the bread and the wine of solace and the overcoming of pain. Asceticism is offered as a suggestion, merely, whereby we presume such solace may be achieved.

Otherwise the poem is rather too rhetorical and the last two lines are too big for the rest of the piece, but the closeness of the experience suggested here is tangible and offers a real opening into faith. This slight rhetoric passes on into the title of another poem, 'Orison', in the same section. Here is the first direct call to God in the poetry: 'Lord, be moved ...' And here, too, Smyth's greatest strength is glimpsed in the use of quite powerful and unexpected adjectives: he speaks of the 'winnowing' candle of prayer. The prayer of this piece is called out of the same awareness of human suffering and the sharing of that suffering by the Christ:

Lord, be moved
when flesh and blood renew your wound
once made irrevocably.

The basic structural imagery of many of Smyth's poems can also be enjoyed in this poem, that of light and darkness, an imagery he can switch about easily to emphasise either sorrow or contentment; (I was going to write Joy, but that yet seems far from the tension and the bleak awareness of the poems); here light wins out: long night succumbs, dawn takes dominion. In these few poems the poet seems to step out from watching from the sidewalk to being in the street, loosening that tense and distant visitation to allow the consciousness of self enter the work. This lifts the poetry to new levels.

Sanctum
Sealed in their reliquary
of pain and gold
the somnolent bones once nailed to hope:

What blind devotion led me
where sign and symbol abolish vacuity?

What contemplation led me here
where the seething bells praise God
and candles tread the air
with improbable serenity?

Who comprehends faith's visitation
or eternal truths in bread and wine?

Black nights of unbelief
deny the dominion of noon.

The fact that most of the poem is written in the form of questions reinforces the sense of wonder at the poet's own faith and
doubt; everything in the poem is shaped in the form of contradiction: the reliquary, of a martyr it would appear, is made of
gold but also houses pain and the bones contained were once
nailed to hope; the phrase 'abolish vacuity', while it is clear, is
still somewhat rhetorical but the message is that a certain blind
devotion, a devotion not linked to reason, has at least done some
good; the bells are 'seething' yet sound in praise, and the candles
offer 'improbable serenity'. Faith comes not as a steady flame,
but as a visitation and even this small belief is lost at the coming
of black night. But the poem works, I feel, because of the absolute honesty of the questioning and the doubting, Smyth's
withdrawn linguistic skills working to hone a darkly personal
work. The sentiments, too, and their expression, will echo
strongly in the mind of any once committed Irish Catholic, suffering in these times the darkness of a once bright belief.

'Sacrifice' has this: 'the spirit whispers to the flesh/ enigmas
of the flesh and spirit', and the poem speaks of human love and
its vocabulary and how words are not sufficient to mend a damaged love, blood is required, the sacrifice of Christ. Later Smyth
writes that 'the saviour brought adamantine mysteries' but
these poems still have a burden of rhetoric and linguistic
overkill: 'O risen morn anoint with radiance/ our averted faces.'
The individual poems, set apart from the others in this collection, still offer what will become the essential Smyth: a tension
between vision and language, an engaged stand-off in perspective, released statements dependent on observed natural phen-
omena and a grace of discovered metaphor that lifts that tendency
to rhetoric onto genuinely poetic planes. The delving into personal religious experience brought new vigour and excitement
to the work at this point in Gerard Smyth's poetic development.

Painting the Pink Roses Black was published by The Dedalus
Press in 1986. In this collection many poems contain references
to religious rituals and habits, and these are taken for granted,
finding their place in the poems as naturally as weather. 'You

cross yourself when you're told ...' 'At night the Virgin in the gilded frame ...' '& the cross with its unmourned Christ/ reminds me that the word love/ is about preparing to die ...' The poems here are also more assured in form, less bleak in their imagery. Yet that underlying darkness remains: 'How empty the world is/ and in it the gigantic throbbing of our hearts.' The poem that gives the book its title is particularly rich:

Fever
The windows of the hospital reflect a lunar calm.
Nightsmoke from the boiler-house
swirls in muted agitation. In a corner
of the fever-ward geraniums that were wilting
bloom – it is the only miracle,
the only sign of a life not thwarted by lassitude.

Soup thick as ointment broods in a bowl,
stiffened bread lies mouldering. The silence now
is a nightingale empty of sound.
The sick child wakes after falling
through the deepness of space:
he feels the leadweight of eyelids
half-opening to the present. At midnight,
when the youngest face wears the oldest expression,
the dark is perfect:
                    it paints the pink roses black.

The darkness here is perfect! Any positive imagery is immediately darkened, save for the geraniums, once wilting, now by a kind of miracle, blooming. Lassitude covers everything. It is the quiet tone, the almost lunar calm of the poem that makes this work so finely achieved. And the sound patterns offer a music that underlies this calmness and definiteness: soup ... broods ... bowl ... mouldering ... And the final movement is just right: midnight, when the whole thrust of human living and suffering has aged the child's face, the final colouring of the scene is taken away, the pink roses become black. Though the poem is so dark, yet there is none of that tension of distance that brooded over the earlier work; it is the tranquillity of the accepted blackness that adds something unique to this work.

The accuracy of observation in other poems continues to delight: 'The man in blue overalls seems to be watching/ for a change in the behaviour of old machinery …' 'The slow walk of father's widowhood/ entered the street …/ everything about him was boarded up'. Then once again, in the final section of the collection, come poems focusing on faith. Saint Thérèse, the little flower, is visited in her quiet suffering, her anguish, affliction, her quiet distress but Smyth sees her, nevertheless, as Job changed to smaller dimensions. This concentration on the black side of this saint's life is to be expected in this poet.

The other poems in this section circle rather than face into the religious theme; there are parts of each poem that read as faith statements; 'Self-radiant child,/ in your child's head a pastoral tenderness;/ in your unfeigned smile/ there's someone back from the dead/ – who's seen the truth/ and solved the mysteries' ('Pentecost'). 'Out of the depths and from echoing hills/ earth's cries/ invoke the unsealed sepulchre/ where death consoles the living' ('Temple'). But these are pieces of the jigsaw and do not fit comfortably into the poems, save, perhaps, for one poem that takes the Good Friday theme and speaks clearly of its requiem music: there is no consolation in the poem, the opposite, in fact, as the final lines of the poem show; the persona of the poet shifts from the I to we and in between are images of effort and decay; the tree in the last stanza even suggests the absence of resurrection, in spite of a momentary sense of tranquillity. Once again there are no resolutions in the piece; it remains tentative but here, even in its groping state, Smyth's taut lines, the accuracy of his images and the determined movement of the piece, are praiseworthy:

Interlude
Looking at thorn I think
of the thorn-covered God. I sit and listen.
An insect-wing is scratching the wall.
My wristwatch, ticking obstinately,
sends out a sound like a clenched
fist hammering and hammering.

In the yard a bony chicken
is picking at patches of sunlight.

Implements of the fields are going rusty
where the moist weather touched them.

Today we are submerged in the requiem
music of Good Friday.
The tree with its back turned to the house
is tranquil, as if it were dead.
Tomorrow
we'll be at each other's throats again.

If the poem lacks faith in the goodness of humanity, perhaps this is a good low point from which Gerard Smyth might rise, using the religious themes he is skirting, towards a more positive outlook? 'Interlude' is the last poem in the collection, *Painting the Pink Roses Black*; it was several years before the next collection, Smyth withdrawing into a silence that, in hindsight, seems predictable: that tension, the watching inwards, the morne view of things. Then *Daytime Sleeper* (Dedalus) appeared in 2002, after a gap of 16 years. But at once there is a new feel to things, a new excitement, a garnered richness, a generous helping of poems and a sense of achieved calm. The caterpillar has become the butterfly, and it is opulently coloured!

As he rooted around in the earlier work to salvage what he felt he could live with, Smyth selected only a few poems and it is wonderful how these seem to take on new vibrancy in the context of his development as a poet. One of these, taken from *Painting the Pink Roses Black*, is 'Childhood House' which shows how the I is allowed into the poems, no longer a disgruntled, gloomy watcher, but an involved self: 'It was milking time in the country,/ the hour I loved. Darkness crowded the henhouse,/ I was afraid to enter.' And the poem 'Epiphany', salvaged from the collection *Loss and Gain*, has the poet watching outwards, too, with a new delight in the things of the earth: 'Look! The orchard –/ the boughs, the fruit …' and 'Look! the clarity of gossamer/ on bowing leaf.' In the 16-year interlude there has been a growth in maturity, in a sense of a more peaceful acceptance of things and, above all, a sense of an involvement of the self in a more meaningful world. Going along with this freshness is a less tense form, a movement of lines that is more graceful and less jerky than before:

I think of this as the beginning of a story
that will take us through the strange calm
of small towns in the small hours,
sheltering places, chambers of rest
(*'On the Way'*)

There is a further looking outwards, with many poems probing the life and work of other writers and artists, like Arvo Pärt,
Lorca, Trakl, James Clarence Mangan ... It is a collection of finely
achieved work and, for those aware of the earlier work, a revelation and a joy. The poems are rich with precise and affectionate
memories of inner city Dublin, touching in this area the richness
of Thomas Kinsella's work. We are looking back, and our looking is filled with peace. It may well be that the earlier poetry was
too involved with place and difficulty to be able to stand back
and gaze, not only with affection but with acuity, on the places
and life of the time. Many of the poems in the centre of the book
display this rich accuracy, as if the disgruntled poet had been
shocked by distance of time and location into objectivity and
love:

Fifties Child
The old boundaries are not here anymore.
They've bricked up the neighbourhood,
houses in which the war was fought
when the war was over. A fifties child, he is homesick
for the chimes that woke him, the rooms
where cold linoleum stuck to the soles of his feet.

This is where he once stood back, stayed at the edge
of the adult world with its perfume
and tobacco smells of aunts and uncles:
some to be trusted, some to be frightened of.

Lovers of singsong and the sound of Sinatra,
they whispered in voices of sad disappointment
and lived through years that were always the end of an era.

The cold linoleum in earlier work would have been a cause
for complaint; here it is nostalgia. No longer is there a standing
back, there is an engaged affection; nor is there a sense of dis-

trust; there is no bitterness, it has been replaced by an occasion-ally wry observation; this is a mature and settled writer, explor-ing location and origin, and it is this that leavens the fine poems that emerge.

As well as this movement away from a querulous self into ac-ceptance of the world as it is, there is, in the poems of *Daytime Sleeper*, a much wider engagement with the world at large, the world beyond Dublin, beyond Ireland. Notes are taken on places such as Prague, Rome, Venice ... and this outward-look-ing awareness gathers to itself a richly observed sense of things way outside the inward-seeking ego.

> And somewhere near the coast
> a funfair stands bereft: the roulette
> and the mechanical ghost
> sheeted where they are left in winter sleep.
> ('On the Way')

Another interesting development in this collection is the growing awareness of the richness of the world heritage of painters such as Rouault, Van Gogh and Gauguin and Hughie O'Donoghue, among others ... It is the looking outwards that helps the work to find its strong and meaningful voice. And the religious themes continue, with this same outward watching at the basis of the works.

> *Thérèse*
> *(for Padraig J. Daly)*
> It was a mutable world.
> Flowers rotted and water grew stale.
> Each day began with ceremony,
> kneeling women sang praise
>
> and heard, far-off,
> the barely audible footsteps on the road
> to Emmaus. Thérèse
> what shudders of doubt cling to you
> as dust was shaken from the empty shroud?
> In your soul-diary:
> anguish, affliction, quiet distress.
> Not the Troubles of Job

and nothing miraculous. Just the mundane
sent to test you.

Is there not a sense of the self of the earlier poet in this work,
in the close identification of poet with saint? If this is as accurate
and as full a portrait of a saint that can be contained in so few
lines, the poem is a result of all the different movements out
from the harrowed self, though bearing with them a memory of
such harrowing, that the poet has achieved. All the references,
from the life of the sisters, through the sense of doubt, to
Emmaus, resurrection and the deep troubles of a normal life,
spring together naturally in the poem; there is nothing forced,
the imagery has sunk to such a depth that it moves as naturally
as the other poems do. And the emphasis is once more on the
close and the small, the everyday things with which this poet
has a Midas touch.

The poems of *A New Tenancy* (Dedalus Press 2004) are content, for the most part, to allow the accuracy of memory and
observation to speak for themselves. Gone is the tendency of the
early poetry to expostulate, to draw inference of bleak conclusion; many of the poems now simply present their offerings and
leave it at that. A great deal, perhaps a little too much, nostalgia
is present for its own sake, an interesting move in the context of
this poet's early work:

Mount Argus
The road forks there where a Celtic Cross
was raised in memory of martyrs shot
in a War of Independence.
Two directions: which one to take?
You always knew and always went
through the palisade of Scots pine
into the shadow of Mount Argus.

Your Santiago where you felt anointed
and walked the stations
from *The Betrayal in the Garden*
to *The Hammering of the Nails*.
I was five or six and led by the hand
to the Christmas animals,
the ox and the lamb.

It was like a gloaming in the candlesmoke.
A world between the worlds
of light and dark.
Nothing stirred except the two of us:
a pair of shadows creaking
in quietness that hung there
like the mummy-cloth of Passion Week.

This method of writing poetry necessitates a sureness and maturity both of self-awareness and life-experience. There is also quietness in the acceptance of the imagery of faith, in the wealth of images offered by Christmas and Easter Week. This gazing backwards in tranquillity offers perfect vignettes of Dublin and other places associated with his friends and family; it is not simple nostalgia, it is the pleasure of language in its discovery and its re-discoveries:

Hallowed with age, everything remains in place:
drawers and boxes stashed with clutter,
the small window of wonder
that frames the good light and the wintry dark.

Awareness shifts in this collection into a group of poems touching on war and its miseries. The poet facing out into the world, observes, and notes and allows the sadness and the knowledge of humanity's bitter legacies to speak for themselves. In this next poem there is an added wonder, the way the poet leaves the religious imagery, too, to speak for itself:

Their Hems Touching the Ground
Young soldiers at sentry points
let us pass into the one-star town
with three ways of life.

Between souvenirs of Palestine
and psalms of the old religion
we are led to the cradle, the nativity crypt,
back to the beginning,
past the beggars, the war cripples.

There are no bringers
of frankincense or myrrh,
no lifting of hosannas into the air.

In Manger Square,
through the babble of Bethlehem,
the fervour of the crowd,
the people from the Beatitudes move,
their hems touching the ground.

This is poetry as witness, a poetry that responds to the words of Czeslaw Milosz in his poem 'Blacksmith Shop':

At the entrance, my bare feet on the dirt floor,
Here, gusts of heat; at my back, white clouds.
I stare and stare. It seems I was called for this:
To glorify things just because they are.

We have come to a poetry that serves almost as journal, as diary, though the language is heightened and the moments are rich and memorably presented. It is a beautifully accomplished poetry, unselfconscious, filled with gratitude for being, and a great distance from the bitterly anxious early poems. Reading and relishing the poems in *A New Tenancy*, one is aware of a fine poet come to rest in his life, content with his memories, with his new home, his work, his family, his faith.

Vladimir Holan was Right
Vladimir Holan was right:
the kitchen is the best place to be
with its coffee aroma, brewing tea,
prattle of the family and purr

of the icebox working its alchemy.
Stored away in its clammy shadows
are shining apples from Adam's garden,
cherries from Argentina.

A place of healing and mending
and clemency when we confess,
where the only empress is the empress
of wonders that never cease.

At the table of drawn-out pleasures,
wars were fought, you read my thoughts,
black headlines were passed between us.
It is here that daybreak makes its first appearance

and tenebrous evening through steamed windows.
Here that we have been talkative,
silent, amorous; pale as consommé,
rosy as ripe tomatoes.

It is tempting always to wonder where the change occurred, from angry and bitter young man, to a settled and mature adult and an accomplished poet. Is it through the discovery of love and family, or the satisfaction of knowing a world of nostalgia … 'Vladimir Holan was right …' is a poem that certainly suggests that love was vital in the development; the accuracy of 'clemency when we confess', and the honesty of 'wars were fought', the intimacy of suggestion in 'black headlines' and the echo, rebounding, of Stevens's 'Only Emperor'. Again it is witness, no great claims are made, no vast philosophies outlined; what matters is the immediacy of the emotion and its accurate portrayal. In the newest poems, a collection from The Dedalus Press, *The Mirror Tent*, the treatment of moments drawn out of the past continues, together with a gaze at other artists and a nod in the direction of a now settled faith. There is, in the new work, a gathering of poems on the theme of personal love, (of which 'Vladimir Holan …') and the facing into such poems offers, no doubt, a clue to the poet's maturity. There is also a delightfully accomplished pair of religious poems.

Lough Derg
Years ago I spent a sleepless night
among sleepwalkers ready to renounce
the world, the flesh, the devil.

It was all Dantesque,
circling and circling the purgatorial beds
in the wet wind and chill from the lake,
to the chant of mingling strangers
ready to make a new beginning.

Black tea, black bread
was the sustenance we were given.
In the first light at five o'clock
the shore appeared out of the dark.
It made us think we were close to God
years ago on Lough Derg.

This appears to me to be something more than a nostalgic look-back; it catches well the mood and bleak disciplines of Lough Derg and echoes accurately the outlook on things religious of the time. It is a great and difficult strength to leave things standing in a poem, and not to draw 'conclusions' or 'lessons'; the lesson here is implied and if the poet has, over time, actually made in his poetry a 'new beginning', then we are the more blessed for the preliminary angers that led to this convincing quietness.

According to Matthew
Falling sparrows, camels passing
through the eye of a needle.
He speaks in metaphors and riddles.
He is a riddle, the Virgin's Son
who stands to pronounce the blunt one-liners
of the Sermon on the Mount:
Blessed are … Come follow me …

In *The Gospel According to Matthew*,
the version by Pasolini,
Christ the agitator hurries through Galilee
healing the stretcher-borne,
casting away the bread of stone
placed before him in temptation.

Christ in the temple speaks in livid gestures:
upending and taking apart
the tables and tills of the money-lenders.
He sits cross-legged to answer the questions
of potentate and plebeian, or with a stick writes
on the ground, defends the slut against the crowd
with a handful of words quite clear to everyone.

Finally, in an as yet uncollected poem, Smyth succeeds in opening up the self to himself and to his readers in a way he has not done before. This works wonderfully well, the catalyst for the movement of the poem being the self-analysis of a poet like R. S. Thomas who has shown the way to burrow deep into the self for awareness that will lead to growth. This short poem encompasses so much that could not have been possible without the cautious development I have outlined above and augurs wonderfully for the future work of this fine poet.

Nicodemus
After the Good Friday ceremony,
the wooden cross without a Christ,
I think of Nicodemus, his night-visits

and how I too am secretive
about the appointments I keep,
always, it seems, in that place

where we go for forgiveness;
the sanctuary described by R S Thomas
as *the ante-room of the spirit.*